Early Childhood Care and I

Early childhood care and education is central to the lives of every family with young children. This insightful book investigates the unique approaches taken by different countries to key issues such as parental leave, childcare, and preschool services. By examining all of these options and the evidence around them, the authors are able to consider how best to provide for young children.

Nine countries, including China, Greece, India, Israel, Italy, New Zealand, Sweden, the UK and the USA, are considered. These countries all have very different policies and provision, and this book examines the ways that these countries are tackling early childhood services and how these services affect young children's experiences and development, for better and worse. The book will answer some of the recurring questions of childcare provision:

- How does a country cope with the childcare needs of families?
- Is day care detrimental to children?
- Does quality of childcare matter?
- Does childcare affect children with different home backgrounds differently?
- How can we best organise parental leave, employment regulations and child-care provision?

This book fills a gap in providing up-to-date information in an area where rapid developments are underway and further changes are being considered. We need to better plan the future of early childhood services and preschool education in relation to children's development, as well as parental employment regulations. Through presenting the situation in various countries and allowing the comparison of alternative approaches, each reader may be able to see new possibilities that transcend the limited experience offered within their own country.

Early Childhood Care and Education is an essential read for anyone interested in both the future and alternative approaches to childhood services and pre school education.

Edward Melhuish is Professor of Human Development at Birkbeck, University of London, UK.

Konstantinos Petrogiannis is Associate Professor of Developmental Psychology at the Democritus University of Thrace, Greece.

Early Childhood Care and Education

International perspectives

Edited by Edward Melhuish and Konstantinos Petrogiannis

Routledge
Taylor & Francis Group

LONDON AND NEW YORK

First published 2006
by Routledge
2 Park Square, Milton Park, Abingdon, Oxon OX14 4RN

Simultaneously published in the USA and Canada
by Routledge
270 Madison Avenue, New York NY 10016

*Routledge is an imprint of the Taylor & Francis Group, an
informa business*

© 2006 Edward Melhuish and Konstantinos Petrogiannis

Typeset in Sabon by
GreenGate Publishing Services, Tonbridge, Kent
Printed and bound in Great Britain by
The Cromwell Press, Trowbridge, Wiltshire

British Library Cataloguing in Publication Data
A catalogue record for this book is available from the British Library

Library of Congress Cataloging-in-Publication Data
Early childhood care and education : international perspectives /
[edited by] Edward Melhuish and Konstantinos Petrogiannis.
p. cm.
ISBN 0-415-38368-4 (hardback) – ISBN 0-415-38369-2 (pbk.)
1. Child care services–Cross-cultural studies. 2. Early childhood
education–Cross-cultural studies. I. Melhuish, Edward C., 1950- II.
Petrogiannis, Konstantinos.
HQ778.5.E22 2006
362.71'2–dc22
2006006416

ISBN 10: 0-415-38368-4 (hbk)
ISBN 10: 0-415-38369-2 (pbk)
ISBN 10: 0-203-96767-4 (ebk)

ISBN 13: 978-0-415-38368-4 (hbk)
ISBN 13: 978-0-415-38369-1 (pbk)
ISBN 13: 978-0-203-96767-6 (ebk)

Contents

Contributors

Virginia D. Allhusen, School of Social Ecology, University of California, Irvine, California, USA

K. Alison Clarke-Stewart, School of Social Ecology, University of California, Irvine, California, USA

C. Philip Hwang, Department of Psychology, University of Göteborg, Göteborg, Sweden

Shraddha Kapoor, Department of Child Development, Lady Irwin College, University of Delhi, Delhi, India

Helen May, Children's Issues Centre, University of Otago, Dunedin, New Zealand

Edward Melhuish, Institute for the Study of Children, Families and Social Issues, Birkbeck, University of London, London, UK

Jennifer L. Miner, School of Social Ecology, University of California, Irvine, California, USA

Tullia Musatti, Institute of Cognitive Sciences and Technologies, National Research Council, Rome, Italy

Konstantinos Petrogiannis, School of Education Sciences, Democritus University of Thrace, Alexandroupolis, Greece

Miriam K. Rosenthal, Graduate Early Childhood Studies, School of Social Work, Hebrew University, Jerusalem, Israel

Li Shenglan, Department of Early Childhood Education, East China Normal University, Shanghai, People's Republic of China

Anne B. Smith, Children's Issues Centre, University of Otago, Dunedin, New Zealand

1 Introducing international perspectives on early childhood care and education

Edward Melhuish and Konstantinos Petrogiannis

The objective of this book is to offer information and evidence on early childhood care and education (ECCE) from an international perspective to those who are, directly or indirectly, interested or involved with young children and their families. Ideological and historical context can explain how a system of ECCE develops within a country, and an understanding of the ECCE system and its characteristics can explain how effects upon children can occur.

The development of ECCE services is intimately linked with the changing role of women, the increase in maternal employment and other social factors (e.g. ageing population, declining fertility, migration, increase of lone-parent families) as these have an impact on countries' policies. Economic factors are also important in two ways. First, without a strongly growing economy a country will not be able to afford the best ECCE services. Second, there is a growing realisation that high-quality ECCE services may well be a critical factor in the economic development of countries in that the human capital created by high quality ECCE is becoming increasingly indispensable in increasingly technological and knowledge-based economies. These two considerations suggest a long-term feedback loop between development in ECCE and economic development.

Some countries have achieved high levels of quality of ECCE services combined with high rates of maternal employment, whereas other countries, despite showing a significant increase of women's employment, did not show much advance in ECCE services. Hence ECCE services do not automatically develop when there is a clear need for them. Other factors such as the ideology and politics deriving from a country's history and culture are important.

The social structures and cultural beliefs of every society are reflected in the broader attitudes of the public and in the ways the governments consider the needs of mothers with young children. The dominant ideology of each country is expressed through policy and partly determines the types, characteristics and the quality of ECCE services. These features have direct and indirect impact on the quality of the experiences of young children and, ultimately, on their development.

This book attempts to relate historical and cultural contexts to the development of ECCE and the place of research on ECCE through a consideration of the situation in nine countries (China, Greece, India, Israel, Italy, New Zealand, Sweden, United Kingdom, United States) from four continents with distinctly different histories and cultures. The situation in countries that have their own tradition and philosophy in the sector of family and child welfare policy is presented as well as the most important up-to-date research evidence concerning ECCE experiences and their effects on young children.

The USA is a country with a long-standing tradition in research regarding early childhood care and education. As a result, the US policy-makers have more detailed information available on the factors known to enhance or impede good child development than other countries. Nevertheless, with regard to supply, quality and affordability of ECCE services for young children, the US is far behind a number of other industrialised countries. The vast research evidence has largely been ignored apart from the case of ECCE programmes for disadvantaged children (e.g. Head Start). In their chapter, Allhusen, Clarke-Stewart and Miner demonstrate how, despite the dramatic increase in maternal employment and the corresponding increase in childcare participation, there is no national policy for increasing the availability of childcare, providing financial backing for families or facilities, or monitoring childcare quality. The result is that today most childcare in the US is informal and unregulated and discrepancies between states have increased. The picture reflects an ideological position, long held in the English-speaking countries, that children under school age are solely the responsibility of the parents, and that the state shall have no role unless the child is at risk.

The chapter by Melhuish describes the long historical development of a similar set of ideologies and governmental policies in the UK. Such policies controlled the development of ECCE in the UK until 1997, when a change of government heralded a new social agenda. There has been a fundamental change, with childcare, preschool education and parental leave being given a high level of priority in government policy and funding. These changes have been accompanied by a parallel emphasis on 'evidence-based policy' with the result that the government's new policies in this area have been heavily influenced by research. The resulting system of ECCE is currently undergoing great turbulence as the country struggles to find a new pattern of services that suits the emerging needs of a changing nation.

Scandinavian countries have long been in the vanguard of progressive social policy, and the fields of ECCE and parental leave are no exception, with the result that other countries often look to the Scandinavian countries for ideas in developing social policy. Scandinavian countries have had the most extensive governmental support for ECCE and parental leave in the world, and their ECCE is amongst the most developed in the world. Hwang presents and discusses policy in relation to ECCE and relevant research in

Sweden. There are two dominant features to the Swedish welfare system: the extent of public childcare and the parental leave provision. The country has established a universal system of childcare and preschool education, and generous parental leave allows parents time with their infants without excessive financial hardship and, when they do return to employment, their childcare needs are catered for and subsidised by the government. But not only are parents' needs taken care of, but also government regulation and funding ensure a prevailing high level of quality of ECCE provision. The extensions to parental leave provision that can stretch up to 18 months after a child's birth have led to a reduction in demand for childcare in the first year of life, when good-quality childcare is most expensive. This in turn releases resources for maintaining quality of services for older children. However, no country is immune from global change and a variety of socio-demographic changes have taken place during the past few decades (e.g. increase in immigration, decreased birth rate, an increase in women in the workforce followed by an increase in unemployment) with consequent changes in patterns of family life. However, the high quality of ECCE provision results in research findings that indicate that children attending day care develop at least as well as children cared for at home.

It is a very different picture in other European countries. In southern Europe there are different traditions to those prevailing in northern Europe. Two countries, Italy and Greece, are considered in this book in that they represent different paths taken in the southern European tradition, where there is an increasing interest in ECCE services.

Italy has a long tradition in the field of early childhood education, and provides an interesting opportunity to study some perspectives on ECCE in modern society, both because of the changes that have taken place in families' demand and because of the history of ECCE provision. The chapter by Musatti discusses the social function of early educational services within the framework of young children's daily lives and their parents' need for social support. Musatti describes early education provision, its development and the issues at stake, and attempts to give answers to parent and child needs. Italy is of particular interest due to the intense socio-economic differences between the north and south, the power of local government, and the pedagogical initiatives undertaken in ECCE. Innovations in Italy in ECCE hold potential lessons for many other countries.

The position of ECCE in Greece is heavily influenced by the traditional structure of Greek families, characterised by a strong sense of inter-generational obligation. This is common in southern European countries. Dramatic economic and socio-demographic changes in the past four decades have led to a progressive change from a collective to a more individualised lifestyle with consequent changing values, conceptions and needs regarding ECCE. Petrogiannis refers to features of the present that are related to significant elements of the past. In common with many countries there are distinct 'care' and 'education' systems controlled by different government departments. This division has consequences for the nature of ECCE provision, e.g. in services offered to parents and children, finance and the training of staff. The prevailing ideology results in a system that suffers from haphazard and poor regulation, and the limited research presents the depressing consequences for the quality of early childcare institutions and possibly for children's development.

Israel has a history completely unlike that of any other country and Rosenthal's chapter illustrates how the country's development and the development of ECCE are inextricably bound together. The country's history leads to an ideology that gives particular emphasis in the acculturation of young children through the tradition, customs, values, beliefs and language of Israel as well as an emphasis on collectivism over individualism. The chapter also presents the evidence on the consequences of the country's policies for the characteristics and particularly the quality of ECCE services, with a consideration of possible consequences for Israeli children's development. The chapter illustrates vividly how ECCE can only be understood in historical and socio-cultural contexts, and current development of services is clearly suffering from the country's economic problems, with a low priority being given to ECCE.

The next two chapters present the situation of ECCE in two of the biggest, and fastest developing, countries of Asia, with their unique demographic and cultural features. Kapoor presents the ECCE situation in India as it has evolved from a particular historical and socio-cultural framework. Traditionally, the child in India is considered to grow naturally and there is little effort to consciously provide or structure the learning environment. Accordingly, the ECCE system is characterised by the minimal participation of very young children in childcare, reflecting an ideology that children's socialisation is the family's responsibility and with traditionally little appreciation of the role of ECCE in child development. Family care is seen as best for the child even when a mother goes out to work. Kapoor argues that it is this feature of Indian society that has been responsible for the lack of state support for ECCE even for the underprivileged population. However, the country is changing at a dramatic pace, and ECCE is increasingly seen as important for economic development. India now has the world's largest integrated early childhood programme providing non-formal preschool education to over 23 million children aged three to six years and aiming to improve the health and development of children.

China has the world's fastest growing economy and social change is phenomenal. Part of the change is the development of kindergartens, a form of ECCE seen as essential to the country's long-term ambitions. Li Shenglan gives an overview of the recent reformation and development of kindergartens in China since 1990. State legislation orders that all provinces, autonomous regions and municipalities across the country not only operate kindergartens but also encourage and support business, enterprise, corporation, resident commission and the individual efforts to run kindergartens.

The author provides an account of the major innovations introduced with regard to programmes and characteristics such as the group sizes and staff–child ratios, enrolment of young children, staff training and qualifications, as well as partnerships of kindergarten, family and community. What is striking is the government's role in every aspect of kindergarten functioning, even down to attempts to specify daily activities. Such an extensive role with plans for universal provision implies enormous public investment in ECCE.

The history of New Zealand with two cultural groups (Māori and Pakeha/'white') coexisting for more than 150 years, has culminated in dramatic changes to ECCE in the country. Issues of biculturalism between Māori and Pakeha are now combined in multicultural diversity that radically affects policy and research. Smith and May describe the history, policy and characteristics of the diverse ECCE provision in Aotearoa–New Zealand and its integrated model of care and education that is supported through government funding, teacher education programmes and a national curriculum (Te Whāriki). Interestingly, this country's policy has been influenced by research in a similar manner to that in the UK. A cumulative body of systematic research has directly influenced government policies towards increasing the status, recognition and funding for ECCE services. The chapter appraises how the unique interplay of research, pedagogy and policy in the advocacy, implementation and evaluation of early childhood care and education has occurred. The result is that the status and recognition of ECCE has increased, with largely positive public attitudes, perhaps because research has supported the value of participation in ECCE for children and families. The high level of public commitment has resulted in innovations in New Zealand that deserve the world's attention.

The book is addressed to those interested in the policy, practice and research evidence on early childhood care and education. It attempts to provide a framework for international comparisons that may enhance the concepts developed within any one country while exposing people to the alternative realities and ways of approaching early childhood care and education apparent in different countries. Students of social policy, social science, psychology and education may all find something useful herein. We hope that this book will contribute to better quality early childcare and education provision and useful knowledge for all those who are involved.

2 Childcare in the United States

Characteristics and consequences

Virginia D. Allhusen, K. Alison Clarke-Stewart and Jennifer L. Miner

Over the past quarter-century, major shifts have taken place in the social demography of the United States. The Utopian view of the two-parent nuclear family living in the suburbs with father working nine to five while mother baked cookies and children played happily in a neatly manicured yard enclosed by a white picket fence has been replaced. Today, when there are cookies they are baked at midnight or bought at the grocery store (also, perhaps, at midnight); there may or may not be a father living at home, but, regardless, the mother is likely to have hung up her apron and found paid employment outside the home, either by choice or by economic necessity. In 1977, approximately 4.3 million American children under age six were cared for by someone other than their mothers for a significant portion of each week. A decade later, that figure had more than doubled to 8.8 million, and by the end of the next decade, 12.4 million children under the age of five were in childcare of some type (Smith, 2002). This figure represents more than half of all preschool-aged children in the United States, and while the climb in childcare use has tapered off, there is no evidence that it will decline any time soon.

In 1970, attendees at the White House Conference on Children voted childcare the most serious problem facing American families. Yet three decades later, despite childcare participation tripling, there is still no comprehensive national policy on childcare. At best, there is a patchwork quilt of programmes and services varying by state, stitched together with a mix of public and private funding, public and private delivery, and a variety of systems for monitoring and regulation. Backing this quilt are long-held cultural beliefs that the family is sacred, that rearing children is the sole responsibility of the family, that the long arm of government has no place in this inner sanctum, and, in addition, ambivalence about whether mommies should be in the workforce. Taken together, the result has been that government has sidestepped responsibility for childcare and, mostly, families have been left to deal with childcare on their own.

Patterns of childcare use in the United States

Two types of care dominate the childcare market: home-based care and center care. Most families with working mothers use some kind of home-based childcare arrangement, partly because many parents of young children prefer a home-like setting for childcare, and partly because center-based childcare is not widely available and is often among the most expensive forms of care. Infants and toddlers of working mothers are usually cared for by their father (20 per cent), another adult relative (28 per cent), or an unrelated adult in that person's home (18 per cent) or, less often, in the child's own home (6 per cent). For older children (three- and four-year-olds), there is a shift toward more formal types of childcare (centers, preschools or nursery schools). Thus, although one-tenth of children under the age of one year are being cared for in centers (Ehrle *et al.* 2001), close to two-thirds of four-year-olds are enrolled in this type of care (NCES, 2002). This pattern of childcare use in the United States has remained remarkably stable over the past 15 years.

The evolution of a childcare 'non-system'

The dramatic increase in the number of children in non-parental childcare over the past three decades has occurred in the absence of any comprehensive national system for increasing childcare, providing financial backing for families or facilities, or monitoring childcare quality. This is not to say, however, that the government has done nothing. From the time women first started to flood the workforce (in the 1960s), the federal government has been involved to varying degrees in financial support and quality regulation. This involvement has been piecemeal, with the country's more than 90 different childcare and early childhood education programmes being managed by 11 different federal agencies and 20 different offices (US General Accounting Office, 1995). Contributors in the private sector have to some extent filled the considerable gaps left in the federal government's attempts to cover American families' childcare needs, but gaping holes still exist, in both financial support and quality regulation.

Financing and provision of childcare

The federal government's role

A variety of childcare programmes were funded in the 1960s, administered by several different federal agencies. Over the course of the next four decades, support for these and later programmes ebbed and flowed, with a decline in funding during the mid-1980s followed by generosity in the mid-1990s. Federal financial support for childcare has taken three basic forms: direct provision of childcare for low-income families (most prominently Head Start), subsidies to help lower-income families pay for childcare, and tax benefits for middle- and higher-income families.

HEAD START

Perhaps the most prominent federal role in childcare has been the Head Start programme. Created in 1965, Head Start is a comprehensive support programme for low-income families. It includes education, health, nutrition and mental health services to children and their families. Historically, Head Start was only available to three- and four-year-old children and funding was available to serve only a small fraction of income-eligible children. Beginning in the mid-1990s, however, Head Start funding was markedly increased, reaching an annual budget of $6.7 billion in 2003 and serving about 60 per cent of eligible children. Additionally, with the emergence of the Early Head Start programme in 1995, there has been a marked increase in the number of children under three receiving Head Start services (Raikes and Love, 2002).

However, Head Start was never intended to provide childcare for the purpose of allowing mothers to work outside the home. On the contrary, one of the founding principles of Head Start was that parents would be intimately involved in the programme, with the hope that such involvement would give them a sense of empowerment. Moreover, few Head Start programmes offer full day care, which working parents usually require.

SUBSIDIES

A second means through which the federal government has provided childcare assistance to lower-income families is via government subsidy programmes. The earliest of these was Title XX (now known as the Social Services Block Grant), begun in 1974. Through this programme the federal government provides states with monies for a variety of human services, including childcare. The 1990s were somewhat of a boom for childcare funding. In 1990 the Childcare and Development Block Grant (CCDBG) was established to help families pay for childcare if they earned less than 75 per cent of their state's median income. In addition, this block grant allowed for a small portion to be set aside for childcare quality improvements. In 1996 the CCDBG was reauthorised and expanded by Congress under the Personal Responsibility and Work Opportunity Reconciliation Act. In an attempt to consolidate federal support for childcare services, several funding sources, including those offered for welfare recipients in job training programmes (Title IV-A JOBS Childcare Program), families who left public assistance for paid employment within the past year (Title IV-A Transitional Program), and families at risk of returning to public assistance (Title IV-A At-Risk Childcare Program) were merged. In 2001 the funds for the expanded CCDBG reached $4.6 billion (Office of Management and Budget, 2001).

TAX BENEFITS

Lower-income families are not the only group to receive federal assistance to pay for childcare. Middle- and upper-income families benefit from two tax credit programmes: the Dependent Care Tax Credit and the Dependent Care Assistance Plan. These two programmes combined represent the federal government's most generous investment in childcare, at approximately $3.5 billion annually (US House of Representatives, 1996). Under the Dependent Care Tax Credit, income-eligible working parents may claim a tax credit of up to $2,400 for one child or $4,800 for two or more children to offset childcare expenses. In 1997 an estimated 6.1 million families claimed this tax credit on income tax (US House of Representatives, 1998). The Dependent Care Assistance Plan allows working parents to deduct up to $5,000 from their gross annual income, thereby reducing their tax burden. Both of these programmes are immensely popular with middle- and upper-income working parents as they allow flexibility in choosing childcare; the childcare provider need not be licensed or registered in order to qualify for either plan.

Contributions from the private sector

Today, the bulk of childcare is sponsored and funded not by the public sector, but by the private sector: employers, charitable organisations, for-profit childcare providers and parents themselves.

EMPLOYERS

Historically, employers have been reluctant to invest in childcare primarily because there is no apparent incentive; they do not need to provide this benefit to attract female employees, and although surveys have indicated that employees would like employers to provide more childcare benefits, they are not demanding that they do so. Consequently, when employers do offer childcare benefits, they are usually modest. The most common benefit offered is access to childcare resources and information phone lines to help employees identify childcare options. A growing benefit offered by some medium- and large-size corporate employers is access to the Dependent Care Assistance Plans, which allows workers to take a tax deduction for childcare expenses. A less common childcare benefit offered to employees in medium and large companies (and only very rarely to those in small companies) is the provision of an on-site or off-site childcare facility for the children of employees. Only about 5 per cent of full-time employees in private industry have access to such a facility (US Bureau of Labor Statistics, 2004). While these types of benefits are not negligible for those employees who receive them, they do not increase the supply of affordable, high-quality childcare. Furthermore, the vast majority of Americans are employed by small businesses who mostly do not and cannot afford to offer these types of benefits to employees.

CHARITABLE ORGANISATIONS

Historically in the US the largest suppliers of childcare have been private, nonprofit providers – institutions and organisations such as the United Way, local churches, and a variety of philanthropic groups. The involvement of these organisations in childcare stems primarily from an interest in providing care for disadvantaged children or for members of a local organisation or church community. Over the last 30 years there has been a decline in the percentage of childcare being sponsored by nonprofit organisations, as the number of for-profit facilities has proliferated. From economic theory, this development is expected; the for-profit sector is sensitive to consumer demands, thus, as the demand for childcare rises, so does the availability of for-profit childcare. Nonprofit facilities, on the other hand, wax and wane depending on funding provided by individuals and charitable organisations, not in response to consumer need for childcare (Cost, Quality and Child Outcomes Study Team, 1995).

FOR-PROFIT CARE PROVIDERS

For better or worse, childcare in the United States is big business. Most childcare operates for profit, primarily in one of two forms: family childcare homes run by entrepreneurs wishing to make extra money at home and childcare centers. Yet even within this framework of trying to profit from the care of young children, it has been suggested that care providers both in centers and in family childcare homes are actually helping to share the cost of childcare in the US, by providing care for children at below-poverty wages and certainly well below the market rate for similar occupations (Cost, Quality and Child Outcomes Study Team, 1995; Galinsky *et al.* 1994).

Family childcare homes are the most numerous, cheapest, and most elastic of for-profit childcare arrangements. There is no need for construction of a facility, no need to set up a complex administrative structure. Childcare homes offer a range of opportunities for the provider, from the most informal and casual taking in of a few children in the neighbourhood to a thoroughly professional effort in a registered, licensed home that may even be part of a network of childcare homes affiliated with a school, university, or childcare center. Most childcare homes tend to be informal, unprofessional, and short-lived. On average, care providers charge about $58 per week for the care of one child (Smith, 2002). Thus family childcare is the cheapest form of childcare outside care by a relative, which is often free or very low cost.

More expensive to start up but also growing in popularity are for-profit centers. Most centers are single-site facilities, but recently, childcare franchises such as KinderCare Learning Centers have steadily increased in number. These franchises might be part of a local, regional or, in the case of KinderCare, national chain of childcare centers. The quality of care offered in all of these centers varies, just as it does in the other childcare arrangements; some for-profit centers offer high-quality care that is educational, individualised and stimulating, whereas others have been found to offer low- or mediocre-quality care. Notably, no differences in overall quality of care were found between for-profit and nonprofit centers in the Cost, Quality and Child Outcomes Study completed in 1995 (Cost, Quality and Child Outcomes Study Team, 1995), after the centers operating in the state with the least stringent standards were removed from the analyses. This study suggests that in states where childcare regulations ensure a baseline of quality, no differences are found between nonprofit and for-profit centers, because both types of center meet the standards set by the state. In states where the childcare standards are lower, however, differences may emerge because for-profit centers operate at the lowest level required in an effort to maximise profits, and nonprofit centers are more likely to exceed the state's requirements.

PARENTS THEMSELVES

In the United States, parents bear the brunt of childcare costs, in keeping with the American ideal of self-reliance. In 2003, parents' childcare expenses averaged $4,000 to $6,000 per year (Schulman, 2000), and childcare costs have been steadily rising in recent years. On average, childcare costs represent about 7 per cent of non-poor families' budgets (more for single parents), but 20 per cent of poor families' budgets (Smith, 2002).

Yet despite the fact that childcare represents such a substantial chunk of many families' budgets, financing childcare is not the only problem these parents face. Even if money were no object, families would still be faced with the enormous challenge of finding childcare of adequate quality.

Childcare quality regulation

At the dawn of the explosion in childcare, the federal government was not just involved in providing funding for childcare services, but also in setting standards for federally funded childcare programmes. At first, because childcare programmes required a state license to receive federal funds, states began to develop their own licensing standards. But by the late 1960s it was obvious that there were substantial differences among the states in their standards. Thus, in 1968 the Federal Interagency Day-care Requirements (FIDCR) were published, establishing requirements for childcare homes and centers. Developed by a well-respected child development expert, Edward Zigler, the FIDCR held the promise of establishing federal childcare guidelines. However, in their first incarnation the guidelines were too broad and nonspecific, making them impossible to enforce. In 1971, the FIDCR were rewritten to be more specific regarding staff training, safety, health, nutrition, educational and social services, parent involvement, adult–child ratios and group sizes. Unfortunately, the new guidelines were vetoed by President Nixon before they could be put into action.

For many years, the FIDCR continued to limp along. Compliance with FIDCR was never mandated, but non-compliance was, at least in principle, grounds for suspension or termination of any federal funding. In practice, however, such action was never taken. Facilities receiving federal dollars were supposed to be evaluated periodically, but no agent for evaluation was ever specified. By 1980 the FIDCR standards were eliminated entirely, a move fueled primarily by conservative American values that viewed mothers as chiefly responsible for childcare and a general fear of communalising child-rearing. Individual states thus inherited sole responsibility for regulating and monitoring childcare programmes, a situation that continues today despite occasional attempts by childcare interest groups and quality advocates to reintroduce national childcare quality standards.

After the FIDCR standards were eliminated, discrepancies between states increased. In a handful of states, childcare funding actually increased, but most states raised fees, cut back services, relaxed their standards for quality, made the standards apply to fewer institutions (e.g. not to church-sponsored or part-time centers), and enforced the standards less stringently and consistently. This led to an increase in the diversity of childcare – a goal of a market economy held dear by most Americans – but it also led to a decline in the quality of care available, particularly for children from low-income households.

Today, most childcare in the US is informal and unregulated. Care in the family's own home or by a relative is completely outside the purview or interest of any government agency; only childcare centers and some (but by no means all) childcare homes, depending on state requirements, are licensed or regulated.

Childcare centers

All states regulate childcare centers, but there is enormous variability in the standards set across states. Adult–child ratios for toddlers, for example, range from 1:3 in states with the most stringent requirement to 1:9 in states with the least stringent requirement (National Childcare Information Center, 2005). There is also wide variability in the educational and training requirements placed on care providers: in some states specific educational and training requirements are in place for caregivers, while in others there are no educational requirements at all for center-based teachers (National Childcare Information Center, 2003).

Childcare homes

Quality standards for childcare homes, like centers, vary a great deal from state to state. States allow anywhere from five to ten young children in a family childcare home with a single caregiver (LeMoine, 2003a). Similarly, there is a wide range of standards regarding caregivers' training and education. Only 16 states require pre-service training or orientation for family childcare providers. Most states require some ongoing annual training after a care provider is licensed, but again the amount of training required varies widely across states, from as little as four hours to as much as 20 hours annually (LeMoine, 2003b). It is likely that the range of quality found in these settings is enormous. To add to this worrisome picture, most home-based arrangements are small and informal; either they are considered exempt from their state's licensing requirements or they operate 'underground' without taking the necessary steps to become licensed. There is no way to know exactly, but estimates are that as much as 90 per cent of the family childcare used in the United States is unregulated (Clarke-Stewart and Allhusen, 2005). In the nine-state NICHD Study of Early Childcare, even among the childcare homes with at least two children unrelated to the care provider and in which the care provider was paid, 82 per cent were not licensed (Clarke-Stewart *et al.* 2002). The fact that family childcare is the most common form of care used by employed mothers for their children under age six years makes it all the more troubling that care in these settings is largely unregulated and of unknown quality.

Research on the effects of childcare on children's development

Practically since the beginning of the escalation of childcare use in the United States, researchers, policy-makers and parents have all wondered about the effects of childcare on children's development. Experts in and out of the field of child development have suggested that childcare is bad for children, especially for infants (Belsky, 1988; Gallagher, 1998). And judging by the somewhat dreary statistics on childcare in the United States, it would not be surprising if this were true. The concern that childcare may be harmful to children's development has been put to extensive empirical testing, not always with consistent results.

The earliest studies of the effects of childcare on children's development, conducted in the late 1960s and the 1970s, were motivated by a concern that childcare in and of itself might be harmful to children. Childcare was a new phenomenon to this generation of Americans, and people wondered whether children's development might be compromised if they spent time away from their mothers; after all, the very idea of young children being separated from their mothers ran contrary to the fundamental American ideal of young children being nurtured tenderly in their mothers' arms. As such, childcare was treated as a uniform entity;

most of these earliest studies were simple in design, merely asking whether any differences could be discerned in the cognitive or social-emotional development of children in childcare compared with those at home, without taking into account variations in the quality of either the childcare environments or the home environments. Perhaps not surprisingly, the results from these studies did not all converge on one simple answer; some investigators found negative effects associated with childcare participation, while others found no relation or even positive relations (Clarke-Stewart and Fein, 1983).

Beginning in the late 1970s, researchers began to recognise the fact that 'childcare' was anything but uniform; it took many different forms. Huge variations existed in the environments where care was offered, the relation of the caregiver to the child (from close relative to a professionally trained care provider), the size of the group (from one-to-one care to groups of 10 or more children), and, perhaps most importantly, the quality of care (from merely custodial to developmentally enriching). Thus evolved a second wave of childcare research, increased in sophistication to take into account these variations. A veritable explosion of childcare research occurred during the 1980s and 1990s, owing perhaps in part to the rapid increase in the number of American children being placed in non-maternal childcare through this period. Fueling this line of research, too, were the continued contradictory findings on the effects of childcare on children's development and the hints from some studies (e.g. Whitebook *et al.* 1990) and press reports that at least some, and maybe most, childcare available in the United States was of questionable quality at best and downright harmful to children at worst.

Variations in childcare quality and outcomes for children's development

As already noted, a massive body of research now exists on the variations in childcare environments in the United States and how the characteristics of these environments are related to children's development. Several different aspects of the caregiving environment appear to be related to children's development. They can be grouped into two main categories: structural features and process features. Structural features refer to the aspects of the childcare environment that can be regulated: adult–child ratios, group size, and caregiver education and training. Process features refer to qualitative aspects of the caregiving environment that are not subjected to regulation: the quality of care provided by the adults in the setting, the quality of the physical environment, and the curriculum of the programme.

Structural features

ADULT–CHILD RATIO AND GROUP SIZE

The ratio of adults to children and the total number of children in the group are the two indicators of childcare quality most likely to affect caregiver–child interaction (see Clarke-Stewart and Allhusen, 2005). Detrimental effects of low adult–child ratios and large class sizes on children's behaviour and development are indicated by associations in many studies. These studies have shown that with less favorable ratios and larger groups, caregivers interact less with the children, are less responsive and less affectionate, spend less time stimulating children cognitively or socially, provide fewer activities, and are more likely to be restrictive and negative. In turn, children who are cared for in large groups or with many children per adult are more likely to look apathetic, cry, act hostile, and are less likely to have secure attachment relationships with their caregivers or their mothers (Whitebook *et al.* 1990).

Results of some studies, however, suggest that while low adult–child ratios (especially one-to-one care) are best for ensuring the quality of infant care, by age three children seem to do best in childcare arrangements with small groups of children rather than in one-to-one types of care arrangements (Galinsky *et al.* 1994). Some researchers have failed to find a significant relation between ratios or group size and caregiving quality for preschoolers (Clarke-Stewart *et al.* 1994; Dunn, 1993), while others have found that ratios and group size are important determinants of caregiving quality even at these older ages (Cost, Quality and Child Outcomes Study Team, 1995; Howes, 1997; Howes *et al.* 1996).

Not only does a large group size or a high child–adult ratio decrease the chance that a child will receive individualised care and attention from the caregivers, it also increases the time that the child spends interacting with other children. Unlike the detrimental effect of diminished adult attention that occurs in large classes, the time a child spends interacting with another child or children in childcare is not necessarily negatively related to the child's development. It may be positively related to the child's level of play, especially if the other child is older: children have been observed to play more maturely with older children in childcare (Dunn *et al.* 1996). There is some suggestion that children in classes with a heterogeneous age mix behave more competently than those in homogeneous groups. In mixed-age preschool classes, children have been observed to participate in more frequent and complex interactions and are more verbal, cooperative, positive, persistent and flexible (Bailey *et al.* 1993).

CAREGIVER EDUCATION AND TRAINING

Many researchers have demonstrated a link between the education and/or training that a caregiver has received and her behaviour with the children in her care. With more training in child development, childcare providers are more knowledgeable, more involved and affectionate, provide more stimulating environments and are less authoritarian (Burchinal *et al.* 2002; Clarke-Stewart *et al.* 2002). In turn, children in the care of educated caregivers are more involved, cooperative, persistent, and learn more (Clarke-Stewart *et al.* 1994; Loeb *et al.* 2004).

Center caregivers with more training are more likely to rely on professional resources for information and to belong to professional childcare organisations; thus one way in which training may lead to high quality care is via the increased reliance of better trained caregivers on professional sources to improve their own performance (see Clarke-Stewart and Allhusen, 2005). Use of professional resources by family childcare providers has also been linked to better quality care: childcare home providers who consider themselves childcare professionals, read books on childcare or child development, attend meetings, and take classes in child development are more likely to engage and teach the children in their care and to provide a more stimulating physical environment. Caregivers who provide family childcare only because no better job is available, or as an informal agreement with friends, neighbours, or relatives are less interactive and stimulating and spend more time on housework (Galinsky *et al.* 1994).

Process features

QUALITY OF CAREGIVING

Not surprisingly, studies show quite consistently that caregivers' behaviour is related to children's behaviour and performance (see Clarke-Stewart and Allhusen, 2005; Vandell, 2004). Children whose caregivers talk to them more and provide intellectually stimulating experiences are advanced in their communication and language skills and score higher on intelligence tests. They play at more complex levels and have more advanced social skills. Children also do better when caregivers are more positive and responsive to their questions, are less critical and directive, and use positive rather than negative reinforcement. Additionally, children are more likely to develop secure relationships with their caregivers when the caregivers are sensitive and answer children's bids consistently and appropriately.

PHYSICAL ENVIRONMENT

The behaviour of both caregivers and children is better when the physical environment is stimulating, safe, and well-organised, when the classroom is divided into interest areas, and when varied, age-appropriate, and educational toys, materials, and equipment are available (see Clarke-Stewart and Allhusen, 2005). However, simply adding novel materials is not in and of itself sufficient for children's intellectual development; rather it is the combination of optimal caregiving in a physical setting of good quality that best promotes children's development (Holloway and Reichhart-Erickson, 1988).

CURRICULUM

Studies of childcare have also shown that children do better in more educationally oriented programmes (those with lessons, guided play sessions, story reading, direct teacher instruction). They spend more time in constructive and complex play with materials and peers and score higher on intelligence and achievement tests (see Clarke-Stewart and Allhusen, 2005). When children spend their time in the childcare center just playing around with other children, they experience less 'rich' play and are less competent in social and cognitive ways (Phillips *et al.* 1987). On the other hand, having too much structured activity also may predict less advanced social and cognitive development (Stipek *et al.* 1995; Stipek *et al.* 1998).

A *third wave of childcare research*

The research conducted on childcare in the United States converges on the fact that features such as adult–child ratios, group sizes, caregiver training and education, caregiving quality, physical setting, and curriculum all play important roles in determining the effects of childcare settings on children's development. Over the years researchers have become more and more sophisticated in their study methods, providing policy-makers and parents with a clearer picture of the state of childcare in the United States and the types of care that are most likely to support children's development. In recent years, however, childcare studies have been designed with even greater complexity and comprehensiveness. This third wave of childcare research is characterised by studies that strive to be more nationally representative, broader in scope, and/or contextual in design.

Three national surveys of childcare have been informative: the National Childcare Survey 1990 (Hofferth *et al.* 1991), the National Profile of Childcare Settings Study (Kisker *et al.* 1991), and the National Household Education Survey (Hofferth *et al.* 1998). The National Childcare Survey was a telephone survey of nearly 5,000 parents with children under the age of 13. It was designed to be nationally representative of the approximately 27 million households in the US (30 per cent of all US households) with children in that age group. Telephone interviewers gathered information on parents' childcare usage, cost of childcare, methods of selecting care arrangements, stability of care, satisfaction with their current care arrangements, and perceptions of childcare availability and policies. This study was coordinated with the National Profile of Childcare Settings Study, launched at about the same time, to provide complementary data gathered from hundreds of childcare providers on caregiver background and training, adult–child ratios, group size, etc. The National Household Education Survey, conducted in 1995, provided similar information regarding patterns of childcare use and features of childcare arrangements being used. This type of survey has been enormously useful in helping researchers and policy-makers learn about the types of childcare arrangements parents are actually using in the United States; until recently, very little was known about the most informal types of care arrangements (for example, care by a relative or neighbour, care by a nanny or sitter in the child's own home). This represented a serious gap in knowledge about childcare, given that a substantial proportion of all childcare being used in the United States falls into these categories of more informal arrangements.

Although the telephone survey studies provided valuable information about childcare use, they were limited in their ability to inform researchers about the *quality* of care provided in those settings. A second group of large-scale studies is useful in filling that void. Observational studies such as the National Childcare Staffing Study (Whitebook *et al.* 1990) and the Cost, Quality and Child Outcomes Study (Cost, Quality and Child Outcomes Study Team, 1995) have added to our knowledge about the quality of center-based childcare, and the Study of Children in Family Day-care and Relative Care (Galinsky *et al.* 1994) provided similar information about family childcare. Owing to their scope, these studies have proved quite useful in drawing attention to the troubling picture of the quality of childcare available in the United States today. The results of these studies have been released to great fanfare in the national media and have garnered a great deal of attention within the scientific community as well as in policy arenas. Even so, they are still somewhat limited in telling us about the full range of care being experienced by American youngsters. First, participants in these studies were drawn from only a few states. Because states vary widely in their childcare regulations, and childcare quality is closely linked to those regulations, it is likely that these studies fail to describe the full range of quality actually experienced by children across the country. Second, participants were recruited only after they were already enrolled in the childcare arrangement, thereby introducing the possibility that parents would select themselves into or out of the samples based on their perceptions of how good their care was. Finally, each of these studies had as a focus some particular question that required that researchers oversample in certain demographic niches. For example, in the Galinsky *et al.* study, children from ethnic minorities, low-income households, and unregulated family childcare homes were oversampled in order to examine the relations between these factors and observed childcare quality.

The most ambitious study undertaken to date is the NICHD Study of Early Childcare and Youth Development, sponsored by the National Institute of Child Health and Human Development (NICHD ECCRN, 2005a). This multi-site longitudinal study – still ongoing – is following over 1,200 children and their families from birth through age 16. Families reside in nine different states, representing the full range of childcare regulations across the country. Although not specifically recruited to be nationally representative, participant families come from a range of racial and ethnic groups and income levels. Families reside in geographically diverse regions of the nation, representing urban, rural, and suburban areas. One- and two-parent families are represented, and educational attainment of the parents ranges from less than a high school diploma to an advanced degree. Perhaps the single greatest unique contribution of this study, however, is the recruitment strategy. Families were recruited from hospital births; children were then observed in whatever childcare arrangements their parents chose for them, thus allowing researchers to observe the full range of care (from informal arrangements in the child's home with a relative or nanny to formal care in organised family childcare homes or centers). This study thus extends earlier studies of childcare in the United States.

The NICHD Study of Early Childcare and Youth Development was designed according to a broad ecological framework; children's social, cognitive, language, and physical development have been tracked over time and across settings that contain the child or influence the child's development. Assessing the child's family context as well as childcare experience allows researchers to control for the self-selection of childcare by parents. This was not possible in most earlier studies, so differences observed may be attributable to family factors rather than childcare factors alone. Results from this study are helping researchers to understand the combined, complementary, and cumulative effects of childcare and family factors in a more complete way. In the following sections we summarise some results of this landmark study.

Estimates of childcare quality

From a policy standpoint, perhaps one of the most important findings to come out of the NICHD study is an estimate of childcare quality in the United States. Observers visited study children in their non-maternal childcare settings when the children were 15, 24 and 36 months of age and rated the overall quality of care on a five-point scale (terrible, poor, fair, good, or excellent). Across the three ages, 11 per cent of all care observed was judged to be of poor quality; only 17 per cent of care arrangements were rated as excellent. Using data from the National Household Education Survey (Hofferth *et al.* 1998), the investigators extrapolated these findings and estimated the quality of care available in the entire country to be slightly worse than that observed in the NICHD study. Thus, although the percentages of high-quality care obtained in the NICHD study were actually better than those reported in other recent large-scale observational studies (e.g. Cost, Quality and Child Outcomes Study Team, 1995; Galinsky *et al.* 1994; Whitebook *et al.* 1990), it is still worrisome that about half of all preschool children with working mothers are apparently spending their days in childcare considered to be of only fair quality or worse.

Attachment security and quality of mother–child interactions

One of the earliest goals of childcare research was to determine whether extensive, repeated separations from the mother threatened the quality of the relationship that infants in childcare developed with their mothers. After dozens of studies producing conflicting results and much rancorous debate, researchers conducting the NICHD study attempted to settle the argument once and for all by carefully examining the quality of infant–mother attachments in conjunction with other child, family and childcare factors. As in previous research, the most powerful predictor of attachment security was maternal sensitivity. No relation was found between attachment security and childcare experience (quality, amount, age of entry into childcare, stability of care, or type of care); however, low maternal sensitivity *in combination with* poor-quality childcare, more than minimal amounts of care, or multiple care arrangements, was related to elevated rates of insecurity.

In a related line of research, the NICHD investigators examined the relation between childcare experience and the quality of mother–child interactions observed when children were six, 15, 24, and 36 months of age. After controlling for selection (income, mother's education), family (marital status, maternal depression, maternal separation anxiety) and child (temperament, gender) factors, it was found that children who spent more hours in care over the first three years were less positively engaged in interactions with their mothers, and their mothers were rated as less sensitive in those interactions. Among the children in childcare, those who were in higher-quality childcare had more sensitive mothers.

Behaviour problems

The issue of children's negative social behaviour (e.g. aggression, noncompliance) has also been of concern. Specifically, researchers have wondered if experience in childcare predisposes some children to be more aggressive, or whether such experience gives them an advantage by giving more opportunities to practise prosocial interaction skills with peers and adults outside the family. In the NICHD study, children's negative externalising behaviour – teasing, bullying, hitting, fighting, disobeying, talking back – was observed and rated by mothers, caregivers and teachers. After controlling for many possible confounds, including geographical location, child's gender and temperament, type and quality of childcare, parents' income and education, it was found that children who had spent more time in childcare with other children were more aggressive and unsociable in childcare when they were two years of age and had more externalising behaviour problems when they were four. When children spent more hours in care each week, from the time they were three months old to the age of four-and-a-half, they were more likely to destroy things, talk back, argue a lot, get in fights, have temper tantrums, and demand attention. And the differences did not disappear when the children left childcare: kindergarten and first-grade teachers also noted more aggressive and disobedient behaviour (NICHD ECCRN, 2005b).

Cognitive and language development

In contrast to the persistent speculation about whether childcare is harmful to children's social development (particularly whether it threatens the development of secure attachment relationships and/or predisposes children to be aggressive), few have suggested that childcare is detrimental to children's cognitive and language development. However, an important limitation of earlier work in this area is that the research was most often conducted in high-quality childcare centers (because they were the most readily accessible to researchers). Perhaps children's cognitive development would be impaired in lower quality centers. The focus of recent research has shifted to examine the relation between cognitive or language development and experience in childcare settings of varying quality. Once again, the NICHD study has been helpful in sorting out not just the contributions of childcare of varying quality, amounts, and types to children's cognitive and language development, but also their contributions over and above the contributions of the family. Researchers controlled for mother's vocabulary, quality of the home environment, observed maternal cognitive stimulation, family income and child's gender. They found that the overall quality of childcare, and particularly the amount of language stimulation provided in the care arrangement, were modestly but consistently related to children's performance on cognitive and language assessments at ages 15, 24, and 36 months. Cumulative experience in center-based care, in particular, was associated with better performance than was experienced in other types of care, after adjusting for the observed quality of the care arrangement.

Summary of NICHD findings to date

Across domains of child development studied thus far, a pattern appears to be emerging from the NICHD data. Family factors such as the mother's sensitivity, family income, and quality of the home environment have a stronger association with child outcomes than childcare factors (including the amount, type, stability, and quality of care). Furthermore, the predictive power of family factors remains even when children have extensive childcare experience (30 or more hours per week over the course of the first few years of their lives). However, childcare is also an important and potentially influential component of the child's life experiences. In particular, the quality of childcare arrangement is associated with cognitive outcomes and the quantity of childcare with behaviour problems – even after family differences and selection factors are controlled statistically. The most recent findings from the NICHD study suggest that higher-quality childcare continues to be linked to higher scores on standardised intelligence tests through third grade, but that relations between amount of time in care and problem behaviours decrease during the early school years (NICHD ECCRN, 2005b).

Conclusions

As we embark on a new century in the United States, we see that childcare and maternal employment are a mainstay of the American way of life, with no evidence of a reversal of this trend in sight. Players in the policy arena have been slow in responding, but within the past decade there appears to have been some acceptance of the fact that childcare is here to stay. Policy-makers have begun to play a more prominent role in assisting families with their childcare needs. Government is becoming more involved in childcare issues, for example, by increasing funding for provision of childcare to lower-income families and providing tax breaks for middle-income families. Industry, too, is beginning to respond to its workers' needs with employee benefits such as paid or unpaid parental leave, childcare resource and referral lines, flexible work schedules, and other such 'family-friendly' policies. A quick glance at the childcare policies and programmes of other industrialised nations, however, reveals that the United States still lags far behind its peers in supporting families' childcare needs. Noticeably absent in the United States is a national-level effort at assuring that the quality of childcare settings available to children and families is adequate – despite the fact that 30 years' worth of research on the effects of early childcare on children's development all converge on one clear fact: childcare quality matters for children's development. Researchers in the field of child development have repeatedly shown which kinds of childcare settings are supportive of children's development, as well as which are potentially detrimental; as an outgrowth of this body of research, standards have been developed to define thresholds of childcare quality that are believed to ensure adequate care (e.g. the National Association for the Education of Young Children Accreditation Standards for centers and for childcare homes). The challenge for policy-makers in the United States in this new century is to recognise that, just as so many other industries in this country are carefully regulated, the childcare industry should be subject to the same level of quality regulation. American children would be well served by such efforts.

References

Bailey, D.B., McWilliam, R.A., Ware, W.B. and Burchinal, M.A. (1993). Social interactions of toddlers and preschoolers in same-age and mixed-age play groups. *Journal of Applied Developmental Psychology, 14*, 261–276.

Belsky, J. (1988). The 'effects' of infant day care reconsidered. *Early Childhood Research Quarterly, 3,* 235–272.

Burchinal, M.R., Cryer, D., Clifford, R.M. and Howes, C. (2002). Caregiver training and classroom quality in childcare centers. *Applied Developmental Science, 6,* 2–11.

Clarke-Stewart, K.A. and Allhusen, V.D. (2005). *What we know about childcare.* Cambridge, MA: Harvard University Press.

Clarke-Stewart, K.A. and Fein, G. (1983). Early childhood programs. In P. Mussen, M. Haith and J. Campos (Eds), *Handbook of child psychology. Volume 2. Infancy and developmental psychobiology* (pp. 917–1000). New York: John Wiley.

Clarke-Stewart, K.A., Gruber, C.P. and Fitzgerald, L.M. (1994). *Children at home and in day care.* Hillsdale, NJ: Erlbaum.

Clarke-Stewart, K.A., Vandell, D.L., Burchinal, M., O'Brien, M. and McCartney, K. (2002). Do regulable features of childcare homes affect children's development? *Early Childhood Research Quarterly, 17,* 52–86.

Cost, Quality and Child Outcomes Study Team (1995). *Cost, quality and child outcomes in childcare centers.* Denver, CO: Department of Economics, University of Colorado.

Dunn, L. (1993). Proximal and distal features of day care quality and children's development. *Early Childhood Research Quarterly, 8,* 167–192.

Dunn, L., Kontos, S. and Potter, L. (1996). Mixed-age interactions in family childcare. *Early Education and Development, 4,* 349–366.

Ehrle, J., Adams, G. and Trout, K. (2001). *Who's caring for our youngest children? Childcare patterns of infants and toddlers.* Washington, DC: Urban Institute Press.

Galinsky, E., Howes, C., Kontos, S. and Shinn, M. (1994). *The study of children in family childcare and relative care: Highlights of findings.* New York: Families and Work Institute.

Gallagher, M. (1998). Day careless. *National Review,* January 26.

Hofferth, S.L., Brayfield, A., Deich, S. and Holcomb, P. (1991). *National Childcare Survey, 1990.* Washington, DC: The Urban Institute Press.

Hofferth, S.L., Shauman, K.A., Henke, R.R. and West, J. (1998). *Characteristics of children's early care and education programs: Data from the 1995 National Household Education Survey, National Center for Education Statistics, 98–128.* Washington, DC: U.S. Department of Education.

Holloway, S.D., and Reichhart-Erickson, M. (1988). The relationship of day care quality to children's free-play behaviour and social problem-solving skills. *Early Childhood Research Quarterly, 3,* 39–53.

Howes, C. (1997). Children's experiences in center-based childcare as a function of teacher background and adult:child ratio. *Merrill Palmer Quarterly, 43,* 404–425.

Howes, C., Galinsky, E., Shinn, M., Sibley, A. and McCarthy, J. (1996). *The Florida Childcare Quality Improvement Study: 1996 Report.* New York: Families and Work Institute.

Kisker, E.E., Hofferth, S.L., Phillips, D.A. and Farquhar, E. (1991). *A profile of childcare settings: Early education and care in 1990. Final report for US Department of Education, No. LC88090001.* Princeton, NJ: Mathematica.

LeMoine, S. (2003a, August). *Definition of licensed family childcare homes.* National Childcare Information Center (NCCIC). http://nccic.org/pubs/definition-fcc.html

LeMoine, S. (2003b, August). *Childcare licensing requirements: Minimum early childhood education (ECE) preservice qualifications, orientation/initial licensure, and annual ongoing training hours for family childcare providers.* National Childcare Information Center (NCCIC). http://nccic.org

Loeb, S., Fuller, B., Kagan, S.L. and Carrol, B. (2004). Childcare in poor communities: Early learning effects of type, quality, and stability. *Child Development, 75,* 47–65.

National Center for Educational Statistics (NCES) (2002). *Digest of Educational Statistics, 2001.* Washington, DC: US Department of Education.

National Childcare Information Center (2003, August). http://nccic.org.

National Childcare Information Center (2005). *Childcare center licensing regulations (April 2005): Child:staff ratios and maximum group size requirements.* http://nccic.org/pubs/cclicensingreg/ratios.pdf

NICHD Early Childcare Research Network (ECCRN) (2005a). *Childcare and child development: Results from the NICHD Study of Early Childcare and Youth Development.* New York, NY: Guilford.

NICHD Early Childcare Research Network (ECCRN) (2005b). Early childcare and children's development in the primary grades: Results from the NICHD Study of Early Childcare. *American Educational Research Journal, 43,* 537–570.

Office of Management and Budget (OMB) (2001). *Budget of the United States Government: Fiscal year 2002.* Washington, DC: US Government Printing Office.

Phillips, D.A., McCartney, K. and Scarr, S. (1987). Childcare quality and children's social development. *Developmental Psychology, 23,* 537–543.

Raikes, H.H. and Love, J.M. (2002). Early Head Start: A dynamic new program for infants and toddlers and their families. *Infant Mental Health Journal, 23,* 1–13.

Schulman, K. (2000). The high cost of childcare puts quality care out of reach for many families. *The Children's Defense Fund.* Washington, DC: www.childrensdefense.org

Smith, K. (2002). Who's minding the kids? Childcare arrangements: Spring 1997. *Current Population Reports: Household Economic Studies.* Washington, DC: US Department of Commerce (pp. 70–86).

Stipek, D., Feiler, R., Beyler, P., Ryan, R., Milburn, S. and Salmon, S. (1998). Good beginnings: What difference does the program make in preparing young children for school? *Journal of Applied Developmental Psychology, 19,* 41–66.

Stipek, D., Feiler, R., Daniels, D. and Milburn, S. (1995). Effects of different instructional approaches to young children's achievement and motivation. *Child Development, 66,* 209–223.

US Bureau of Labor Statistics (2004). *Employee benefits in private industry, 2003.* Washington, DC: Department of Labor (USDL–03–489).

US General Accounting Office (1995). *Early childhood programs: Multiple programs and overlapping target groups.* Washington, DC: Author (95–4FS).

US House of Representatives, Committee on Ways and Means (1996). *Overview of entitlement programs: The 1996 green book.* Washington, DC: Author.

US House of Representatives, Committee on Ways and Means (1998). *Overview of entitlement programs: The 1998 green book.* Washington, DC: Author.

Vandell, D.L. (2004). Early childcare: The known and the unknown. *Merrill-Palmer Quarterly, 50,* 387–414.

Whitebook, M., Howes, C. and Phillips, D.A. (1990). *Who cares? Childcare teachers and the quality of care in America. Final report: National Childcare Staffing Study.* Oakland, CA: Childcare Employee Project.

3 Policy and research on early childcare and education in Greece

Konstantinos Petrogiannis

Almost four decades ago, it would have been inconceivable for a Greek mother to leave her child in someone else's care. Her childcare needs would have been met by a close relative or neighbour, and together they would have formed a 'collaborative team' (Doumani, 1990). However, the dramatic socio-economic changes since the early 1950s and the sequential waves of urbanisation, particularly in Athens, have had a strong impact on family structure and traditional community life (Gizelis *et al.*, 1984; Moussourou, 1990, 1998).

It is broadly documented that southern European families interact more frequently and have a substantially greater sense of inter-generational obligation than families in the rest of Europe (Bozini-Antinach, 2002). Greece is a typical example since often grandparents move closer to their working children in order to contribute to the care of their grandchildren and minimise the financial strain experienced by new families (Georgouli *et al.*, 1993; Symeonidou, 1990). In this way, they form a type of extended family analogous to the traditional living conditions found in rural communities 40 years previously (Georgas, 1999). However, social changes are making it more difficult for relatives to provide direct support to parents with young children and therefore increasing the need for day care. This increasing need has also been fuelled by a number of other social trends: lone-parent families (mostly single mothers) now account for approximately 5.6 per cent of Greek households (Kogkidou, 2005); divorce rates are increasing, although Greece has one of the lowest rates among EU countries (Ditch *et al.*, 1996); and the size of Greek family units is in dramatic decline (Bagavos, 2005). The increased availability, and economic and social benefits, of day care services have proved important incentives for young couples (Sarikaki, 2001). However, the most significant social trend affecting a heightened demand for childcare provision is the increase in maternal employment.

Demographic changes in Greece

Greece, along with Spain, Italy and Malta, has one of the lowest female employment rates in the EU with only about 45.2 per cent of the female population aged 15–64 in work. Female unemployment rates in Greece (17 per cent for full-time work and 5 per cent for part-time employment) are some of the highest in the EU. Nevertheless, within Greece, the employment rates for women have significantly increased since 1988, and they will continue to increase as Greece competes with European levels of female participation in the workforce (Eurostat, 2005, 8 Sept.).

It should be noted, however, that Greek women's employment is affected by child-bearing as many mothers stop working after the birth of their first child (Symeonidou, 1989). The rigidity of the market (no part-time opportunities, no long-term maternity leave) in combination with the absence of retraining programmes for women who have been, for an extended period, out of the labour force whilst rearing children, makes it difficult for mothers to return to work. In addition, the perceived role of the mother is in flux, oscillating between aspects of collectivism and individualism. Current cultural pressures are moving Greek culture away from traditional forms of life that privilege the group over the individual and exhibit gender divisions between the public and private spheres, towards a more individualistic ideology. Whilst the Greek family is still the tight-knit 'southern (European) family model' (Bozini-Antinach, 2002) providing support for mothers in a way that acts as a counterweight to the state's very weak welfare provision or the expensive private childcare arrangements (Symeonidou, 1989; Bozini-Antinach, 2002), cultural changes continue to affect women's role and their employment patterns (Dragonas *et al.*, 1997).

However, as more women with young children go out to work, the capacity for family childcare diminishes. Employment rates for older women are also increasing with roughly 24 per cent of women aged 55–64 now in work (Eurostat, 2005, 12 April). It can no longer be assumed that relatives will continue to provide childcare to the same extent as they do now. Consequently, as the childcare provided by relatives decreases, childcare services, both public and private, will need to increase.

To summarise, demographic conditions, values and ideas have changed progressively over the last 20 years. The change from a collective to a more individualised lifestyle has meant new ideas, values, attitudes and needs have been developed. Young women are better educated and have started to compete with men in the labour market. An increasing demand for supplementary, non-familial, preschool childcare has developed because of these changes in lifestyle: the loosening of family ties, the distance between young parents and their family of origin, the increase in divorce and growing numbers of single-parent families, the diminished family size, the change in values, the intense urban migration (Bagavos, 2001) and the progressive change in educational policy. Supplementary day care services, whether formal or informal, part time or full time, are essential for the modern Greek mother.

Early care and education services

The variety of childcare arrangements in Greece is rather limited compared to other western European countries. Relatives, and grandparents in particular, remain by far the most commonly used form of alternative 'cheaper' care. If no relatives are available then there are two potential alternatives: 'babysitting' in the child's own home, or group care such as nurseries, kindergartens and preschools. Babysitting can be difficult and frustrating because it is temporary, changeable, expensive, and there are no officially approved or registered babysitters. Nurseries, kindergartens and preschools provide a more economic form of early childhood care and education and grow more popular every year. According to the most recent estimations 110,000 children aged between five months and five years – representing more than the 20 per cent of the population of this particular age group – attend one of the 3,000 nurseries (KEDKE-EETAA, 2005; Tsoulea and Kaitanidi, 2005). 'Other family care' is not thought to exist on any significant scale and there is no information on 'own home care' similar to that found in other European countries, such as childminders or family day care, au pairs, playgroups, or organised childcare etc.

The history of early care and education in Greece starts in the 1830s with the charitable formation of orphanages. Before 1995 early childhood care and education institutions went through five phases of development (Papathanassiou, 1997) and by 1996 we were in a sixth phase following the transfer of the former state nurseries to local authorities.

There are four kinds of early childhood care and education institutions that can be loosely divided into two categories: very early childcare for children from as young as two months; and care and education for slightly older children. The very early nurseries are: *vrephikos stathmos,* infants' nurseries for children aged two months (or seven months for the public sector nurseries) up to two-and-a-half years of age; and *vrephonipakos stathmos,* infants' and toddlers' nurseries for children aged two months up to compulsory school age (six years). Nursery care for children aged two-and-a-half upwards is provided by *pedikos stathmos* (kindergartens), which cater for children up to compulsory school age; and preschools called *Nipiagogeion,* for children of four years old up to compulsory school age. All these types of early education and care must be officially approved and registered with the appropriate authority.

Nipiagogeion (preschools) operate under the Ministry of Education typically for three-and-a-half hours a day (9am to 12:30pm) and are run by preschool teachers. They are the first (optional) level of the Greek education system, providing educational services based on the national curriculum. Preschools follow the same schedule as primary schools and parents are responsible for catering for their children. Private sector preschools are also registered with the Ministry of Education.

The two levels of *stathmos (vrephonipakos* and *pedikos),* have mixed educational personnel – nursery teachers, nursery assistants, preschool

teachers – and traditionally offer custodial care with some education services (based on national curriculum for preschools) for up to eight or nine
hours a day, five days a week. They are now officially under the supervision
of local authorities and governed by the Ministry of the Interior. Nurseries
that are not publicly funded must get official approval and be registered
with the local authorities. To be given approval, nurseries must fulfil certain
criteria, which are mainly focused on the structure and safety features of the
nursery facilities and staff. The adult–child ratio, for example, is defined as
one educator and one assistant to 25 children for the preschool classes
(*pedikos stathmos*), and either one educator and one assistant to eight
infants/toddlers, or two educators and one assistant to 12 infants/toddlers.
However, there has been no relevant Greek research to justify the criteria
and standards of the laws concerning space and safety. Within nurseries,
children are divided, in most cases, into mixed gender groups. The head
teacher has almost exclusively administrative tasks and duties.

These group-based types of childcare are provided by a variety of agents:
private, company or syndicate and municipal. There are approximately
1240 privately operated nurseries attended by approximately 60,000 children. The total cost of €3000–5500 per year (Tsoulea and Kaitanidi, 2005;
Kouklaki, 2003) is paid by parents with only a limited tax exemption.
Company- or syndicate-run nurseries (of which there are approximately
30–40) are set up in accordance with the law, which states that all companies, in both public and private sectors, with 300 or more employees, must
fund, establish and operate a day nursery for their employees within or near
to the company's workplace. From 1996 onwards, responsibility for state
nurseries has been transferred from the Ministry of Health and Welfare to
municipalities in an attempt to decentralise the administrative system and
engage local communities. Although the Ministry of the Interior publicly
subsidises these municipal nurseries, the subsidies only cover basic operational costs (Tsoulea and Kaitanidi, 2005). Today there are 1975 municipal
nurseries in the country (KEDKE-EETAA, 2005), and 78,000 healthy children aged eight months to six years are registered per year, selected
primarily on socio-economic criteria. There is extremely low provision for
handicapped children or children with other special needs and tuition fees
range between €550 and €1200 annually. With the increasing demand for
early childhood care and education, more municipal nurseries are needed
(Tsoulea and Kaitanidi, 2005).

Despite a number of changes that have taken place since the early 1990s
aimed at supporting families with very young children by facilitating
women's employment (Papadopoulos, 2002), childcare services have only
been minimally altered (Anagnostopoulou and Papaprokopiou, 1998). The
whole system appears to suffer from haphazard and poor regulation
(Foskolos, 2001; Stathakou, 1997). Both the government and local authorities attribute this poor regulation and inspection of childcare to an
absence of trained supervisory staff (Foskolos, 2001). This lack of

resources is indicative of the low priority given to early care and education in Greece.

The division between early childcare and education

There are considerable differences between nurseries and preschools with regard to: the content of the services offered to parents and children; the type of organisation and administration of the facility itself; the financing; the professional training of staff (Laloumi-Vidali, 1998); and managerial ideology.

Reviewing the regulations for nurseries since their official recognition in the 1930s, it could be argued that they reflect an ideology of custodial care aiming at ensuring the health and safety of young children, whereas preschools provide education.

Apart from the lack of state service organisation, there is also little government funding given to operate nurseries. The state overlooks the conditions prevailing in the country, which leads to policy choices not corresponding to the modern needs of the Greek urban family. For example, between 1941 and 1960 a number of state nurseries were established in areas with few preschool children with the aim of serving local political interests, despite the fact that, during that same period, tremendous urbanisation and a rise in female employment were producing childcare needs in other areas that were ignored (Papathanassiou, 1997; Papaprokopiou, 2003). In 1935 regulations were devised for nurseries that didn't change for 40 years. Even though the preschool national curriculum of 1977, and then 1988, tried to introduce a 'child-centred' programme for nurseries, public nurseries still tend to focus on care rather than education (Papaprokopiou, 2003; Papathanassiou, 1997), though there are notable exceptions in, for example, the municipality of Athens (Papaprokopiou, 2003).

Therefore, for a number of historic reasons, a division was created with two parallel structures: one for early childhood care (formerly under the Ministry of Health and Social Welfare and recently under local authorities); and one for early childhood education (under the Ministry of Education). The division of the two structures is made official by the government's decision to support preschools and phase out public (municipal) nurseries.

This 'split model' exists in other countries as well (David, 1993; Zambeta, 1998). However, whereas in many other countries the children's care/welfare institutions have had their remit expanded to encompass education, in Greece the original division of care and education remains, making it hard for services to implement early care and education centres.

Even following the new law of 2001, there remains:

> a question of whether local authorities have realised how important it is for the development of children that the new services do not perpetuate the split model but develop a multifunctional community institution if they want to develop quality targets in services for young children.
>
> (Laloumi-Vidali, 1998: 22)

Research evidence

As mentioned earlier, policy changes were not introduced on the basis of relevant research data. Governmental decisions usually rely upon intuition or the dominant political ideology and factors related to the effectiveness of the system are often ignored (Laloumi-Vidali, 1998). Research into the enduring ingredients of good-quality childcare environments (Textor, 1998) that nurture children's intellectual, social, emotional and physical development, though justified by the increasing demand for childcare, remains underdeveloped, receiving neither adequate encouragement nor support. The lack of information on the quality of childcare in Greece has been widely documented (e.g. Papathanassiou, 1997; Papaprokopiou, 2003; Petrogiannis, 1995, 2001; Mantziou, 2001; Municipality of Athens, 1998).

The few research studies that have been conducted converge on certain points despite different methodologies and time periods. The first report concerning the quality of day nurseries comes from the study of Tsiantis and his colleagues (1988, 1991) that was carried out to develop a global quality measure taking into account the intercultural features of a variety of day care systems. It has been demonstrated in Greece (Petrogiannis and Melhuish, 1996) that 'global quality measures' such as the Infant and Toddler Environment Rating Scale (ITERS) (Harms, Cryer and Clifford, 1989), the Early Childhood Environment Rating Scale (ECERS) (Harms and Clifford, 1980; Harms, Clifford and Cryer, 1998), the Assessment Profile for Early Childhood Programs (Abbott-Shim and Sibley, 1987) and the Childcare Facility Schedule (Dragonas *et al.*, 1995; WHO, 1990) are highly correlated, indicating that these measures assess similar aspects of day care environments.

Lambidi and Polemi-Todoulou (1992a, b) studied preschool children aged three to four-and-a-half years who attended day nurseries in Athens, to assess the quality of childcare in day nurseries using ECERS. Sixty day care centres of all types (state, municipal, private and syndicate-funded) were included in the study. These care centres were divided into three groups according to their size (fewer than 40, 41–80, and 80-plus children). There were significant differences between private, state and municipal nurseries, reflecting a particular ideological orientation for each one. Space, for example, is a serious problem for many private and public-sector nurseries and this is recognised by parents (AMDC, 2003) and staff (Tsakiri, 1999). The lack of appropriate buildings, especially in cities, contributes to this problem, but space also refers to the quality and layout of furniture and materials inside the building. According to Papaprokopiou (2003), who observed former state nurseries, the arrangement of furniture and materials reflects pedagogical views that aim to restrict child movement and maintain a 'quiet class'. This implies a systematic effort to control children's behaviour and restrict their natural curiosity. This pedagogic system is almost exclusively observed where the children are seated in chairs and the free choice of materials is limited. In another study, Papathanassiou (1997) observed that there was little relationship between the curriculum and actual nursery practice.

In the Lambidi and Polemi-Todoulou study (1992a, b), the private nurseries reflected a child-centred orientation, with younger caregivers, better caregiver-to-child ratios, and less concern for the personal and professional needs of caregivers, despite demanding a high standard of care provision. The state nurseries reflected an orientation towards the operational aspects of caregiving, with older head teachers and caregivers, lower caregiver-to-child ratios, but more concern for the professional needs of the staff. Management only expected staff to provide routine care with less play and other educational activities than at private nurseries. Finally, in the municipal-funded nurseries there was a balance between these two extremes, with more child-oriented activities, which were expressed through dramatisation and role-play, a sufficiency of play materials, and 'play-corners' in the classroom, as well as a greater interest in the professional and training needs of the staff.

The ECERS assessment of the 60 nurseries showed that nurseries gave more emphasis to those aspects of organisation related to routine care, cleanliness, safety – which is considered by parents to be very important (see also Kritikos, 2001) – and supervision. However, they gave less emphasis to educational activities, dramatisation and role-play, and the provision of play materials. They also seemed to take little interest in caregivers' professional needs, as they had no staffroom and no staff training. Group size and number of caregivers were important. Lambidi and Polemi-Todoulou (1992a, b) found that in the private nurseries the average group size was between 16 and 20 children. The municipal and syndicate nurseries had classes of either 16–20 children or 21–30 children. On the other hand, in more than half of the state nurseries there were classes with more than 30 children, and in around 65 per cent of state nurseries there were more than 40 children per class. Added to the fact that there were one to two caregivers in each class, the problems of the state nurseries, with overly large groups and poor adult–child ratios, become obvious. Other studies found similar patterns (Petrogiannis, 1995; Mantziou, 2001).

Lambidi and Polemi-Todoulou's study brought to light another problem in the state nurseries: an ageing staff. In the state nurseries, 30 per cent of the caregivers were 40–50 years old and 47 per cent were 31–39 years old. The younger caregivers were employed in the private and municipal nurseries. Eighty per cent of private nursery caregivers, and 88 per cent of municipal, nursery caregivers were under 30 years old. The authors listed three reasons: municipal nurseries were recently established and therefore have only recently employed staff; private nurseries have a policy that encourages a high turnover of staff; state nurseries follow the public sector pattern of providing employees with permanent, full-time contracts.

Overall, the Lambidi and Polemi-Todoulou study (1992a, b), observed a higher quality of care and education in the syndicate-funded and private nurseries. The state nurseries were of lower quality in terms of space, materials and educational programmes. They found that emphasis was given to the 'human factor' over and above the organisation of the physical environment. Routine care, cleanliness and supervision were characteristic priorities of state nurseries. Educational activities and the professional needs of the caregivers were considered to be secondary priorities. Such findings are consistent with the work of Tsiantis *et al.* (1988), and the later work of Mantziou (2001) in northern Greece, although with slightly higher overall scores in ECERS. Petrogiannis (1995) found an overall low quality of childcare in 25 centres in Athens. The highest quality score was given for social interaction, as found in the Lambidi and Polemi-Todoulou study (1992a, b). In addition, it was found that adult-to-child ratios and overall quality of childcare scores were associated, and that in lower quality centres, caregivers exhibited harsher and overly controlling discipline towards them. When a caregiver supervised fewer children, they were less likely to discipline them. Similar evidence was found by Mantziou (2001).

In contrast with childcare systems with an educational orientation (e.g. Britain; David, 1992), the Greek public nurseries emphasise routine care. Supervision alone, without the energetic and directive involvement of the staff in educational activities, is less demanding for the caregivers. For example, as Papaprokopiou (2003) has indicated, 'free time' and/or 'organised' activities were rarely properly organised. Interviews with nursery teachers revealed that nurseries were structured into routine activities, but that these activities were not organised. The teachers showed a lack of pedagogical thought and they made no effort to improve nursery conditions (Papaprokopiou, 2003). Papaprokopiou understood these findings as evidence of a generally controlling attitude towards children's behaviour. Similar findings were reported by Papathanassiou (1997). Teachers tended to blame nursery problems (such as low adult-to-child ratio and the grouping of children, regardless of their age, into one single class) on staff shortages, an argument made repeatedly over the years (Tsakiri, 1999).

Most important, however, is that the typical 'custodial care routine' does not allow for parent involvement. It is characteristic that the national curriculum of 1988 had limited references to the importance of the parental role (Papathanassiou, 1997). Indeed, the few studies of former state nurseries indicated that the presence of parents was very rare and restricted to special occasions (e.g. during Christmas or Easter) (Papaprokopiou, 2003; AMDC, 2003). According to Papaprokopiou, this means that nursery teachers are isolated in a way that helps neither parent nor child. In Papaprokopiou's study (2003), nursery teachers thought that parents were not interested in their child's care and education. Even though Tsakiri's study (1999) showed that parents were keen to cooperate with nurseries, their interest was mostly confined to questions about whether their child 'did eat or not in the nursery [...] nothing else' (Papaprokopiou, 2003). Other studies have revealed similar findings: parents collaborate with nursery staff only when it concerns the physical well-being of their child; they do not collaborate in, or question, their child's educational experiences. The Laloumi-Vidali (1998) study, concerning parents' perceptions and satisfaction with the early childhood services, had some interesting findings. Parents placed little importance on 'recreation' and 'collaboration with parents', confirming the earlier findings of Papaprokopiou (2003). Laloumi-Vidali's study (1998) showed that parents are most willing to collaborate with early childhood professionals about aspects of childhood care rather than education, even though it has been shown that parents expect preschool children to have access to combined early childhood care and education (Laloumi-Vidali, 1998; Tsakiri, 1999; Kritikos, 2001) reflecting a holistic, integrated approach to early childhood services. Parents support the role day nurseries play in children's socialisation and their 'mental development and social adaptation' (AMDC, 2003; Tsakiri, 1999; Laloumi-Vidali, 1998; Kritikos, 2001), but they continue to place little importance on the 'Relationships between preschool services and the local community' (Laloumi-Vidali, 1998). Though Laloumi-Vidali's study (1998), indicates an opposite conclusion, the low value parents give to the school's relationship with them and the local community implies that parents are unaware of their rights under the relevant laws (AMDC, 2003).

Ongoing in-service training is another area highlighted by Greek childcare research that can improve the quality of early childhood care and education. In Tsakiri's study (1999) both parents and teachers saw the training of staff as a high priority. The 'Synergie' project, implemented in a small number of nurseries within the municipality of Athens and in Pistoia, Italy (Anagnostopoulou and Papaprokopiou, 2003; Iozelli, 1998; Ntoliopoulou, 2000), showed that where ongoing training is supported by the local authority, both community links and professional standards improve.

Finally, an important area of research refers to the potential relationship between the quality of provided care and child outcomes. How the childcare environment relates to early development has been a topic of longstanding interest. In their attempts to understand the influence of day care on children's development, researchers have come to understand that the influence is enmeshed in a multiple of contextual layers that jointly conspire to produce particular child outcomes (Clarke-Stewart and Fein, 1983; Phillips and Howes, 1987).

When both day care and family characteristics are used to predict children's development, the combination explains more of the variance in a child's behaviour than either day care or family characteristics alone (Howes and Stewart, 1987). Following this line of thought, Petrogiannis (1995) conducted a study with 123 children, 60 with, and 63 without, nursery care experience. He focused on their individual characteristics and on structural, contextual and process aspects of both home and day care environments.

The findings suggested that there were consistent effects of both environments on language and partly on social-emotional development.

Home-cared children had higher cognitive and linguistic scores, but were more excitable when interacting with the female researcher, which is understandable given the wider social experience of the day care children. When considering only the group-cared children, it was found that the day care history of the child, the overall quality of the in-home environment, and the overall quality of the out-of-home environment, were correlated with aspects of cognitive and language development. How the mother understood and approached the maternal role was critical for their social development.

More recently, Mantziou (2001) studied the effects of nursery organisation, looking at the types of educational activities, and measuring the quality of early childcare by recording the way children ask questions, specifically 'identification', 'substantial/transformational', or 'routine' questions. The study was carried out in 17 day nurseries with a sample of 70 children between four-and-a-half and five-and-a-half years of age. The findings revealed that positive teaching behaviour and higher quality care provoke children into asking more 'substantial' questions. 'Substantial' questions require more advanced levels of thought, reflecting and enhancing children's autonomous learning. Children in lower quality care were more likely to ask 'identification' questions, which focus on a more superficial gathering and labelling of information and experience. According to Mantziou, the children in lower quality care asked a limited number of 'substantial' questions for a number of reasons: the 'climate' of the classroom did not promote interaction between the children; nursery teachers used an 'authoritative' style to control children's behaviour, a finding that agrees with earlier studies (Papaprokopiou, 2003); nursery teachers displayed a lack of the appropriate pedagogical knowledge and techniques needed to provoke different kinds of questions; and nursery teachers had low expectations of the children's questioning abilities.

Conclusions

In Greece, early childhood care and education is characterised, primarily, by a division between care and education services. This division, reflecting historical and socio-economic conditions, continues to affect the pedagogical practices of day nurseries and preschools, especially those in the public sector. Since the state has not taken a clear position on the form and content of early childhood care and education services, the state reinforces the ideological division between the 'education' of preschool children and the 'care' of infants and toddlers (Papaprokopiou, 2003). In this divided system, where parents and staff choose between education and care, young children are not experiencing equal preschool learning opportunities. Local communities used to have very little impact on early childhood care and education due to the centralisation of the administrative system. The new decentralisation will certainly enforce an awareness of the issue, although unless local communities directly address the problems of early childhood care and education the quality of services will not improve. With an introduction of care and education standards, a new education philosophy, adequate funding, and good relations between services, parents and local communities, the quality of state early childhood care and education services could be improved. Good quality nursery provision presupposes the involvement of parents as catalysts for child development. A partnership between parents and preschool provides children with an essential continuity of experience, and can allow the preschool to influence how effectively parents perform their role (Siraj-Blatchford, 1995). Preschool services in Greece will improve if local authorities can develop a model of preschool provision that identifies and assesses both the needs of children and the expectations of parents (Laloumi-Vidali, 1998). If new policy can be developed to identify and satisfy parental and children's needs, future problems related to parental pressures can be avoided. If preschool policy-makers do not correctly assess the needs, values and expectations of parents, there could be negative consequences for children (Laloumi-Vidali, 1998). The new conditions provide a unique opportunity for parents, professionals and local authorities to improve nursery provision, sharing the responsibilities and setting the right priorities. The research literature suggests that the establishment of clear aims, objectives and shared priorities is the major determinant of progress (Ball, 1994; Bertram and Pascal, 1995). While adequate funding provides the means of achieving targets, this is of little use without any consideration of the quality of provision.

Another area requiring further Greek research is the effect preschool experience has on children's development. Contemporary researchers recognise the necessity of taking into account not only the quality of the day care environment, but also the quality of the home environment, the individual characteristics of children, and the history of children's experience with day care, since family and day care environments have mutual influences on each other, and complementary influences on child development. The few Greek studies that have been conducted in this area indicate that further research is needed to determine the developmental consequences of children's experiences in Greek early childhood care and education institutions, both public and private. In order to provide for children's long-term optimal development, 'structural' changes to services are needed. All research to date into Greek early childhood care and education confirms a need for a radical re-evaluation of childcare policies and a commitment to continuing in-service teacher training.

'Good' nursery provision needs constant reassessment. Its definition varies with time and socio-cultural conditions. In an era of dramatic demographic and socio-political change across Europe, including the recognition of multicultural groups (Fthenakis, 1998), policy-makers, at either the national or local authority level, need to base changes in early childhood care and education on relevant, current research that indicates how service provision could work to optimise child development. The whole early childhood care and education system must be worked out in a systematic way, with clear targets. It must be adapted to current conditions in order to provide the right experiences, and match the needs, provision and outcomes for children.

References

Abbott-Shim, M. and Sibley, A. (1987). Assessment profile for early childhood programs: preschool, infant, and school age. Atlanta, GA: Quality Assist.

AMDC–Athens Municipality Developmental Corporation (2003). Study for the condition of Athens day nurseries – Analysis and conclusions. Unpublished technical report. Athens: Municipality of Athens.

Anagnostopoulou, E. and Papaprokopiou, A. (1998). Crisis in the welfare system and young children's quality of life in the preschool settings. In I. Konstantopoulou (Ed.), *Family – Europe – 21st Century: Prospects and Institutions*. Proceedings of the European Forum for Child and the Family. Athens: Foundation for Child and the Family/Nea Synora Livanis).

Anagnostopoulou, E. and Papaprokopiou, A. (2003). The planning of the 'Synergie' project. In EADAP (Ed.), *Towards a cooperative and participant training in preschool education* (pp. 59–66). Athens: Gutenberg.

Bagavos, C. (2001). The situation of families in Greece. Available at http://www.mmo.gr/pdf/library/Greece/gm_01_greece_bagavos.pdf.

Bagavos, C. (2005). Demographic dimensions of families and households changes in Greece – A first approach. In L. Moussourou and M. Stratigaki (Eds.), *Issues of family policy* (pp. 31–72). Athens: Gutenberg.

Ball, C. (1994). *Start Right: The importance of early learning.* London: RSA.

Bertram, T. and Pascal, C. (1995). Questions of quality. In P. Gammage and J. Meighan (Eds.), *Early childhood education: The way forward* (pp. 53–74). Derby: Education Now Books.

Bozini-Antinach, M. (2002). *Working women–mothers in southern Europe: Reconciling female roles in the turn of the twentieth century.* EUI–Florence. http://www.lse.ac.uk/collections/EPIC/documents/C2W2Bozini.pdf

Clarke-Stewart, K.A., and Fein, G.G. (1983). Early childhood programs. In P.H. Mussen (Ser. Ed.), M. Haith and J. Campos (Vol. Eds), *Handbook of child psychology* (v. 2, pp. 917–1000). New York: J. Wiley.

David, M.E. (Ed.) (1993). *Educational provision for our youngest children – European perspectives.* London: Paul Chapman.

David, T. (1992). What do parents in Belgium and Britain want their children to learn in the early years? Paper presented at the World Congress in Early Childhood Education, August, Arizona, USA.

Ditch, J., Barnes, H. and Bradshaw, J. (Eds) (1996). *Developments in national family policies, 1996. European Observatory on National Family Policies.* University of York–Social Policy Research Unit. York, England: University of York.

Doumani, M. (1990). Greek family: From the collective organisation to interpersonal relations. In S. Tsitoura (Ed.), *Care for the family* (pp. 11–15). Proceedings of the Hellenic Society of Social Psychiatry and Health Promotion Congress, Athens.

Dragonas, T., Petrogiannis, H. and Adam, H. (1997). Working women, their emotional wellbeing and pregnancy in Greece. *Journal of Reproductive and Infant Psychology, 15,* 239–256.

Dragonas, T., Tsiantis, J. and Lambidi, A. (1995) Assessing quality day care: the Childcare Facility Schedule. *International Journal of Behavioural Development, 18,* 557–568.

Eurostat, (2005, 12 April). News release 49.

Eurostat, (2005, 8 September). News release 112.

Foskolos, G. (2001). Day nurseries of insecurity. *Ethnos, 28,* September (p. 41).

Fthenakis, W.E. (1998). The socializing role of early childhood development and education in the 21st century. Paper presented at the European Policy Conference, Amsterdam.

Georgas, D. (1999). Psychological dimensions of the modern family. *The Greek Review of Social Research, 98–99,* 21–47.

Georgouli, I., Chandanos, D., Kondyli, E. and Chatzivarnava, M. (1993). Solidarity between the generations: Relations and support between older and younger members within the Greek family. Paper presented in the Panhellenic Conference of the EKKE 'Ageing and society', November, Athens.

Gizelis, G., Kaftantzoglou, R., Teperoglou, A. and Filias, V. (1984). *Tradition and modernity in the cultural activities of the Greek family: Changing patterns.* Athens: EKKE.

Harms, T. and Clifford, R.M. (1980). *Early Childhood Environment Rating Scale.* New York: Teachers College Press.

Harms, T., Cryer, D. and Clifford, R.M. (1989). *Infant/Toddler Environment Rating Scale.* New York: Teachers College Press.

Harms, T., Clifford, R.M. and Cryer, D. (1998). *Early Childhood Environmental Rating Scale – Revised.* New York: Teachers College Press.

Howes, C. and Stewart, P. (1987). Child's play with adults, toys, and peers: An examination of family and child-care influences. *Developmental Psychology, 23,* 423–430.

Iozelli, S. (1998). The responsibility of local authorities in the organisation of services for preschool children: Strategic and qualitative choices. The educational policy of Pistoia. In: Municipality of Athens (Ed.), *Local authorities and day nurseries – Reflections and prospects.* Proceedings of conference, 12–13 June, Athens.

KEDKE-EETAA (2005). Study of subsidies distribution of public child and infant day nurseries of the Local Authority Organizations. Unpublished technical report. Athens: YPESDA-KEDKE.

Kogkidou, D. (2005). Changes of family organisation – Single parent families: A challenge for family policy in Greece. In L. Moussourou and M. Stratigaki (Eds), *Issues of family policy* (pp. 123–160). Athens: Gutenberg.

Kouklaki, D. (2003). Preschools like colleges. *Ta Nea,* 4 September, p. 22.

Kritikos, G. (2001). Early childhood education – Children living with grandmother at home. *Ethnos,* 29 April, p. 31.

Laloumi-Vidali, E. (1998). Parental expectations of early childhood services for preschool children: The case of policy change in Greece. *International Journal of Early Years Education, 6(1),* 19–30.

Lambidi, A. and Polemi-Todoulou, M. (1992a) The preschool child: State institutions, settings and procedures of adjustment in the Modern Greek reality. *Psychologica Themata, 5(4),* 325–347.

Lambidi, A. and Polemi-Todoulou, M. (1992b) Social development of preschool children – Assessment in the day-care setting and the family. Paper presented at the Annual Conference of the Hellenic Psychological Association, Athens.

Mantziou, T. (2001). Children's questions, day nursery quality and mother's emotions. Unpublished doctoral dissertation. University of Athens/Department of Preschool Education.

Moussourou, L.M. (1990). *Urban family and social modernisation.* In S. Tsitoura (Ed.), *Care for the family* (pp. 2–22). Proceedings of the Hellenic Society of Social Psychiatry and Health Promotion Congress, Athens.

Moussourou, L.M. (1998). Europe in front of 21st century. Tendencies and developments that influence the family. In I. Konstantopoulou (Ed.), *Family – Europe – 21st century: Vision and institutions* (pp. 53–61). Proceedings of the European Forum for the Family. Athens: Nea Synora.

Municipality of Athens (Ed.) (1998). *Local authorities and day nurseries – Reflections and prospects.* Proceedings of conference, 12–13 June, Athens.

Ntoliopoulou, E. (2000). *Modern programs for preschool children.* Athens: Typothito.

Papadopoulos, T. (2002). *Family policy in Greece.* Technical report. University of York–Social Policy Research Unit. http://www.bath.ac.uk/~hsstp/TP-Publications/TP_Family_Policy_Greece_2002.pdf

Papaprokopiou, N. (2003). Public day care centres: Yesterday, today, tomorrow. In EADAP (Ed.), *Towards a cooperative and participant training in preschool education.* Athens: Gutenberg.

Papathanassiou, A. (1997). Programs and activities in the state day nurseries of the Ministry of Health and Welfare. Doctoral dissertation. Ioannina: University of Ioannina.

Petrogiannis, K. and Melhuish, E.C. (1996) Aspects of quality in Greek day care centres. *European Journal of Psychology of Education, 11,* 177–191.

Petrogiannis, K. (1995). Psychological development at 18 months of age as a function of childcare experience in Greece. Unpublished doctoral dissertation. Cardiff: University of Wales.

Petrogiannis, K. (2001). Day care experience and its effect on the psychological development of 18 months old children. In Petrogiannis and E.C. Melhuish (Eds), *Preschool age: Care – Education – Development* (pp. 349–393). Athens: Kastaniotis.

Phillips, D. and Howes, C. (1987). Indicators of quality in childcare: review of research. In D.A. Phillips (Ed.), *Quality in childcare: What does research tell us?* (pp. 1–20). Washington, DC: NAYEC.

Sarikaki, A. (2001). *Institutional reactions towards low fertility trends in Greece.* Proceedings of 'The Second Demographic Transition in Europe – Euroconference on Family and Fertility Change in Modern European Societies: Explorations and Explanations of Recent Developments', 23–28 June, Bad Herrenalb, Germany.

Siraj-Blatchford, I. (1995). Expanding combined nursery provision: Bridging the gap between care and education. In P. Gammage and J. Meighan (Eds), *Early childhood education: The way forward.* Nottingham: Education Now Books.

Stathakou, E. (1997). Day nurseries and ... Herod. *Apogevmatini,* 14 December (pp. 77–78).

Symeonidou, H. (1989). Life cycle events and women's employment. *Synchrona Themata, 40,* 61–70.

Symeonidou, H. (1990). *Fertility and employment of women in the greater Athens area.* National Centre for Social Research, Athens.

Textor, M.R. (1998) International perspectives on quality childcare. *Early Childhood Education Journal, 25,* 167–171.

Tsakiri, T. (1999). A survey of parental, teachers', and local authority's perception of nursery provision within a single district of Athens. Unpublished Masters thesis. London: Institute of Education.

Tsiantis, J., Caldwell, B., Dragonas, T., Jegede, R.O., Lambidi, A., Banaag, C. and Oakley, J. (1991) Development of a WHO Childcare Facility Schedule (CCFS): A pilot collaborative study. *Bulletin of the World Health Organisation, 69(1),* 51–57.

Tsiantis, J., Demenaga, N. and Lambidi, A. (1988) Preliminary observations from the evaluation of the WHO Childcare Facility Schedule in Athenian day-care centres. *Iatriki, 54,* 57–62.

Tsoulea, R. and Kaitanidi, M. (2005). Lottery to find a place in a day nursery. *Ta Nea,* June 13, p. 14.

World Health Organisation (WHO) (1990). *WHO Childcare Facility Schedule with user's manual.* Geneva: WHO Division of Mental Health.

Zambeta, E. (1998). *Early childhood education in Europe – A comparative approach.* Athens: Themelio.

4 Policy and research on preschool care and education in the UK

Edward Melhuish

The culture of a country both determines and is partly determined by its employment and childcare patterns. Today's patterns of employment and childcare have evolved from a complex series of antecedents and it is useful to have a historical perspective on how the UK has changed (see Melhuish and Moss, 1992). This chapter will provide such a perspective before considering the dramatic changes in policy post-1997, and also then provide a summary of research on childcare in the UK, some of which has influenced the policy changes that have occurred.

Historical perspective

The nineteenth century in Britain was an age of industrialisation. Briefly, Britain was the 'workshop of the world' and during this period there was a transfer of labour from agriculture to industries sited in towns. Industrialisation led to a dislocation of home and work and this dislocation had profound effects upon maternal employment and childcare.

The 1851 census records an employment rate of 24 per cent for married women. Thereafter it began to decline and was not reached again for another 100 years (with brief exceptions in World Wars I and II). By 1911 only 14 per cent of married women were employed. This decline in married women's employment was reflected in the Trades Union Congress of 1877 who adopted the aim 'to bring about a condition ... where wives should be in their proper sphere at home, instead of being dragged into competition against the great and strong men of this world' (cited in Thompson, 1988, p. 197).

Such opposition to married women's employment was rife. The Interdepartmental Committee on Physical Deterioration (1904) argued that 'employment of mothers in factories is attended by evil consequences to themselves and their children'. Given the climate of opinion it is no surprise that there was virtually no publicly funded day care. The main source of day care was relatives, and there were a few childminders, who were not well-regarded.

In the nineteenth century, childminding merges into the institution of the 'dame school', where women looked after children in their own homes.

There were around 3,000 dame schools in 1819 catering for 53,000 children, aged two to seven years (Whitbread, 1972). Dame schools existed mainly to care for children while parents were employed, and they declined as maternal employment declined.

The first day nursery opened in London in 1850, but as the fees were high, such establishments were not successful. Early in the twentieth century voluntary day nurseries started to appear and the National Society of Day Nurseries, founded in 1906, represented 30 nurseries. The First World War increased maternal employment and nearly 200 day nurseries were publicly funded by the Board of Education. After the war this boost proved temporary and in 1936 there were only 104 public day nurseries.

In the latter half of the nineteenth century there was a growth in schools and also in three- to five-year-olds attending them. Most primary schools admitted some three- and four-year-olds. This early schooling provided an alternative to dame schools and hastened the demise of the latter. The 1870 Education Act made schooling compulsory from the age of five, but gave parents the right to earlier education. By 1870 a quarter of three- and four-year-olds attended school, and this increased to 43 per cent by 1900. However, after 1901, education authorities were permitted to refuse admission to children under five, and by 1931 attendance for three- and four-year-olds was down to 13 per cent.

This under-five schooling was bleak, with huge classes, strict discipline and largely unqualified teachers. The alternative was to develop schooling suited to the needs of young children. The Board of Education (1908) argued the case for nursery education for working-class children, but with little success. Later the Hadow Report (Consultative Committee on Infant and Nursery Schools, 1933) proposed that whereas children under five should ideally be at home, nursery education should be provided if the mother worked or the home was unsatisfactory. There was some expansion of nursery education and in 1938 there were 118 nursery schools, but the outbreak of World War II halted further expansion.

Middle- and upper-class women in the nineteenth century were typically not employed. Yet they often delegated childcare to nannies. Gathorne-Hardy (1972) stated: 'by the end of the century [nineteenth] you were barely middle class if you did not have a nursemaid for your children'. The heyday of the nanny was 1850 to 1930, and at their height there may well have been 500,000 nannies (Gathorne-Hardy, 1972, p.181). Nannies were not to enable mothers to work, but rather to enable them to pursue 'interesting' activities.

During the Second World War, female employment and childcare expanded rapidly with state funding. By 1944 there were 1,559 day nurseries taking 71,500 children. After the war, circumstances changed, and a government circular of 1945 stated,

... in the interest of the health and development of the child no less than for the benefit of the mother, the proper place for the child under two is at home with his mother ... the right policy to pursue would be to positively discourage mothers of children under two from going to work.

(Tizard *et al.*, 1976, p. 73)

The same circular advocated nursery schools for two- to five-year-olds, and stated that special day nurseries should be,

supplements to meet the special needs of children whose mothers are constrained by individual circumstances to go to work or whose home conditions are in themselves unsatisfactory from the health point of view, or whose mothers are incapable for some good reason of undertaking the full care of their children.

(Ibid.)

Public day care places fell markedly from 71,500 in 1944 to 21,140 in 1969. Nursery education also had low priority, and in the late 1980s there was preschool education for around 25 per cent of three- to four-year-olds, almost all of it part time. This inadequate preschool provision stimulated the growth of playgroups for three- to four-year-olds. The first playgroups were parent-run but voluntary groups, and local authorities became involved so that by 1988 there were 17,000 playgroups for 400,000 children in England. Playgroups were typically part time and compensated for the lack of state preschool provision. Their short hours, often two-and-a-half hours per day, meant that employed mothers could only use them together with other childcare, such as childminders or relatives. Such low levels of childcare were associated with lower maternal employment for mothers of under-fives. In the 1980s around a quarter of mothers of under-fives worked and half of these worked less than 20 hours per week.

In the 1980s changes became perceptible. Demand for women in the workforce increased, and families' consumption patterns increasingly needed two incomes. By 1987 employment for mothers of under-fives increased to 35 per cent, and childcare appeared on the political agenda. Governments still regarded childcare as a private issue (except for children 'at risk'), but the increase in childcare use required some government response. This occurred in the 1989 Children Act that tightened up the regulation of childcare. Some of the guidance related to this legislation was influenced by government-funded research that had occurred in the 1980s, the London Day-care Project (Melhuish *et al.*, 1991). The lack of state provision yet with burgeoning demand for childcare led to expansion of private day nurseries, and to some extent of childminders and even nannies, who were now used by middle-class women to enable them to continue to pursue their careers. This expansion of private childcare continued through the 1990s.

Throughout the twentieth century, British childcare for under-fives reflected a split between care and education. Day care for under-fives was the responsibility of the Department of Health and preschool education for three- to five-year-olds was the responsibility of the Department of Education. State involvement was limited to nursery schools and classes, providing for around 18 per cent of three- and four-year-olds (concentrated in disadvantaged areas), and day care for a few children from 'at risk' home backgrounds in local authority day nurseries. Overwhelmingly, childcare and preschool education were provided by the private and voluntary sectors, with parents bearing the cost. Also a large proportion of provision was part time. The patchwork system of provision persisting into the 1990s reflected the ideology that childcare is a private issue and the state should not play a role except in exceptional circumstances.

1997 onwards

Maternal employment

By international standards the rate of female employment in the UK currently is relatively high. It has increased from 56 per cent in 1971 to around 73 per cent today, with a closing of the gap between female and male employment to around 13 per cent difference (OECD, 2005). Only Canada, Austria, Switzerland, the Scandinavian countries and Iceland have higher employment rates among women aged between 25 and 54. However, women are much more likely to work part time. While only 10 per cent of men work part time, the figure for employed women is 44 per cent. Women have also been increasing their participation in managerial and professional jobs from 25 per cent to 33 per cent over the past 10 years.

Maternal employment has also been increasing steadily. In 1981 only 24 per cent of women returned to employment within a year of childbirth. By the early twenty-first century this proportion had increased to 67 per cent. Much of this employment is part time and part-time employment is linked to number of children. For employed women aged 25 to 54 without children only 24 per cent work part time. This increases to 47 per cent for women with one child and 63 per cent for women with two or more children. The OECD (2002) report shows how the link between part-time employment and motherhood is much stronger in the UK than other OECD countries.

In parallel with changes in female and maternal employment there has been increasing polarisation of employment, with a growth in 'work-rich' households where all adults work mirroring a rise in 'work-poor' households where no one works. Single breadwinner households have fallen substantially. There has been a parallel increase in lone-parent families with an increase in the proportion of children in lone-parent households from 8 per cent in 1972 to around 23 per cent in 2002. Worklessness is higher among lone-parent families and the rise in lone parenthood has been a significant factor behind the increasing number of children living in poverty since the 1970s, and growing up in poverty is linked to poorer child development with consequences lasting into adulthood. Work is the best route out of poverty, and childcare can remove barriers to work, which may help families break out of the cycle of poverty and worklessness thus supporting social mobility and equality of opportunity. New Labour has taken these messages to heart and its initiatives encourage mothers, including lone mothers, into work (Driver and Martell, 2002).

Early years policy

In 1997 a Labour government took office with a markedly different agenda from preceding governments. It was committed to evidence-based policy, and an example of legislation being influenced by research is the expansion of preschool education. In 2004, the government made a publicly funded, part-time preschool place a statutory right for all three- and four-year-old children. The government's papers make clear reference to the convincing evidence provided by the Effective Provision of Preschool Education (EPPE) project (described later) in influencing this policy. The New Labour government also had a strong commitment to equal opportunity issues including women's rights. Hence parental leave and childcare provision became increasingly central in the political agenda so that women's employment disadvantages would be reduced.

The New Labour commitment to the early years is indicated by rises in expenditure on the early years from around £2 billion in 1997–8 to almost £3.7 billion five years later (National Audit Office, 2004). This commitment is encapsulated in a Ten Year Childcare Strategy (HM Treasury, 2004), which draws together previously separate strands of policy, and was driven by three central principles:

1   The importance of ensuring every child has the best possible start in life;
2   The need to ensure that parents, particularly mothers, can work and progress their careers;
3   The legitimate expectations of families to control the choices they make in balancing work and family life.

In line with its commitment to eradicate child poverty, the UK government set a target of a 70 per cent lone parent employment rate by 2010, with some progress occurring. Between 1997 and 2004, the lone parent employment rate increased by 8 per cent to 54 per cent – the highest rate on record. Many workless lone parents find it difficult to return to employment, and childcare is an important facilitating factor.

Ensuring low-earning parents can access childcare and engage in employment is critical in breaking cycles of poverty and promoting social mobility. There is a case for subsidising childcare costs for parents with low earnings to support parental employment, which may lead to improved outcomes for disadvantaged children. In addition, good quality early years provision can have long-term benefits to children and help redress the impact of growing up in poverty. Hence children from disadvantaged backgrounds should have access to good quality childcare.

Statutory force to deliver the key commitments in the Ten Year Childcare Strategy was initiated with the Childcare Bill (2005), which provides for:

- A new duty on local authorities to improve the outcomes of all children under five, and close the gaps between groups with the poorest outcomes and the rest, by ensuring early years services are integrated and accessible;
- A new duty on local authorities to secure sufficient childcare to ensure it meets the needs of their local communities, in particular those on low incomes and with disabled children;
- An extended duty on local authorities to ensure people have access to the full range of information they may need as parents;
- The introduction of the Early Years Foundation Stage to support the delivery of quality integrated education and care for children from birth to age five;
- A reformed regulatory framework for early years and childcare to reduce bureaucracy and raise quality.

The Childcare Bill is a landmark in that as well as laying the foundation for childcare provision it is the first legislation to acknowledge a responsibility to reduce social inequality. This latter point illustrates how the issues of improving childcare and reducing social exclusion are interwoven in much government thinking.

Childcare places

Changes in maternal employment, particularly since the 1980s, resulted in increased demand for childcare and an expansion in private day nurseries. Currently, over 200,000 children under three years old attend a day nursery. The National Childcare Strategy was launched in 1998 in England to increase the number of affordable, good quality childcare places. In total the government has created 1.2 million childcare places since 1997 (an increase of 525,000), in a wide range of settings including in nurseries, with childminders and in before- and after-school clubs. Many new places are in disadvantaged areas where often there was little or no childcare in the past.

The Neighbourhood Nursery Initiative was introduced in 2000 to expand childcare provision in the 20 per cent most disadvantaged areas in England. The intention was to reduce child poverty through increasing childcare so parents could return to training or employment. Places were provided through new nurseries or additional openings at existing nurseries.

By 2004, 1,279 Neighbourhood Nurseries were open, providing over 45,000 new childcare places in disadvantaged areas.

In 2004 the government introduced free part-time (12.5 hours a week) early years education for all three- and four-year-olds, which is used by almost all parents. Children aged three and four are entitled to five 2.5-hour sessions of early education per week for 33 weeks per year. In practice, children who take up a place in school receive a free entitlement equivalent to 38 weeks a year and four-year-olds in school reception classes receive free full-time education. From 2006, for three- and four-year-olds the free entitlement to 12.5 hours a week of early education will be extended to 38 weeks for all. From 2007, this free entitlement will extend to 15 hours a week, with a goal of 20 hours a week for 38 weeks by 2020. There will be flexibility to use the free entitlement across a minimum of three days.

Research indicating long-term beneficial effects for early childhood programmes for disadvantaged children impressed the government and Sure Start Local Programmes (SSLPs) were set up to reduce child poverty and social exclusion (Glass, 1999). The first SSLPs began in 1999, with 260 SSLPs underway by 2001, and a total of 524 SSLPs existing by 2004. They were targeted on families with children from 0–4 years of age in the 20 per cent most deprived communities. Their foundation recognised that disadvantaged children are at risk for compromised development and this has profound consequences for the children, their families and communities, and for society at large. Thus, SSLPs aim not only to enhance well-being during the early years but, thereby, to increase the chances that children will enter school ready to learn, be academically successful in school, socially successful in their communities and occupationally successful when adults. Indeed, by improving early in life the developmental trajectories of children known to be at risk of compromised development, SSLPs aim to break the intergenerational transmission of poverty, school failure and social exclusion. However, the local autonomy of SSLPs resulted in great variation between them in the range, quantity and quality of services provided. Some would provide substantial childcare and others very little. An evaluation of the impact of SSLPs on children and families indicates mixed results (see NESS Research Team, 2005a, b).

Changes are underway. The 524 SSLPs will become Children's Centres by the end of 2006 and come under local authority control. In addition, many nurseries in the Neighbourhood Nurseries Initiative will become Children's Centres and additional Children's Centres will also be established, with a target of 3,500 by 2010, with a Children's Centre in every community.

Children's Centres are one-stop shops joining up services for young children and their families, including childcare integrated with early learning. Children's Centres should provide seamless holistic integrated services and information, with access to teams of professionals. Children's Centres will link all childcare and provide help to parents with childcare needs.

Children's Centres should build on the lessons learnt from Sure Start Local Programmes in being community-based, responsive to local needs and tackling early disadvantage. Many Children's Centres will offer some childcare and where they do not, staff will help parents access other childcare. Centres will also help parents access other services including:

- Early education and childcare, in group settings, with childminders, or at home;
- Parenting and family support;
- Health advice, including health visiting and midwifery;
- Preventative services for children with additional needs early in a child's life, including outreach into communities;
- Support for parents to move into work and training.

While there should be a Children's Centre in every community by 2010, the full range of services, in particular early years care and education, will only be mandatory in the 30 per cent most deprived communities. For the other 70 per cent of communities Children's Centres need only provide information to parents. With Children's Centres under local authority control, a local authority may decide to exceed their legal duty and provide early years care and education in communities outside the 30 per cent most deprived. The Childcare Bill (2005) does place a duty on local authorities to secure sufficient childcare to meet the needs of working parents. Local authorities may provide childcare themselves or in partnership with private and voluntary providers, schools and Children's Centres, with the aim of ensuring access for all to high-quality childcare.

Childcare for school-aged children

It is planned to enhance childcare provision for five- to 14-year-olds through extended schools. The law has been changed to allow schools to set up community facilities. Extended schools may provide services themselves or in partnership with the private and voluntary sectors. By 2010 all parents with children aged five to 11 will be offered affordable school-based childcare on weekdays, 8am to 6pm, all year round, and all secondary schools will open on weekdays from 8am to 6pm, all year round, offering activities such as music and sport.

Financial support to parents for childcare

The UK government has reformed financial support for families since 1997. Underlying state support follows the principle of progressive universalism – support for all but more help for those who need it most. Childcare subsidies occur on both the supply side and the demand side. On the supply side, payments are made direct to the childcare provider. On the demand side, payments are made to parents to help with the cost of childcare, with payments greatest for those with lower incomes.

Help towards childcare costs was originally introduced in 1994, and was improved with Working Families' Tax Credit in 1999 and from 2003 further help was available under the Working Tax Credit (WTC) scheme. Help is available to parents working at least 16 hours a week; in a two-parent family both must work at least 16 hours a week. In 2005 the contribution towards childcare costs was a maximum of 70 per cent of costs for parents on low incomes, up to £175 per week for one child and up to £300 per week for two or more children, depending on household income. In 2006 the maximum proportion of costs covered increased from 70 per cent to 80 per cent.

Tax credits vary with number of children, childcare costs and household circumstances. For parents with two children, working at least 30 hours a week and with childcare costs at the limit, their tax credits award would taper away to zero at a household income of around £55,000.

Lone parents may receive additional help with childcare costs under the New Deal for Lone Parents. Measures have also been introduced to increase employer support for childcare, both to stimulate supply and to increase affordability for employees. From April 2005, employers may offer up to £50 per week of support for childcare costs free of tax and National Insurance contributions.

Parental leave

Paid maternity leave has been extended from 18 to 26 weeks, with the right to a further 26 weeks of unpaid leave. In 2005 the level of Statutory Maternity Pay (SMP) and Maternity Allowance (MA) increased to £106 per week, with SMP paid at 90 per cent of earnings for the first six weeks. Paid paternity leave was introduced in 2003, with fathers eligible for two weeks' part-paid leave after their child's birth. These changes build on 13 weeks of unpaid parental leave introduced in 1999 for parents of children up to age six. In addition to these pay and leave entitlements, from 2003 parents acquired rights to request flexible working arrangements. Employers are obliged to consider these requests seriously, and must provide good business reasons if they turn them down. In the year following its introduction, almost a quarter of parents with children under six requested to work flexibly. One million asked and almost 800,000 requests to work flexibly were accepted by employers fully or partly.

Paid maternity leave allows most mothers to take six months off work. The right to 26 weeks' additional maternity leave allows mothers to retain the right to return to work for longer, but since there is no maternity pay for these six months it may not provide a real choice for those without other income, for example a partner in work, employer support or savings. Thus many mothers feel forced to return to work for financial reasons before they want to. Also fathers want to play a greater role in caring for their children. The constraints of work often mean that they have to work through their child's infancy. The introduction of paternity leave from 2003 gives fathers the option of taking two weeks' paid leave when their child is born.

Quality of childcare

The government has responded to research evidence showing that the quality of childcare is variable, and that this can undermine parents' confidence, and at its worst can have harmful impacts on children's development. Turnover of childcare providers is high, which has an impact on quality. In 2004, 17.7 per cent of childcare providers closed during the year.

In its Ten Year Childcare Strategy (HM Treasury, 2004) the government recognised three levers that can help improve the quality of childcare provision:

- robust regulation and inspection to enforce standards and inform parental choice;
- a high quality workforce;
- informed parental choice about services, and input into service delivery.

The ten-year strategy aims to improve the effectiveness of these levers in delivering higher quality. Quality can be improved through regulation and improving the childcare workforce.

Regulation

Regulation of childcare ensures minimum quality standards. In 2001 responsibility for regulation and inspection was transferred from local authorities to the Office for Standards in Education (Ofsted). National standards and a national registration authority resulted in a more consistent approach to childcare regulation.

Since 2003 Ofsted has been linking the inspections of childcare providers with the inspection of nursery education, a function it has had since 1998. The Childcare Bill (2005) provides for a more integrated early years inspection framework. Under this framework Ofsted plans to end prior notification of inspection, and will publish all early years education and childcare inspection reports on its website, including those on childminders. More information on quality will help parents make informed decisions and give greater confidence in the providers chosen.

Evidence from Ofsted indicates almost all childcare is at least satisfactory, with more than half of nurseries and playgroups providing good quality care. Most providers of free part-time early education for three- to four-year-olds are ranked as good, and nearly a third as very good.

Childcare workforce

The childcare workforce ranges from poorly paid unqualified staff to qualified teachers. Lower-qualified and lower-paid staff are concentrated in private and voluntary settings, which have higher staff turnover and recruitment difficulties. In day nurseries 30 per cent of staff are unqualified and turnover is around 20 per cent per annum.

The government is committed to reform the childcare workforce. The aim is to:

- Ensure that full day care settings are led by graduate-qualified early years professionals;
- Improve the qualifications and status of early years and childcare workers. More will be trained to degree level. There will be a single qualifications framework and greater opportunities for workers to increase their skills. The role of the early years professional will be strengthened and home-based care will become more integrated with group provision;
- Provide training opportunities for childminders and other home-based carers that enable more to improve qualifications;
- Work in partnership with other providers and develop long-term careers as part of the children's workforce.

With regard to the latter, there are two models for early years professionals under consideration:

1 An early years teaching qualification – training routes are established, with teachers taking undergraduate and postgraduate routes to qualified teacher status, and some employment-based routes also exist.
2 A new profession combining learning with care, along the lines of the Danish 'pedagogue' model. This has no tradition in the UK, and work would be necessary to establish new training. However, the opportunity would exist to develop this model to suit the early years framework, and give 'pedagogues' the flexibility to exist alongside teachers in schools.

Research evidence

Early years provision in the UK as elsewhere is split between childcare for the under-threes and preschool provision, often with more educational input for children age three years upwards. Research reflects this dichotomy.

Research on childcare from 0–3 years

Early research was oriented towards possible detrimental effects of child-care and was influenced by Bowlby (1951), who stressed the possible harm of repeated separations from the mother during infancy. An example is Moore (1975) who studied children who had experienced day care in the 1950s. He compared a day care group with a 'no day care' group. For boys only there were significant differences indicating worse literacy at age seven associated with infant day care. At adolescence there were effects for behaviour with greater aggressive non-conformity, excitability and less timidity being shown by the boys in the day care group.

Several studies focused on childminders, the second most common form of day care after relatives. Mayall and Petrie (1977) and Bryant *et al.* (1980) both reported more responsive interactions between mothers and two- to three-year-olds than between childminders and the same children. Mayall and Petrie also claimed that childminded children were below age norms for language development, but as there was no comparison group their conclusion of poor language development associated with childminding was unjustified. Raven (1981) tested this idea more thoroughly with matched childminder and comparison groups and found no differences in language development.

Cohort studies

The UK has a tradition of longitudinal cohort studies that follow thousands of children from birth. Data from such studies have been used to investigate the effects of early maternal employment and childcare upon children's development. Gregg *et al.*, (2005) analyse data from a cohort of children born in 1991–2 in Bristol. They find evidence that full-time maternal employment in the first 18 months of life was associated with small adverse effects upon educational attainment and literacy at seven years of age, after controlling for demographic factors. There was some suggestion that the effects may be stronger where childcare is provided by unpaid friends or relatives, rather than by paid childcare. Part-time employment had no adverse effects. Similar results related to adverse effects of early maternal employment have been found by Joshi and Verropoulu (2000) from earlier cohort studies, and Ermisch and Francesconi (2001) found evidence that such effects upon educational attainment may persist up to 18 years of age.

London Day-care Project

This study (Melhuish, 1991) was the most comprehensive UK study of early childcare up to 2000. It investigated the impact of employment and childcare decisions on 255 women and children in dual-earner households having their first child. There were four sub-groups. Three sub-groups consisted of women who intended to return to full-time employment after maternity leave and use a relative, childminder or day nursery for childcare. The fourth sub-group consisted of women not returning to employment.

Observations of mother–infant interaction when the child was five months of age, before childcare commenced, revealed an intriguing difference related to mothers' employment decisions. Where the mother would not return to employment there was more mother–child interaction with boys than girls: this did not occur amongst other women. Possibly women not returning to employment differentiated between boys and girls more than women who returned to employment, and may reflect different views on gender roles (Melhuish *et al.,* 1991).

At 18 months of age, Melhuish *et al.* (1990a) observed children's experiences in the home; with a relative or childminder; and in nursery; and differences emerged in behaviour and interactions between childcare environments. Communications were most frequent in the home, followed by care by relative, then childminder, with least in nurseries. Responsiveness and affection followed a similar pattern. Observations when the children were three years old revealed similar differences between the home, relative, childminder and nursery environments in the amount and quality of interaction experienced by the child.

Did differences in quality between childcare environments have an impact upon children's development? There were differences in language development associated with different types of childcare. The nursery group had lower language development at 18 months of age (Melhuish *et al.,* 1990b), and these results were due to differences in communications and responsiveness between settings. Also, unstable care was associated with poorer communication and responsiveness. These results are consistent with the explanation that the quality of childcare has effects, and that the effects seem to be strongest on language development. Different aspects of development are sensitive to environmental influence at different ages and are most sensitive when at their most rapid rate of development. At 18 months of age, word combinations are starting to be acquired and there is rapid development of language. Hence language development is particularly susceptible to environmental influence at this age. At another age another aspect of development may become susceptible to environmental influences such as childcare experience. These effects of the quality of childcare upon language development, observed as early as 18 months of age, were persistent in the longitudinal follow-up of these children at three and six years of age (Melhuish, 1993).

This study also found short-term effects of type of childcare on socioemotional development. At 18 months of age, children's reactions upon separation from the mother became more negative for group care. The children with nursery care were less concerned with an unfamiliar person and showed less orientation to people and more a negative mood (Melhuish, 1987). At three years of age, the nursery children were less timid and more sociable and showed more prosocial behaviour. By six years of age there were no differences in socio-emotional development related to infant childcare. Hence, unlike the effects upon language development, the socio-emotional effects were not long-lasting.

Families, Children and Childcare Study

This recent study follows 1,200 children in north London and Oxford from birth to four years of age, investigating the effects of childcare upon child development. Early reports concern mothers' decisions and perceptions in the first year. Although very early use of childcare (three months post-birth) was more common amongst disadvantaged families, increasing childcare use during the first year by advantaged families meant that when children were 10 months old childcare use was greater amongst advantaged families. Mothers using childcare believed more in the benefits of maternal employment and also rated their child as less 'adaptable' (at three months) or more 'fussy' (at 10 months) (Sylva *et al.*, in press). For mothers returning to employment, those using the child's father or grandparent for childcare reported most satisfaction with their arrangements, and those using day nurseries reported less. Communication about issues such as feeding and sleeping appeared to be most favourable with childminders (Barnes *et al.*, 2006). Also mothers expressed concerns about communication with caregivers, their desire to keep control of their infants' lives, worries about infants' safety and stimulation in childcare (Leach *et al.*, in press).

Preschool childcare from age three

Many studies have reported benefits for children associated with preschool centre experience (see Melhuish, 1993, 2004; Sylva and Wiltshire, 1993). The Child Health Education Study indicated that children with preschool education had better educational outcomes (Osborn and Milbank, 1987). Jowett and Sylva (1986) found that working-class children who had attended a nursery class did better in primary school than playgroup graduates, suggesting the value of an educationally orientated preschool. Shorrocks *et al.* (1992) examined National Assessment results from seven-year-olds. Children who had attended preschools achieved higher scores in English and maths tests. A comparison of four types of preschool – nursery schools, nursery classes, playgroups and day nurseries – by Hutt *et al.* (1989) found only slight differences, with children from day nurseries (particularly boys) making more bids for attention than children who had started school coming straight from home. In turn, these verbal bids gained them more verbal attention. Sylva *et al.* (1980) found more developmentally enhancing activities in nursery schools than playgroups, suggesting that type of preschool is important.

While cross-sectional designs are often used to explore the impact of preschool provision, longitudinal designs allow the separation of preschool influences from those related to children's personal and family characteristics. Two recent large-scale studies utilise such designs to investigate effects of preschool provision upon children's development. They are the Effective Provision of Preschool Education (EPPE) project in England and the Effective Preschool Provision in Northern Ireland (EPPNI) project. Both studies use similar methods for measuring childcare and children's development and use longitudinal designs that allow child and family background factors to be controlled in analyses, and produce largely compatible results.

EPPE and EPPNI projects

These longitudinal studies of children from age three upward investigate the contribution to children's development of individual and family and preschool characteristics. Both projects focus on:

- the effects on children of different types of preschool provision;
- the interaction between child, family and preschool factors in affecting children's development.

The EPPE project also addresses the characteristics of effective preschools (e.g. interaction, pedagogy), in that the use of multi-level modelling allows the investigation of the effects not only of child, socio-economic and family characteristics, but also of specific preschool centres.

The EPPE sample was selected from the six types of preschool in England: playgroups, municipal day nurseries, private day nurseries, nursery schools, nursery classes, and integrated centres (combining care and education). The sample consisted of 2,857 children from 141 preschool centres plus 314 children with no preschool-centre experience, giving a total of 3,171 children. Data were collected on the children's cognitive, language and social development at three, five, six and seven years of age; family characteristics and home environment; and the preschool characteristics and quality.

The EPPNI project studied the development of over 800 children annually from three to eight years of age, their home backgrounds and the preschool settings they attended. It involved 700 children from 80 preschool settings in Northern Ireland (nursery schools/classes, playgroups, private day nurseries, reception classes and groups (i.e. three- to four-year-olds in school settings)) and a sample of 'home' children (who had no preschool-centre experience).

Findings from the EPPE and EPPNI projects

When the children were three to four years old, their development was related to the home learning environment and their experience of childcare over the first three years (after controlling for the influence of individual and demographic factors).

These studies introduced an interesting measure called the Home Learning Environment. Parents were asked about various activities in the home offering learning opportunities to the child (library visits, reading, painting/drawing, teaching alphabet, letters/numbers, songs/poems/rhymes). Using information on the frequency of such learning opportunities the Home Learning Environment measure was constructed. Higher levels of the Home Learning Environment were associated with better outcomes for all cognitive, language and social behavioural factors, and these effects were detectable at three years of age and persisted through to at least seven years of age. Moreover, the effects of the Home Learning Environment were found to be as strong or stronger than any other factor investigated in the studies (Melhuish *et al.*, 2001a, 2001b, 2005; Sammons *et al.*, 2002, 2003; Sylva *et al.*, 2004).

In addition, at three to four years of age, both studies found previous childcare related to social development. Childcare was measured in terms of the total amount of care by a relative (e.g. grandmother), individual care (e.g. childminder) or in a group (e.g. day nursery). Where children had received higher levels of relative care (usually grandmothers) they showed less antisocial behaviour and more cooperative behaviour. Also for a small number of children with very high levels of individual childcare (e.g. with childminders) there were indications of more antisocial behaviour, while those children with moderate to high levels of group care showed higher levels of antisocial behaviour (Melhuish *et al.*, 2001a, b). The effects of extensive early group care were still present at seven or eight years of age (Sammons *et al.*, 2004; Melhuish *et al.*, 2005).

In both studies, when children started school the effects of preschool experience became apparent. Children with no preschool experience were rated as poorer on cognitive measures and independence, cooperation and sociability. Also they were more likely to be 'at risk' of developing a special educational need. Hence children without preschool experience may be at a disadvantage when they start primary school. For children with preschool experience there were effects upon their development linked with type, quality and duration of preschool.

TYPE

In England, nursery schools and integrated centres had better cognitive and social development outcomes, and nursery classes had better social development outcomes. In Northern Ireland, nursery schools and classes generally had the better cognitive and social outcomes for children. These effects appeared to be linked to the higher qualifications of staff (more qualified teachers) and the higher observed quality of these settings.

QUALITY

Quality of preschool was measured using three observational instruments: the ECERS-R (Harms *et al.,* 1998), ECERS-E (Sylva *et al.,* 2003) and the Caregiver Interaction Scale (Arnett, 1989). Both studies found effects of quality upon cognitive and social development. Overall quality was related to better child cooperation, and two aspects of quality (language/reasoning and social interaction) were associated with better cognitive, language and social behavioural outcomes. Also better child interactions were related to better literacy and numeracy and social development. Where preschool quality was better there was evidence of some reduction in children's anti-social behaviour.

DURATION

In both countries, whether children attended preschool part time or full time did not affect their development, with part-time and full-time attendance being associated with equal benefits. However, in England the number of months of attendance was important (there was little variation in this measure in Northern Ireland). From two years of age upwards, more months of attendance were associated with better cognitive development and greater sociability. These effects persisted until seven years of age (Sammons *et al.,* 2004; Sylva *et al.,* 2004).

The studies also found that disadvantaged children did better if they attended a preschool with children from a wide range of social backgrounds rather than a preschool catering mostly to other disadvantaged children. Advantaged children did equally well whether in preschools with children from mixed backgrounds or in preschools with mostly advantaged children (Melhuish *et al.,* 2005; Sylva *et al.,* 2004).

The EPPE methodology, based upon multi-level modelling, allowed the estimation of the effectiveness of individual preschools. Qualitative studies of those effective preschools revealed several differences relevant to practice (Siraj-Blatchford *et al.,* 2003). In interactions there was more 'sustained shared thinking' in the more effective preschools, in that there was more working together to solve a problem, clarify a concept or extend an activity. Also effective centres had a more equal balance of child-initiated and adult-initiated interactions. Staff in effective centres showed better knowledge of the curriculum and of child development. Generally the better-qualified staff provided the best learning support for children, but less-qualified staff were better at this if they worked alongside more qualified staff. Effective centres also were more likely to have clear policies for dealing with behaviour problems. It was also the case that parent involvement appeared to be greater in the more effective centres.

Differences between England and Northern Ireland

High-quality preschool care was related to better intellectual and social/behavioural development for children, and is likely to be affected by staff qualifications and training. The quality of preschool environments in Northern Ireland and England was broadly similar. However, playgroups in Northern Ireland were of higher quality than in England, and their staff also had better training and qualifications. This strongly suggests that improved staff training can improve quality of preschool provision. Also the higher quality and better child outcomes for nursery schools/classes are likely to be related to higher staff qualifications in these centres.

The persistence of beneficial preschool effects was more evident in Northern Ireland than in England in that preschool was associated with superior attainment in literacy and mathematics, and some aspects of social development (e.g. the preschool group were consistently less anxious) until age eight. Also there were still persisting effects related to type and quality of preschool in the EPPNI study that were stronger than in the EPPE study. At age eight, in comparison with the home group, beneficial effects were still evident for children from nursery schools and classes, slightly less so for children from playgroups, less again for children from reception classes, but had largely disappeared for children from private day nurseries and reception groups. Also effects upon cognitive and social development related to the quality of preschool diminish with time in primary school but are still present at age eight years (Melhuish *et al.,* 2005).

Conclusions

The historical development of policy for childcare has followed a path guided by ideology and labour market pressures. Until very recently the predominant ideology as in many other countries has been to regard home as the best place for young children and mothers, and childcare before school as a private concern. This has been changing rapidly post-1997. The new policies related to infant childcare, preschool education, parental leave, government financial support for childcare, and the regulation and improvement of the quality of childcare may well produce more change than occurred in the previous century. While this new policy direction is heavily influenced by the government's ideology it is noteworthy that the policy has also been driven, at least partly, by research findings. This effect of the interest in evidence-based policy is a very new feature of government decision-making and it remains to be seen how permanent it will be.

It might have been thought that UK membership of the European Union might have had a greater impact in this area, but it would appear that it is yet to occur. While the UK has occasionally looked enviously at the wealth of provisions in the Scandinavian countries, influences from abroad have been minor, with policies driven by domestic ideology and influenced mostly by British research, with occasional influences from US research (as in the case of Sure Start Local Programmes).

Early research was influenced by the predominant ideology but from the 1980s the issues of quality of care and how that interacts with family factors in affecting children have come to the fore in British research. It is also apparent that the scale of research studies is increasing, with more recent studies having sample sizes in the thousands. This increase in scale has to a large extent been driven by increased sophistication in research methodology, but it has been made possible because of increased funding from a government that appears to be interested in the results of such studies. It is also the case that the larger scale of studies has made their findings much more convincing to the government and others who might previously have been sceptical. Another aspect of recent policy is the greater integration of policies as reflected in the Ten Year Childcare Strategy and the Childcare Bill, and this has started to bring about greater integration of provision, with the old dichotomy between care and education for young children being challenged, which is what research evidence has been indicating for some time.

British research reveals evidence of the effects of preschool childcare and education upon children's development. The quality, quantity and type of childcare are all important from infancy to starting school, and effects can persist well into the school years and possibly beyond. The effects of childcare under three years of age (particularly under two) can be negative or positive, but the effects of childcare (preschool provision) post-three is almost always positive, with the extent of the positive effects partly determined by duration, quality and type of provision. Also the studies reveal the importance of home background, which has effects about twice as strong as childcare effects. In particular the Home Learning Environment generally has one of the strongest and most consistent and persistent effects of all variables upon children's development.

References

Arnett, J. (1989). Caregivers in day-care centres: Does training matter? *Journal of Applied Developmental Psychology, 10,* 541–552.

Barnes, J., Leach, P., Sylva, K., Stein, A., Malmberg, L-E., and the FCCC team (in press). Infant care in England: Mothers' aspirations, experiences, satisfaction and caregiver relationships. *Early Child Development and Care,* 176.

Board of Education (1908). *Report of a consultative committee on the school attendance of children below the age of five.* Parliamentary Papers, 1908, 82.

Bowlby, J. (1951). *Maternal care and mental health.* Geneva: World Health Organisation.

Bryant, B., Harris, M. and Newton, D. (1980). *Children and minders.* London: Grant McIntyre.

Childcare Bill (2005). Available at: www.publications.parliament.uk/pa/cm200506/cmbills/080/06080.i-v.html

Consultative Committee on Infant and Nursery Schools (1933). *Report of the Committee (Hadow Report).* HMSO: London.

Driver, S. and Martell, L. (2002). New labour, work and the family. *Social Policy and Administration, 36,* 46–61.

Ermisch, J. and Francesconi, M. (2001). *The effects of parents' employment on children's lives.* Bristol: Policy Press.

Gathorne-Hardy, J. (1972). *The rise and fall of the British nanny.* London: Hodder and Stoughton.

Glass, N. (1999). Sure Start: The development of an early intervention programe for young children in the United Kingdom. *Children and Society, 13,* 257–264.

Gregg, P., Washbrook, E., Propper, C. and Burgess, S. (2005). The Effects of a Mother's Return to Work Decision on Child Development in the UK. *The Economic Journal, 115,* 48–80.

Harms, T., Clifford, R.M. and Cryer, D. (1998). *Early Childhood Environmental Rating Scale – Revised.* New York: Teachers College Press.

Hutt, S.J., Tyler, S., Hutt, C. and Foy, H. (1989). *Play, exploration and learning.* London: Routledge.

HM Treasury (2004). *Choice for parents, the best start for children: a ten year strategy for childcare.* London: HM Treasury.

Interdepartmental Committee on Physical Deterioration (1904). *Report on Physical Deterioration.* Parliamentary Papers 1904, 32.

Joshi, H. and Verropoulu, G. (2000). *Maternal employment and child outcomes.* Smith Institute Report.

Jowett, S. and Sylva, K. (1986). Does kind of research matter? *Educational Research, 28 (1),* 21–31.

Leach, P., Barnes, J., Nichols, M., Goldin, J., Stein, A., Sylva, K., Malmberg, L-E., and the FCCC team (in press). Child care before 6 months of age: a qualitative study of mothers' decisions and feelings about employment and non-maternal care. *Infant and Child Development.*

Mayall, B. and Petrie, P. (1977). *Minder, mother and child.* London: University of London Institute of Education.

Melhuish, E.C. (1987). Socio-emotional behaviour at 18 months as a function of day-care experience, temperament and gender. *Infant Mental Health Journal, 8,* 364–373.

Melhuish, E.C. (1991). Research on day-care for young children in the United Kingdom. In E.C. Melhuish and P. Moss (Eds), *Day-care for young children: International perspectives* (pp. 142–160). London: Routledge.

Melhuish, E.C. (1993). Preschool care and education: Lessons from the 20th for the 21st century. *International Journal of Early Years Education, 1,* 19–32.

Melhuish, E.C. (2004). *A literature review of the impact of early years provision upon young children, with emphasis given to children from disadvantaged backgrounds:* Report to the Comptroller and Auditor General. London: National Audit Office. Available at: http://www.nao.org.uk/publications/nao_reports/03–04/268_literaturereview.pdf

Melhuish, E.C., Mooney, A., Martin, S. and Lloyd, E. (1990a). Type of day-care at 18 months: I Differences in interactional experience. *Journal of Child Psychology and Psychiatry, 31,* 849–860.

Melhuish, E.C., Lloyd, E., Martin, S. and Mooney, A. (1990b). Type of day-care at 18 months: II Relations with cognitive and language development. *Journal of Child Psychology and Psychiatry, 31,* 861–870.

Melhuish, E.C., Moss, P., Martin, S. and Mooney, A. (1991) How similar are day-care groups before the start of day-care? *Journal of Applied Developmental Psychology, 12,* 331–345.

Melhuish, E.C. and Moss, P. (1992) Day-care provision in Britain in historical perspective. In M.E. Lamb, K.J. Sternberg, P. Hwang and A. Broberg (Eds) *Childcare in Context: Cross-cultural Perspectives.* New York: Erlbaum.

Melhuish, E.C., Sylva, K., Sammons, P., Siraj-Blatchford, I. and Taggart, B. (2001a). *The Effective Provision of Preschool Education Project, Technical Paper 7: Social/behavioural and cognitive development at 3–4 years in relation to family background.* London: Institute of Education/DfES.

Melhuish, E., Quinn, L., Sylva, K., Sammons, P., Siraj-Blatchford, I., Taggart, B., McSherry, K. and McCrory, M. (2001b). *The Effective Preschool Provision in Northern Ireland Project, Technical Paper 2: Cognitive and Social/behavioural Development at 3–4 years in Relation to Family Background.* Belfast, NI: Stranmillis University Press.

Melhuish, E., Quinn, L., Hanna, K., Sylva, K., Siraj-Blatchford, I., Sammons, P. and Taggart, B. (2005). *The Effective Preschool Provision in Northern Ireland Project, Summary Report.* Belfast, NI: Stranmillis University Press.

Moore, T.W. (1975). Exclusive early mothering and its alternatives: The outcome to adolescence. *Scandinavian Journal of Psychology, 16,* 255–272.

National Audit Office (2004). *Early Years: Progress in developing high quality childcare and early education accessible to all.* Report by the Comptroller and Auditor General. London: NAO. Available at www.nao.gov.uk/publications/nao_reports/03–04/0304268.pdf

NESS Research Team (2005a). *Early Impacts of Sure Start Local Programmes on Children and Families.* Surestart Report 13. London: DfES. Available at http://www.ness.bbk.ac.uk/documents/activities/impact/1183.pdf

NESS Research Team (2005b). *Variation in Sure Start Local Programmes Effectiveness: Early Preliminary Findings.* Surestart Report 14. London: DfES. Available at http://www.ness.bbk.ac.uk/documents/activities/impact/1184.pdf

OECD (2002). *Employment Outlook.* Paris: OECD.

OECD (2005). *Employment Outlook.* Paris: OECD.

Osborn, A.F. and Milbank, J.E. (1987). The effects of early education: a report from the Child Health and Education Study of children in Britain born 5–11 April 1970. Oxford: Clarendon Press.

Raven, M. (1981). Review: The effects of childminding: How much do we know? *Child: Care, Health and Development, 7,* 103–111.

Sammons, P., Sylva, K., Melhuish, E.C., Siraj-Blatchford, I., Taggart, B. and Elliot, K. (2002). *The Effective Provision of Preschool Education Project, Technical*

Paper 8a: Measuring the impact on children's cognitive development over the preschool years. London: Institute of Education/DfES.

Sammons, P., Smees, R., Taggart, B., Sylva, K., Melhuish, E.C., Siraj-Blatchford, I. and Elliot, K. (2003). *The Effective Provision of Preschool Education Project, Technical Paper 8b: Measuring the impact on children's social behavioural development over the preschool years.* London: Institute of Education/DfES.

Sammons, P., Sylva, K., Melhuish, E., Siraj-Blatchford, I., Taggart, B, Elliott, K. and Marsh, A. (2004). *The Effective Provision of Preschool Education (EPPE) Project: Technical Paper 11: The continuing effect of preschool education at age 7 years.* London: Institute of Education.

Shorrocks, D., Daniels, S., Frobisher, L., Nelson, N., Waterson, A. and Bell, J. (1992). *ENCA 1 project: The evaluation of National Curriculum Assessment at Key Stage 1.* Leeds: School of Education, University of Leeds.

Siraj-Blatchford, I., Sylva, K., Taggart, B., Sammons, P., Melhuish, E. and Elliot, K. (2003). *Technical Paper 10 – The Effective Provision of Preschool Education (EPPE) Project: Intensive Case Studies of Practice across the Foundation Stage.* London: DfEE/Institute of Education, University of London.

Sylva, K. and Wiltshire, J. (1993). The impact of early learning on children's later development. A review prepared for the RSA enquiry Start Right. *European Early Childhood Education Research Journal, 1 (1)*, 17–40.

Sylva, K., Roy, C. and Painter, H. (1980). *Childwatching at Playgroup and Nursery School.* London: Grant McIntyre.

Sylva, K., Siraj-Blatchford, I. and Taggart, B. (2003). *Assessing Quality in the Early Years Early Childhood Environment Rating Scales Extension (ECERS-E) Four Curricular Subscales.* Stoke on Trent, UK and Stirling, USA: Trentham Books.

Sylva, K., Melhuish, E., Sammons, P., Siraj-Blatchford, I. and Taggart, B. (2004). *The Effective Provision of Preschool Education (EPPE) Project: Final Report. A Longitudinal Study funded by the DfES 1997–2004.* London: DfES.

Sylva, K., Stein, A., Leach, P., Barnes, J., Malmberg, L-E., and the FCCC team (in press). Family and child factors related to the use of non-maternal infant care: An English study. *Early Childhood Research Quarterly.*

Thompson, F.M.L. (1988). *The rise of respectable society.* London: Fontana.

Tizard, J., Moss, P. and Perry, J. (1976). *All our children.* London: Temple Smith.

Whitbread, N. (1972). *The evolution of the nursery-infant school.* London: Routledge & Kegan Paul.

5 Children's and parents' needs and early education and care in Italy

Tullia Musatti

This chapter discusses the social function of early childhood education and care services in Italy within young children's daily lives, and parents' need for support in the care and education of their children. The chapter goes on to describe early education and care provision, its development and current issues and then makes suggestions for the future.

The daily life of young children

The experience of being an only child

Italy has a very low birth rate – less than two per female in recent decades. The birth rate decline is due, not to a rejection of parenthood, but to fewer children born in each family. The percentage of mothers in the fertile age group has not changed appreciably in recent decades, while there has been a considerable reduction in the number of second and third childbirths. This phenomenon has important implications for firstborn children in that many of them will be their parents' only child. For even more children, being an 'only child' characterises the experience of their early childhood. In the late 1980s, one quarter of under-14s were only children, together with 37 per cent of the under-sixes and 46 per cent of the under-threes. Moreover, the age gap between the first and second child is quite large and so whenever a child under the age of three is not the only child in her family and has a brother or a sister, the latter has already attained school age.

Being an only child means not only being unable to enjoy the important experience of a sibling relationship at an early age but also having to cope alone with a world composed exclusively of adults – and the adults are getting older. There has been an increase in the age at which women and men become parents; the majority of parents with young children are over 30 and, since life expectancy has increased, grandparents and great-grandparents are more likely to be present. The latter phenomenon, found in numerous European and non-European countries (Segalen, 2000), is true for Italy where 98 per cent of children under the age of 15 (ISTAT, 2001) have at least one living grandparent. This is important for the experience of young children in that one or more grandparent is continuously present as, though they rarely live with the child's family, they usually live in the same city, often close by. In sum, the attention, expectations and anxiety of a greater number of adults are often concentrated on a single young child.

The young child's daily experience

During the working week, if children do not attend childcare, their life is lived mainly at home and in contact with a single caregiver – mother, grandmother or babysitter. For the majority of children, before they enter childcare, their only experience of social contact with other children takes place in public playgrounds for relatively short periods of time and only occasionally (Musatti, 1992; Musatti and Pasquale, 2001; Rullo and Musatti, 2000). Musatti (1992) found that parents', and particularly mothers', social and employment status produced significant differences in toddlers' daily experiences. Paradoxically, children who spent less time in play interactions with adults and more time watching TV were the children of non-working mothers who spent long hours alone at home with the young child. It is also their mothers who ensured fewer hours of peer interaction in playgrounds. Subsequent studies analysed the mothers' opinions regarding these long days spent alone with the child (Musatti and Picchio, 2005; Picchio and Musatti, 2001a; Rullo and Musatti, 2005). As already indicated by previous authoritative studies (Dolto, 1981; Tizard, 1978), these analyses showed that long periods alone with the child, which also marks the experience of working mothers during non-working hours, can cause maternal stress and feelings of intolerance towards the child and a refusal by mothers to accept an educational role. Furthermore, regardless of the time spent with their child, mothers, particularly those with only children, were strongly aware of the need for their own child to meet other children (Rullo and Musatti, 2005).

Parents' need for social support in childcare and education

The studies cited above and the experience of practitioners who come into contact with parents agree that parental awareness of the educational needs of their children is accompanied by increased anxiety about their own educational responsibilities. Awareness of children's educational needs is an important component of modern parenting, which is now characterised by a greater need for social support. New needs for emotional and psychological support in coping with parenting have emerged alongside the increasing need for childcare support.

Support in childcare during mothers' working time

With mothers' increased participation in the labour market, childcare needs have increased. Despite constant difficulties in accessing the labour market, there is considerable participation in the labour force by mothers of children under three, more than 40 per cent of whom work (Fine-Davis *et al.*, 2004; Musatti, 1992), which is average for Europe. The presence of women in the labour market has gradually increased in terms of numbers employed, employment demands and job quality. A feature of Italian women's employment is that women's access to the labour market is supported by their education more than is men's. Although there are regional differences, a recent survey (ISTAT, 2003) found that in northern and central regions 63.2 per cent of mothers of children under two years old work compared to 32.5 per cent in the southern regions, yet women's desire to find a job outside the home is very strong in the whole country. How do working mothers solve the problem of providing day care for their children during working hours?

The ISTAT survey shows that only 22.4 per cent of toddlers' mothers use a public or private day care centre (*nido*), because of inadequate provision. As an alternative to the *nido*, as there is little family day care, childcare in the child's home is the only option. Private options range from unpaid care within the family (mother, grandmother or other relative) to a paid person who cares for the child at home (i.e. a babysitter). The most frequent choice, made by 54.5 per cent of toddlers' mothers, is having the childcare by a grandmother, while only 11 per cent of working mothers leave their child with a babysitter. This data confirms the trend in childcare choice identified by a previous survey (Musatti, 1992). This survey showed that although grandmothers' help is provided to all working mothers, mothers working full time at low-level jobs use it more frequently. The mother's employment status, income and degree of flexibility of her job largely determines her choice. When the income is low, with inadequate money to pay for full-time childcare, the only alternative to quitting employment is to use the extended family network. For higher earners, working conditions are more rewarding and the use of private, highly paid care is possible. Fathers' income also seems to affect the choice of childcare.

Grandparents' support in childcare

A third of all Italian children under three are cared for by a grandparent for some hours every day (ISTAT, 2001). However, grandparent care has psychological and cultural implications that are worth exploring.

Childcare by grandparents mostly only covers working hours, though sometimes other needs are supported. Grandparents help non-working mothers far less frequently (Musatti and D'Amico, 1996; Musatti and Pasquale, 2001; Sabbadini, 1999). Grandparents provide an important support even when children attend a *nido*, when the hours do not fit working schedules. In the past grandparents and parents were often in conflict over the *nido* choice, but nowadays the availability of childcare provision interacts with the availability of grandmothers in a more complex way (Musatti and Pasquale, 2001; Sepe, 2000). The use of educational provision may nevertheless still clash with old conceptions of inter-generational bonds. However, as women become grandmothers later in life and as their working life is extended, grandmothers have a growing awareness of children's educational needs, making them view the *nido* as favourably as parents.

Childcare tends to be provided by maternal grandmothers, although if the paternal grandmother provides childcare, she is involved to the same degree. There are deep emotional bonds between mother and grandmother. These overshadow other factors such as the proximity of maternal and paternal grandparents. Working mothers of lower socio-economic status (SES) make use of grandmother care more frequently; grandmothers of lower SES, regardless of the mother's status, perceive care of the grandchild as a duty and provide the majority of grandmother childcare (Musatti and D'Amico, 1996). In addition, the grandmother's involvement in childcare is always accompanied by intense emotions and positive feelings (Budini Gattai and Musatti 1999). The intense grandmother–grandchild relationship interacts with both the pre-existing grandmother–mother and developing mother–child relationships in complex ways (Picchio and Musatti, 2001b). It seems that modern life is also transforming mutual aid within extended families. Ongoing changes also affect intimate aspects of mother–grandmother relationships regarding the care and education of the young child. The grandmother's role in the extended family has changed and the inter-generational transmission of knowledge concerning the child's care and education has broken down and lost much of its value. As a result the grandmother has suffered a loss of power and authority in the eyes of the mother. Likewise, the mother has lost a point of reference and material and psychological support for practical and strategic choices in the education of the young child.

Parents' need for emotional and psychological support

Changes have also occurred in the attitudes and values involved in parenting, accompanied by new psychological and cultural conflicts. The increase in the number of working women has engendered strong expectations for more equal sharing of tasks between couples. This equality is not achieved very often and this is often a source of conflict for couples. The expectations of sharing, as well as a growing emphasis on the relational aspects of parenthood (Eme, 1999), clash with the traditional division of parenting roles between father and mother. Furthermore, a highly explicit social expectation exists concerning parenting, above all during early childhood. Parenting becomes a self-realisation challenge for the individual. However, there is also awareness that a child's upbringing will escape parental control and that culture intrudes on the parent–child relationship, for example, affecting ideas of physical contact and methods for putting to bed, etc.

Parents' demand for educational services

Parents' increasing demand for childcare arises from all the above elements, as parents appear to attribute to the preschool services the function of satisfying needs beyond simple care. There is some evidence in support of this hypothesis. First, the demand for childcare is spread across all social classes regardless of the material need for working mothers to have childcare during working hours. Also, whenever preschool is available, all parents regardless of mothers' employment request it.

Analysis of parental demand for services that accept children under the age of three indicates that parents are not only looking for childcare. As the *nido* is a public provision, all local governments have established rules regulating access. In most cities, children reported by social services and children with psychological or physical problems have absolute priority, and other children are selected mostly on the basis of mother's employment and family income. Although no child is excluded a priori, in almost all cities only a certain percentage, and certainly fewer than the number of working mothers, get a *nido* place. So, the question arises: which families use this public provision?

Some answers come from surveys of *nido* users (Ingrosso, 1988; Musatti, 1992; Musatti and Pasquale, 2001; Sepe, 2000; Trifiletti and Turi, 1983). The analysis of mothers' employment status shows no significant change over the years. Although more working mothers were found among the *nido* users than in the general population, the substantial number of non-workers among the *nido* users (between 14 and 22 per cent) does not correspond to the number of socially disadvantaged children accepted by the *nido* centres. In all centres, permanently employed mothers represented about two-thirds of the working mothers, as in the general population. Musatti (1992) found in the Emilia-Romagna region (where children attending the *nido* represent a significant percentage of the under-threes) choosing the *nido* is more likely for permanently employed mothers. Also the *nido* mothers' educational level is higher than that of non-*nido* mothers and increases substantially over the years, in keeping with the increase in the education of all Italian women. These findings reflect the fact that women with low education are often excluded from the labour market and thus have a low priority of access to the *nido*. Overall, the surveys showed that no specific category of mothers is likely to be favoured in gaining access to the *nido*. The *nido* appears to be an educational provision that is both requested, and used, by families of different socio-economic status, albeit with a prevalence of dual-earner families.

Since there has been a growing number of immigrant families with young children, the question was raised about their childcare needs. A recent survey of *nido* demand by immigrant families in Rome (Mayer *et al.*, 2003) showed that it is equivalent to the demand made by Italian families.

Whenever the mothers' reasons for choosing to use the *nido* are examined, we find a growing number of answers that attribute an educational value to the *nido* as a place which nurtures the child's social and psychological development rather than simply a solution to childcare needs (Sabbadini, 1999). These answers are more frequent among non-working mothers and better educated mothers (Musatti, 1992). Another interesting element that emerges (Musatti and Pasquale, 2001; Sepe, 2000) is the high degree of satisfaction expressed by parents with the *nido* experience. This degree of satisfaction is greater than that expressed by mothers for other forms of childcare at home.

The answer to parents' demand for childcare

Childcare for young children in Italy became a significant phenomenon after the Second World War. Kindergartens, now called *scuola dell'infanzia*, have existed in Italy since the beginning of the last century. In the first half of the twentieth century, they were run mainly by charitable and religious agencies and sometimes by municipal authorities. After the Second World War, and especially in the 1960s, many local authorities opened preschools for three- to six-year-olds to meet families' needs. However, it was only in 1968 that a state-run *scuola dell'infanzia* was set up. Scuola dell'infanzia rapidly spread over the entire country, helping to ensure basic schooling for over 90 per cent of three- to six-year-olds. Although over half the children today go to state schools, the intervention of local government, private religious and non-profit-making agencies is still important, particularly in the large cities. The educational nature of the scuola dell'infanzia was outlined in 1991 and reiterated in recent national education reforms. However, although these reforms acknowledge that the scuola dell'infanzia is the first step of the educational process and call for universal provision for all three- to six-year-olds, the funds have not been forthcoming. In recent years, the national government has instead proposed lowering the entry age to two-and-a-half years old and that for primary school from six years to five years old. This proposal was rejected by the National Association of Italian Municipalities (ANCI) and by all professional associations of teachers and educators, who claim that educational contexts should match children's needs at the various ages. In recent years, financial subsidies from the national government were provided to private schools. Many local governments attempted to set up a local network between schools in the public (local and national government) and private sectors, aimed at coordinating enrolment procedures and in-service staff training.

The educational provision for under-threes is more recent and far less extended. In 1971, the *nido* was established as a public service for children under three by a national legislative act in reaction to campaigns by trade unions and the women's movement. This act made the municipal and regional authorities responsible for the planning, construction, regulation and management of the *nido* centres. Owing to different local policies, most were in the north and central regions. The majority of *nido* centres were opened between 1975 and 1985. In the following 15 years the economic crisis that hit the country, the curtailment of national funding and the substantial financial constraints on local governments brought expansion to a halt. However, even in these years there was a small increase in the number of centres due to the increase of parental demand. A national survey in 2000 by the Centro nazionale di documentazione per l'infanzia e l'adolescenza (2002) found that, although the *nido* accepted 7 per cent of the total number of under-threes, in several cities in the central and northern regions, the *nido* centres catered for 20 to 30 per cent of this age group. Paradoxically, the number of parental requests was related to the number of *nido* provided in each region. In recent years, pressure from families, whose requests were increasingly unsatisfied, stimulated a new expansion of *nido* provision in many cities (as in Rome, where 50 per cent more places were created in the past three years). Pressure has also increased at the national level, where there are calls for new funding and a law that recognises the educational identity of the *nido*.

At the beginning there were vague expectations about the education the *nido* would provide. The history of the *nido* has been characterised by the gradual acquisition of educational status. In the early years many *nido* teachers thought of their profession as a mission of great cultural and political significance. Taking their work seriously, beyond the image perceived by users, meant they were willing to acquire professional skills in early education (Ongari and Molina, 1995; Ongari *et al.*, 1996, 1999). This was then supported in the national labour contract for teachers in *nido* centres when it allocated teachers paid time devoted to in-service training.

In the following years, local governments who were running *nido* and scuole dell'infanzia, gradually took on staff with professional expertise in the field of education (Musatti and Mayer, 2003). In the 1990s, as in other European countries, the hiring of professional educational staff spread throughout most municipalities running *nido* centres (Baudelot *et al.*, 2003). This class of personnel, denoted *coordinatore psicopedagogico o educativo* (pedagogic or educational coordinator), occupy different positions in the municipal administration, as well as performing management tasks. They provide professional support for the educational practices of the *nido* and the scuola dell'infanzia and coordinate the educational services in the city. In sum, coordinators have an important role in enhancing the quality of services. Many local governments have also produced educational orientation documents for *nido* centres.

During the first decade, the *nido* experience was supported by several research initiatives. Breaking with the psychoanalytical tradition, the aim was to investigate the positive aspects of the experience of socialisation outside the family, the possibility of multiple attachments and the importance of a reference teacher for each child inside the *nido*. In these years, in parallel with international scientific interest, numerous investigations were made of peer interactions by Italian researchers (Musatti and Mantovani, 1983).

These investigations demonstrated early positive interactions between peers with attendant cognitive and emotional implications, and looked at the causes of aggressive behaviour among children.

Attention was focused on the relations between the *nido* and the family. The *nido*, while giving priority to children of working mothers, was viewed as a provision offered to the whole community and was strongly linked to the culture of the local community. Most local governments regulated the *gestione sociale* (social management) of the *nido,* as they had previously done for their scuole dell'infanzia. This meant that they encouraged family and local community involvement. The value of parents' involvement was constantly mentioned at in-service training, as was the need for good communication between family and the *nido*, and not just between the individual teacher and the individual parent (Falcinelli and Falteri, 2005; Foni, 1997; Restuccia Saitta and Saitta, 2002). Special attention was also paid to the child's transition from family to *nido*. *Inserimento,* which is how the child adapts on entry to the *nido*, has been the focus of much research. Most cities with an active policy for children and families indicate procedures for inserimento, sometimes even in regulatory acts. Inserimento is a typical topic for Italian research and innovative practices (Cassibba, 1994; Cassiba *et al.,* 2000; Fava-Vizziello *et al.,* 1992; Mantovani *et al.,* 2003; Varin *et al.,* 1996). On the whole, the *nido* has represented an important window on the new needs of parents regarding social support. It is no coincidence, therefore, that the new educational services aimed at satisfying these needs were created inside the *nido* world.

New types of educational provision

The establishment of new types of educational provision emerged in Italy from a background of practices and research that differed substantially from other European countries (Mantovani and Musatti, 1996). Public provision was run by local governments, which, on the basis of the experience acquired in the management of *nido* centres, succeeded in finding new solutions to the new family demands. Both national and regional governments have implemented specific forms of funding to allow these services to be started by local governments. In 2000 the survey conducted by Centro nazionale di documentazione per l'infanzia e l'adolescenza (2002) found 500 new services run by local governments or by the private sector with public funding.

The new provisions have important links with the *nido* centres. The resources of the existing *nido* are frequently used: their premises and personnel, as well as their professional know-how regarding education and relations with parents. The new provisions employ teachers with working experience in *nido* centres, are monitored by the same coordinators as *nido* centres, and frequent joint in-service training sessions are run. Although the new provisions show a variety of different practices, they may all be grouped into two main functional categories. The first of these, Centro per Bambini e

Genitori (Centres for Children and Parents), stems from the first provision set up in Italy in 1986, Tempo per le Famiglie, in Milan, the result of collaboration between the local government and the Bernard van Leer Foundation. In this case, the under-threes are received together with their parents, in an extremely flexible organisational setting, by teachers who act as facilitators of communication between children and adults. The second type of provision arose out of the Area Bambini experience in Pistoia from 1987. In this case, stable groups of children aged 18 to 36 months were taken in for half a day, two or three times a week. Here, the teachers were given the role of promoting autonomous play and positive interactions among children. This type of provision was given the name of Spazio Bambini (Children's Places).

Both types of provision are aimed at meeting new family needs, although for a more restricted set of needs than the *nido*. While they do not provide childcare, they aim at combating the daily solitude of parents, helping parent and child at home, as well as providing opportunities for discussing parents' experiences. Centro per Bambini e Genitori are designed to directly involve the parents in sharing their own experience, while Spazio Bambini set out to offer parents an occasion for considering the development, capacities and psychological needs of their children from a fresh perspective. In the early years, there was intense debate on which type of provision was best suited to children and parents' needs. Experience has subsequently shown that they are complementary. Comparison of users' experience of services showed that parents were very positive for both types of service (Galardini *et al.*, 1993; Picchio and Musatti, 2001a; Musatti and Picchio, 2005).

Conclusions

The analysis of demands for early childcare prompts a few general conclusions. First, the relevance of offering the parents of under-threes a variety of care and educational choices has been confirmed (Melhuish and Moss, 1991). Also, extended public provision of centres should respond to parents' demands for ensuring equal access to, and quality of, childcare. Lastly, it is clear that the options must include not only responses to material needs but also responses to the psychological needs of socialisation and support during parenting. All these issues contribute to the ongoing debate on childhood and family policy in this country. The same issues also deserve consideration in specific research projects and innovative practices.

References

Baudelot, O., Rayna, S., Mayer, S. and Musatti, T. (2003). A comparative analysis of the function of coordination of early childhood education and care in France and Italy. *Early Years Education, 11*, 105–116.

Budini Gattai, F. and Musatti, T. (1999). Grandmothers' involvement in grandchildren's care: Attitudes, feelings, and emotions. *Family Relations, 48*, 35–42.

Cassiba, R. (1994). L'uso dell'Attachment Q-Set nella valutazione dell'attaccamento alla madre e all'educatrice di asilo nido. *Età Evolutiva, 48,* 42–50.

Cassiba, R., Van Ijzendoorn, M. and D'Odorico, L. (2000). Attachment and play in childcare centers: Reliability and validity of the attachment Q-Sort for mothers and professional caregivers in Italy. *International Journal of Behavioural Development, 24,* 241–255.

Centro nazionale di documentazione per l'infanzia e l'adolescenza (2002). I servizi educativi per la prima infanzia. *Quaderni del Centro nazionale di documentazione per l'infanzia e l'adolescenza, 21.*

Dolto, F. (1981). La Boutique verte: histoire d'un lieu de rencontres et d'échanges entre adultes et enfants, in F. Dolto, D. Rapoport, and B. This (sous la direction de), *Enfants et souffrance.* Paris: Stock, pp. 137–156.

Eme, B. (1999). *Les modes d'accueil de la petite enfance ou l'institution de la parentalité.* Paris: CRIDA – LSCI.

Falcinelli, F. and Falteri, P. (Eds) (2005). *Le educatrici dei servizi per la prima infanzia.* Bergamo: Edizioni Junior.

Fava-Vizziello, G., Palacio Espasa, F. and Cassiba, R. (1992). Modalités de réorganisation des enfants de 9 à 30 mois suite à la séparation des parents à la crèche. *Neuropsychiatrie de l'Enfance, 40 (8–9),* 431–448.

Fine-Davis, M., Fagnani, J., Giovannini, D., Højgaard, L. and Clarke, H. (2004). *Fathers and mothers: dilemmas of the work–life balance.* Dordrecht: Kluwer Academic Publishers.

Foni, A. (1997). Le educatrici di fronte alle domande dell'utenza (pp. 21–27). In A. Foni (a cura di), *Il comune come ente gestore. Proposte dai servizi educativi per la prima infanzia.* Roma: Edizioni delle Autonomie Locali.

Galardini, A.L., Giovannini, D. and Musatti, T. (1993). Area Bambini. I nuovi servizi per l'infanzia a Pistoia. *Bambini, 9,* 1–32.

Ingrosso, M. (1988). *Stelle di mare e fiocchi di neve. Le famiglie di fronte all'evento nido. Un'indagine in Emilia-Romagna.* Firenze: La Nuova Italia.

ISTAT (2001). *Parentela e reti di solidarietà. Indagine Multiscopo sulle famiglie 'Aspetti della vita quotidiana',* Roma, ISTAT, 'Informazioni', n. 22.

ISTAT (2003). *Indagine campionaria sulle nascite.* Roma: ISTAT.

Mantovani, S., Restuccia Saitta, L. and Bove, C. (2003). *Attaccamento e inserimento: stili e storie delle relazioni al nido.* Milano: Franco Angeli.

Mantovani, S. and Musatti, T. (1996). New educational provision for young children in Italy. *European Journal of Psychology of Education, XI,* 119–128.

Mayer, S., Musatti, T. and Rullo, G. (2003). Le famiglie straniere e la domanda di nido a Roma. In G. Favaro (a cura di) *Culture d'infanzia.* Milano: Franco Angeli.

Melhuish, E.C., and Moss, P. (Eds) (1991). Current and future issues in policy and research. In E.C. Melhuish and P. Moss (Eds). *Day care for young children* (pp. 199–215). New York: Routledge.

Musatti, T. (1992). *La giornata del mio bambino. Madri, lavoro e cura dei più piccoli nella vita quotidiana.* Bologna: Il Mulino.

Musatti, T. and D'Amico, R. (1996). Nonne e nipotini: lavoro di cura e solidarietà intergenerazionale. *Rassegna Italiana di Sociologia, 37,* 559–584.

Musatti, T. and Mantovani, S. (Eds) (1983). *Bambini al nido: gioco, comunicazione e rapporti affettivi.* Bergamo: Juvenilia.

Musatti, T. and Mayer, S. (2003). *Il coordinamento dei servizi educativi per l'infanzia. Una funzione emergente in Italia e in Europa.* Bergamo: Edizioni Junior.

Musatti, T. and Pasquale, F. (2001). *La cura dei bambini piccoli nei Comuni di Città di Castello e Gubbio,* in *Cura dell'infanzia e uso dei servizi nelle famiglie con bambini da 0 a 3 anni,* a cura di L. Cipollone, Quaderni del Centro Infanzia e Età Evolutiva, Regione Umbria, Perugia, pp. 41–101.

Musatti, T. and Picchio, M. (2005). *Un luogo per bambini e genitori nella città. Trasformazioni sociali e innovazione nei servizi per l'infanzia e le famiglie.* Bologna: Il Mulino.

Ongari, B. and Molina, P. (1995). *Il mestiere di educatrice.* Bergamo: Junior.

Ongari, B., Schadee, H.M.A. and Molina, P. (1996). Lavorare al nido: soddisfazione e immagine del lavoro con i bambini nelle educatrici. *Ricerche di Psicologia, 20,* 7–39.

Ongari, B., Schadee, H.M.A. and Molina, P. (1999). Un'analisi strutturale della rappresentazione sociale della professione di educatrice di nido. *Età Evolutiva, 63,* 73–80.

Picchio, M. and Musatti, T. (2001a). A tu per tu con il bambino piccolo: le parole delle madri. *Psicologia clinica dello sviluppo, n. 5,* pp. 241–260.

Picchio, M. and Musatti, T. (2001b). Autour du petit-enfant: entre mères et grands-mères. *La revue internationale de l'éducation familiale, n. 5,* pp. 45–56.

Restuccia Saitta, L. and Saitta, L. (2002). *Genitori al nido.* Milano: La Nuova Italia.

Rullo, G. and Musatti, T. (2000). *La vita quotidiana dei bambini tra 1 e 3 anni nella Città di Terni,* Rapporto Tecnico, Roma, Istituto di Psicologia, CNR.

Rullo, G. and Musatti, T. (2005). Mothering young children: childcare, stress and social life, *European Journal of Psychology of Education,* Vol. XX, n. 2, pp. 107–119.

Sabbadini, A.L. (1999). Modelli di formazione e organizzazione familiare. Convegno 'La famiglia in Italia', March, Bologna.

Segalen, M. (2000). *Sociologie de la famille.* Paris: Armand Colin.

Sepe, C. (a cura di), (2000). *Progetto pilota 'Riorganizzazione e potenziamento della rete di servizi alla prima infanzia del Comune di Roma'.* Roma: Comune di Roma.

Tizard, J. (1978). *Nursery needs and choices.* In J. Bruner and A. Garton (Eds) *Human growth and development.* Oxford: Clarendon Press.

Trifiletti, R. and Turi, P. (1983). Immagini, interpretazioni ed attese della famiglia di fronte al nido: una ricerca condotta in Toscana e in Umbria. In Gruppo Nazionale Permanente di Lavoro e di Studio sugli Asili Nido, Regione Toscana, and Comune di Pistoia (Eds), *Il bambino di fronte ad una famiglia e ad una società che cambiano.* Bergamo: Juvenilia.

Varin, D., Molina, P. and Ripamonti, C. (1996). Sensitive periods in the development of attachment and the age of entry into day care. *European Journal of Psychology of Education, 11,* 215–229.

6 Policy and research on childcare in Sweden

C. Philip Hwang

Several years ago an English journalist described Swedes as being lazy, sick and totally unable to enjoy anything nice in life. In addition, Swedish cars are wrecks, Swedes dress sloppily and, if you do not want to work, you do not need to – but you are still fully paid. Finally, he described family policy in Sweden: 'Just imagine a country where mothers as well as fathers can stay at home 13 months, with almost full pay after a baby is born, or a country where the state pays several thousand Euros for every child that goes to a day care centre – this would be totally impossible in Britain.'

How did the Swedish public react to this article? Surprisingly, most people agreed with his description of the Swedes. Yes, we are lazy, too many people are sick, and we are unable to enjoy the good things in life. There was only one issue where people disagreed with the article: very few were negative about family policy in Sweden. On the contrary, most people took for granted parental leave, the possibility of staying at home with a sick child and publicly funded day care. Even though this was some years ago, the Swedish public would probably react the same today.

This chapter will describe family policy in Sweden in relation to care for children under school age (six years). This includes different forms of public childcare, but also a parental leave programme. Later, the chapter examines the research evidence relating to Swedish childcare and children's development.

Demographic changes

Family patterns have changed dramatically in Sweden in recent decades. During the late 1990s, the number of immigrants decreased and fewer children were born. From 2002, however, there has been a slight increase in population due to the increase in births (Statistics Sweden, 2004). The fertility rate in 2000–2005 was 1.6 children. The average age of first-time mothers has increased by three years since the 1970s. In 2003 the average age for women was 29 years and for men 31 years when their first child was born (Statistics Sweden, 2004). Changes in marriage patterns and increasing divorce have resulted in new kinds of families. Families with children make up 24 per cent of households (41 per cent of whom are families with cohabiting parents). Most often, families have one child or two children. Fewer families consist of three or more children. Most parents are married or cohabiting, and one in five families is a lone-parent household, mainly headed by a woman (Statistics Sweden, 2004).

The proportion of women in the workforce rose dramatically between 1970 and 1990, and decreased after that. During the 1990s unemployment increased, and the proportion of women who were full- and part-time employees decreased. Employment rates for women aged 20–64 were 79 per cent in 2003, with an unemployment rate of 3 per cent. For men, the unemployment rate reached its peak in 1993, then decreased until 2002. Employment rates for men aged 20–64 were 84 per cent in 2003, with an unemployment rate of 4 per cent (Statistics Sweden, 2004). While in the past there was one wage earner per family, the most common pattern in Sweden today in a two-parent family is that both parents are employed, the father full time and the mother part time.

A final comment: despite the fact that most men and women are gainfully employed, Sweden's labour market remains one of the most sex-segregated in the world, with women and men occupying jobs traditionally associated with their sex, and women seldom in power positions. In about two-thirds of households, women still have more responsibility for childcare than men, and women are more likely to work part time, take parental leave and make adjustments to their work in response to family demands (Haas and Hwang, 2000).

Parental leave

There are various ways societies can assist with childcare. A parental leave system is an obvious alternative or supplement to out-of-home care. Most European countries now have parental leave systems of varying lengths. Sweden has developed what is probably the most extensive parental leave system. One result is a dramatic decrease in demand for out-of-home care during infancy. The overwhelming majority of Swedish parents stay home with their infants during the period covered by parental leave (13 months are reimbursed at 80 per cent of salary), and many families also stretch out the time they get paid for staying home by accepting a lower rate of payment during three extra months (Hwang and Broberg, 1991).

The parental leave programme developed in the 1970s. Until then, Sweden had provision for maternity leave that had been extended on several occasions since it was introduced in 1931. In 1974, however, Sweden introduced a system of parental leave which allowed either parent to stay home from work for six months after the birth of a child, or to divide this time as they chose. This programme developed in response to three major concerns: worry about a low birth rate; the need to encourage women's employment (as the programme gives fathers the opportunity to stay at home and mothers to go back to work); and the desire to liberate men from gender stereotypes. Interestingly, the well-being of children was not among the main reasons for introducing the programme.

Swedish parents are entitled to 480 days of leave compensated with a benefit. The parental leave system involves measures ensuring parents are able to care for their young child. Fathers are granted 10 paid days off from work to be with their newborn or adopted children within their first two months of life. All fathers and mothers are awarded two (non-transferable) months each of paid parental leave and have the right to share nine months of paid parental leave with each other, for every child (averaging 80 per cent of salary, up to a 'ceiling' of €32,800 per year). Collective agreements frequently provide a benefit supplement so that parents receive their full or almost their full salary for the parental leave period. Parents are also entitled to an additional 90 days at a flat rate payment of approximately €20 per day.

Parental leave is flexible; it can be taken full time or part time, all at once or in chunks, any time until a child's eighth birthday, while parents retain the right to return to the same or equivalent job after the leave. Fathers as well as mothers also have paid time off to care for sick children and have the right to reduce their regular workday from eight to six hours (with a corresponding reduction in wages), both in private and public sectors, until children reach school age.

Families with multiple births are entitled to additional paid leave (in the case of twins, an additional 90 days at 80 per cent of earnings and 90 days at a flat rate). If only one parent has custody of the child, she/he can use all the parental leave.

Parental leave benefit is financed through employer contributions and general taxation. The benefit is taxed, provides pension credits and entitles the employed recipient to a minimum of five weeks' annual paid vacation.

During 2003, nearly half a million parents used parental leave (Statistics Sweden, 2004). The proportion of fathers using parental leave has increased along with the expansion of entitlement to leave. In 1987 fathers took about 7 per cent of the total parental leave days, increasing to about 10 per cent over the next decade; from January 1997 to February 2004 men's share of paid parental leave increased from 9.9 per cent to 17.5 per cent, with a further increase to 18.7 per cent by December 2004. The introduction of a father quota in 1995 (each parent awarded one non-transferable month) and its extension in 2002 (to two non-transferable months) have both led to more fathers taking leave. With regard to leave for caring for a sick child, fathers and mothers are more similar in the number of days taken: 36 per cent of the eligible days are taken by fathers and 64 per cent by mothers. Fathers with more education take more parental leave as do fathers whose partners have higher levels of education or income. Fathers taking no leave are more likely to have been born outside Sweden. The right to work reduced hours is mainly used by mothers.

Public childcare

In Sweden, parents' employment entitlements, with their encouragement to fathers to take more responsibility for children, and public childcare are seen as part of an integrated childcare system. One consequence of the parental leave scheme and its gradual extension is that the age of admission to childcare has risen: very few Swedish children are now placed in childcare during their first year and around 18 months is a common starting age. The legislation also allows parents to work reduced hours. This was motivated in part by concern with the length of time that many children spent in childcare. Finally, a system of maximum fee was introduced in 2002. This system is not compulsory for the municipalities, but most agreed to participate. The maximum fee system means that parents pay between 1 to 3 per cent of their annual income for day care or family day care (3 per cent for the first child, 2 per cent for the second child and 1 per cent for the third child). There is also a 'ceiling' set for the cost of first, second and third child etc. per month. The aim of this reform is equality between children and between municipalities, but it has also led to more children entering into groups (Pramling and Sheridan, 2004).

Owing to parental leave, most parents (mothers or fathers) with a child under one year are at home. In 2003, 75 per cent of all one- to five-year-olds were in day care centres. Comparable figures for 2002 and 2001 were 72 per cent and 68 per cent (the slight increase in 2002 was because children at home with parents who were on parental leave due to the birth of a sibling became entitled to attend day care). Broken down into age groups, the figures are: 40 per cent for one-year-olds, 78 per cent for two-year-olds, and 83 per cent, 88 per cent and 89 per cent for all three-, four- and five-year-olds. As is obvious, a higher percentage of older children are in childcare.

The different types of childcare

As mentioned above, there are several different types of childcare in Sweden. These include:

- day care centres (for all children with working parents, parents who study, are on parental leave or unemployed);
- preschool (all four- and five-year-olds are entitled to 525 hours free of charge;
- so-called 'open day care centres' (mothers' clubs) where the municipality provides premises and a preschool teacher to assist parents who are at home with their children, regardless of age;
- family day care (carers are paid to look after non-related children in their own homes).

At day care centres, children usually receive full-time care while their parents are employed. The number of day care centres has increased over recent decades. As mentioned above, 75 per cent of children in this age group are in day care (Skolverket, 2004). Non-public provision, such as parent cooperatives, has increased in Sweden, along with provision from non-profit organisations, companies and others (Skolverket, 2004). Seventeen per cent of all children in day care receive provision in a non-public centre, while 9.4 per cent of all children in family day care receive provision in a non-public family day care centre. Most of these day care centres consist of parent cooperatives where parents have set up the centre with financial support from the municipality. Parent cooperatives became equivalent to municipal day care in 1988 and have since been entitled to state support. Around 30 per cent are run by a workplace, and various other non-profit providers run the remaining centres.

Non-public provision exists mainly in cities and suburbs and is less common in municipalities with big industries. In 63 of 290 municipalities, non-public care was, however, not available (Statistics Sweden, 2004).

The number of open day care centres has decreased drastically in recent years, and in the past two years more than 20 per cent have closed down. In the autumn of 2003 there were 551 open day care centres, compared with 708 in the autumn of 2002. Since 1997, 45 per cent of all open day care centres in Sweden have been closed. Opening hours vary, and in some municipalities all centres are open more than 16 hours per week. In 2003, 52 per cent of all open day care centres were open more than 16 hours per week. As there is no formal application procedure, there are no records of how many children attend open day care centres.

The implementation, orientation and quality of Swedish childcare

The Preschool Educational Programme, published in 1987, clearly defined the division of responsibilities between national and local authorities. Up until 1996, the National Board of Health and Welfare had responsibility for all preschool services and allocated state grants for day care services to the municipalities. Each municipality was responsible for the development of public day care in accordance with national guidelines. According to a 1985 law, all municipalities were to increase public day care to ensure that by 1991 there was provision for all children over 18 months who needed day care. In the summer of 1990, however, only 67 per cent of municipalities indicated that they would be able to achieve this requirement. From July 1996, responsibility for childcare was transferred to the Ministry of Education in order to strengthen the educational aspects of day care.

Prior to 1996, the National Board of Health and Welfare had responsibility for all childcare services in the public sector. Because of reliance on this board, rather than on the Board of Education, day care services had been more influenced by ideas and values in the health sector than by goals in the education sector, and, traditionally, there had been a reluctance to introduce too much school-like activity into day care centres and kinder-gartens. In accordance with the Education Act of 1998, however, the National Agency for Education now regulates day care centres.

While there remains a concern to avoid becoming like schools, for those children in day care, the educational content of care should ensure that day care institutions cooperate with parents in order to 'give children ample and comprehensive opportunity to develop their emotional and intellectual potential and become open and considerate individuals, capable of empathy, cooperation with others, and of learning to seek knowledge for themselves and forming their own opinion' (quoted in European Commission, 1996).

The National Board of Health and Welfare issued central guidelines to guarantee that the expansion of municipal day care centres met certain quality requirements. The effects of these guidelines have been unmistakable. Swedish day care centres are of a high standard with respect to formal or structural aspects of quality. Legislation in 1995, 1998, and 2001–2003 further improved the requirements in staffing, group size and other aspects of quality of day care and family day care. In addition, from the first of January 2003, all municipalities are according to the law required to provide childcare (day care or family day care) as soon as possible, i.e. within three to four months after the parents have applied for a place (Pramling and Sheridan, 2004).

Design of premises for day care centres

There are detailed structural requirements to be met by day care centres. The guidelines are meant to guarantee that the expansion of day care is not achieved at the expense of quality. As a result, all Swedish day care centres contain child-sized furniture and fittings, have a room for gross motor activity, a room for more sedentary and fine motor activity, a corner for games involving water, and a 'cosy corner' where the children can sit quietly and look at books, etc. Most foreign visitors are struck by how well the premises of Swedish day care centres meet their stated purpose.

Staffing and staff training for day care centres

Staff working with children under the age of six must, in principle, have successfully completed training either as a childcare attendant (barn-skötare) or a preschool teacher (förskollärare). To train as a childcare attendant, it is necessary to have completed compulsory education (nine years of schooling) and to be at least 16 years old. The course lasts three years and provides students with basic knowledge of child rearing and development. Preschool teacher education consists of a post-secondary course of study that lasts a further three years. Students must be at least 18 years old, with 11 years of schooling, and may start the course after successfully completing the childcare attendant course. Educational levels among staff are, therefore, high, with few lacking formal education for working with children.

Well-educated staff is a key factor for quality when it comes to giving children the best possible conditions for learning (see e.g. Kärrby, 1996; Gustavsson and Myrberg, 2002). Unfortunately, there is presently a shortage of skilled preschool teachers. This is both a question of recruiting new people into initial teacher training and also one of upgrading what were previously called nursery nurses or childcare attendants (*barnskötare*).

In 2003, there were 65,498 employees in various types of alternative care in Sweden (public and non-public). This is an increase of almost 2000 employees compared with the year before (2002). According to Skolverket (2004) the number of employees is expected to rise in the coming five to ten years owing to a larger number of children in the population. With regard to the so-called open day care centres, there is an opposite trend, with 734 employees in 2003, a decrease of 127 employees from 2002. Only 475 employees are involved in open day care centres today.

Group size and adult–child ratio in day care centres

Children in day care centres are usually divided into mixed age groups. These can consist of children up to age three (27 per cent of all one- to three-year-olds are in this age group), sibling groups (usually children aged three to six) or extended sibling groups, which can include children of preschool age as well as younger schoolchildren from six to nine years. Most day care centres have four groups of children with an average group size of 17.2 children. (Skolverket, 2004). Day care groups for one- to three-year-olds are normally smaller in size compared to groups with older children. In 2003, almost half (47 per cent) of these groups contained between 14 and 16 children. There has been a steady overall increase in group size between 1990 and 2002. In 1990, there were on average only 13.8 children per group; in 1995, 16.5 children and in 2002, 17.4 children in each group. As the figure for 2003 was 17.2, it might be that the trend towards increasing group size has stopped (Skolverket, 2004).

A better indication of quality than group size is probably number of children per employee. In the early 1980s there were nearly four children per employee compared to 5.6 in 1996 (Statistics Sweden, 1997), and 5.4 in 2003 (which is approximately the same as in 2001 and 2002) (Skolverket, 2004).

Day care centres are normally open from Monday to Friday. Children are provided with two or three meals a day and participate in activities which, for example, introduce them to natural history, culture and society. All activities are planned in cooperation with parents and based largely on the children's backgrounds, interests, previous experience and special needs.

Day care centres vary considerably in size. Typically, they have three or four groups and around 50 to 60 children. The availability of places for children under three years varies between municipalities, but as mentioned above the municipalities are required by law to provide day care (and family day care) within three to four months after the parents have applied for a place (Skolverket, 2004).

In 'toddler groups', most children are under three years old. Since the youngest child is generally 15 to 18 months old, this means that all the children are close to each other in age. Until some years ago, this was by far the most common grouping for children under three.

In 'sibling groups', children are between three and six years old. The groups contain an average of 15 to 18 children and three staff members (two teachers and a childcare attendant). 'Extended sibling groups' span the whole preschool age range; they are required to contain no more than 15 children, and to have at least three staff members. This type of grouping has become more common in recent years.

Municipal family day care

Municipalities also support family day care, provided by carers who are paid to look after non-related children in their own homes; this municipal family day care is used by 33,700 (7 per cent) one- to five-year-olds. When broken down into age groups the figures are as follows: 5 per cent of all one-year-olds, 8 per cent of all two- to four-year-olds, and 7 per cent of all five-year-olds are in family day care. There has been a gradual decrease in children in family day care. For instance, there were 3,800 children fewer in 2003 compared with 2002 (Skolverket, 2004). Within the municipal system, the childminders (*dagmammas*) are recruited, paid, supervised and supported by the municipality, which also arranges placement of children. Some children are cared for by nannies in the child's own home. Some nannies live in, but mostly they come in during the day.

Local authorities control most family day care. In 2003, there was a total of 7,687 family day carers (Skolverket, 2004). A number of family day carers do, however, operate unofficially. The family day care system is most used in rural areas, where three times as many children attend compared with urban areas.

There are national regulations for organised family day care. In addition, municipalities are responsible for setting their own regulations and requirements for qualifications. In the organised schemes, a person who is responsible for the quality of service must supervise family day carers. In a number of municipalities, family day carers are attached to local centres whose manager acts as a supervisor.

Over the past 10 years, the overall education level has increased for childminders, but, in the last few years, it has decreased again. Between 1999 and 2003, 70–72 per cent of all family day carers had some kind of training for working with children. A majority of these carers have received training as childcare attendants (*barnskötare*). The employee–child ratio in family day care is slightly lower than in day care centres, and has decreased during the time period 1998–2003, from 5.6 to 5.2 (Skolverket, 2004).

Family day carers receive a monthly salary based on the number of children in attendance, which includes paid holiday, pension contributions and sick pay on the basis of a full-time position equivalent to caring for a certain number of children (Kärrby, 1996). This fixed monthly salary, however, is conditional on the childminder caring for at least four non-related children full time or providing an equivalent number of hours of care for children attending part time. Indeed, many childminders must look after eight to ten children part time to qualify for their salaries. One of the reasons that childminders enrol so many children on a part-time basis is that many municipalities exclude part-time attendance at day care centres, arguing that places at these centres are too expensive to be filled part time only.

Since family day care is usually carried out in the childminder's own home, the quality can vary a great deal. Childminders are given equipment grants to purchase toys, etc., and family day care home assistants ensure a minimum quality of family day care. The main responsibilities of the family day care home assistant are to investigate, assess and choose childminders; place children; provide childminders with guidance, advice and support; organise and coordinate childminders' activities; and develop activities for childminders and children. It is increasingly common for four to six childminders in the same area to bring their children together regularly in special premises, for example, in mothers' clubs or in day care centres. Since the children get to know other childminders and children in these groups, it is easier to find a substitute if a childminder needs to take time off.

Financing Swedish childcare

In the view of the national authorities, childcare is a right that may be enjoyed by all families with children, if they wish. Consequently, the cost to the individual family of obtaining places in day care service must not be so high as to deter them from exercising this right. This has led to a heavy reliance on public funds to finance childcare.

The total cost for childcare (excluding family day care) is €3.6 billion, which means that the cost for each child is approximately €10,000. The corresponding figure for family day care is €340 million, which means that the cost for each child is approximately €8,000. Seventy-five per cent of the total cost for day care, and 84 per cent of the costs for family day care, consists of salaries to employees. The cost for places in municipal day care centres is divided so that the state and the municipality each contributes, while parents pay an average of 8 per cent of the real costs. The state's contribution to the cost of places in family day care homes is rather less, with parents paying up to 10 per cent (Skolverket, 2004). In addition to municipal centres and family day care homes, substantial financial support is also given by the municipalities to day care centres run by parent cooperatives or non-profit private organisations.

The state's share of childcare costs is covered by social insurance contributions that all employers must pay to the government. Municipalities' share of costs come from municipal taxes levied on companies and individuals. Sweden is characterised amongst the Nordic countries by its relatively large employer and employee contributions, which provide 55 per cent of total costs. Included here is parental leave, of which 86 per cent is funded by employers through a collectively paid social insurance fee, and the remaining 14 per cent by the state (Rostguard and Fridberg, 1998).

Research on childcare

Sweden has national regulations, a national curriculum and norms for staffing levels and training, group size, daily routines and design of the day care environment. This does not mean that all day care centres are identical. There are wide variations in group composition, atmosphere and the staff's experience and working methods; but these variations are within certain specified limits. If we compare day care centres and ordinary homes, it seems probable that variations between different home environments are much wider than between different environments in day care centres (Gunnarsson et al., 1987).

The circumstances of childcare in Sweden mean that there is a generally high quality of care with limited variation in quality. Kärrby and Giota (1994; 1995) found that the Early Childhood Environment Rating Scale (ECERS) is useful in describing the quality of care in day care centres in Sweden. They also related ECERS scores to parental views of quality. One programme of research (Bjurek et al., 1996) has considered the relation between resources in man-hours and space available, to the quality of care as measured by ECERS. Overall, there was little relationship between resources and ECERS. However, this did not apply across socio-economically deprived areas, where high quality required a high level of resources.

Some studies have investigated the quality of children's experiences in childcare. Ekholm et al. (1995) described three climates in childcare centres reflecting differences in adult and child collaboration, and factors affecting this collaboration. A later study (Hedin et al., 1997) found that where there was more adult–child collaboration, children collaborated with each other more, and showed higher levels of prosocial behaviour. Staff training related to organisational factors affecting climate may therefore have benefits for child development.

Most early day care studies were retrospective in design, and they did not report any important differences between children with different childcare histories. An early systematic Swedish childcare study was carried out by Stukát in the middle of the 1960s. This study focused on the influence of kindergartens on children's development. There were few differences between children with and without kindergarten experience. In the case of social and emotional development, the only difference was that nursery-school children tended to manage better by themselves. The differences were not large. In the case of intellectual development, nursery-school attendance appeared to have some favourable effects. Nursery-school children tended to have better elementary knowledge and skills (e.g. oral command of language, sense of locality and vocabulary), but did not, however, perform better on tests on reading, spelling and arithmetic, or on teachers' ratings of school performance. Svenning and Svenning (1979) studied the effects of preschool experience on school-aged children, using parent questionnaires. Children were compared with respect to parental attitudes, achievement tests and grades. There were small differences between children with different day care experience but large differences were found between children from different family backgrounds.

Hårsman (1984) studied the adjustment process in infants who were placed in day care centres at between six and 12 months of age (the study was carried out in the 1970s when paid parental leave was not yet in practice). Over six months, observations of children in the day care centre initially indicated signs of depression. Hårsman also found differences on personal–social development favouring children cared for at home. Children in day care were more clingy than children cared for at home initially. After about two months these signs began to disappear and after five months there were no differences between the groups. These results suggest that early centre day care exposes children to stress and puts excessive demands on their ability to adapt. The results do not say anything about possible long-term effects. Hårsman also found large individual differences between different children's ability to adapt to centre day care. Some children recovered fairly quickly while others had still not done so at the end of the study.

Later studies have used longitudinal designs when trying to measure the effects of out-of-home care on children's development. Söderlund (1975), who studied a group of seven- to nine-months-old children in Stockholm, carried out one of the first longitudinal studies. Children's development was assessed before entering organised childcare and when they were 18 to 24 months old. Children in centre day care achieved higher scores on motor development than did children in family day care or in home care. In a later follow-up of these children (Rudebrandt and Thörn, 1979), four groups of 12 children each were compared. Three of the groups comprised children with stable childcare histories: i.e. children cared for in the home only, children continuously enrolled in centre day care, and children continuously enrolled in family day care. The fourth group consisted of children with experience of different forms of childcare. Children who had experienced multiple forms of out-of-home care scored lowest on developmental scales, whereas there were no differences between children with different but stable day care histories.

One of the most comprehensive longitudinal studies was carried out by Cochran and Gunnarsson (Cochran, 1977; Cochran and Gunnarsson, 1985; Gunnarsson, 1978; Larner, 1982). The research focused on 60 children who had been in centre day care since one year of age. Their development at five years of age was compared with that of 60 children who had either been cared for at home or in family day care. Yet another follow-up study was carried out when the children were nine to 10 years old (Larner, 1982). At the age of one, no differences were observed between the children in centre day care and children cared for at home, nor were there any group differences in the emotional closeness of mothers and children. The results obtained from the later follow-up studies showed very small differences between the groups, between-group differences being much smaller than differences within the groups. Sex differences were most pronounced. Girls cared for at home were more 'obedient', while girls in day care centres were more likely to manipulate adults in order to get their own way. In this respect girls with day care centre experience were similar to boys cared for at home. The boys in centre day care were by far the most peer-orientated group, and they had very little contact with adults. One problem with this study is that no distinction is made between children cared for at home by their parents and those in family day care; they are regarded as a single group. Another shortcoming was that children in centre day care were only studied in their day care centre environments whereas children cared for at home were only studied at home.

The Gothenburg Childcare Project was set up to assess the effects of out-of-home care on children's social, emotional and intellectual development. When this longitudinal study was started by Hwang and Lamb in 1981, the effects of contrasting care arrangements had not yet been studied, and scientists thus had to generalise from the results of retrospective studies focused on short-term effects. As a result, this study was designed to explore prospectively the short- and long-term effects of early entry into out-of-home care on psychosocial and cognitive abilities, with characteristics of the child, family and childcare setting also taken into account. Among the potential influences considered were the nature and quality of in-home and out-of-home care, perceived social support, various indices of socio-economic status, and children's temperament.

Of the 145 children in the study, none had begun out-of-home care before the research team visited them at an average age of 16 months. Children were divided into three groups: those who were to begin in centre-based day care (N=53); those who were offered care in municipal family day care homes or where parents made their own arrangements with private childminders (N=33); and, finally, a group which did not enter day care (N=59). So far, each of the participating 145 children has been visited 30 times over a 22-year period. In the last wave of data collection, 130 of the young adults participated. This study has so far generated almost 30 papers published in international journals (see, for example, Broberg et al., 1989; Prodromidis et al., 1995; Broberg et al., 1997).

In the first and second visit to the homes, assistants assessed family background, social networks, care arrangements, quality of the home environment, relative parental involvement, child's temperament, and their initial response to the visiting adult. Thereafter, some of the children obtained centre placements, others were instead offered places in family day care settings, and the remainder continued at home in their parents' care. Children enrolled in centre-based day care or family day care entered these settings within two weeks of the first home assessment. Six weeks later, their childcare facilities were visited to obtain observational and interview data about the care arrangement and its quality (Phase I).

One (Phase II) and two (Phase III) years thereafter, the families were visited again, and similar assessments were performed in Phases IV and V. Family and centre-based day care facilities were also visited to collect data about the quality of care and the children's behaviour in those settings. The fourth (Phase IV) and fifth (Phase V) waves of data collection took place prior to elementary school and when the children were in second grade, respectively. During these visits, the children's verbal and mathematical abilities were tested while data about paternal involvement, children's personal maturity, peer play skills, and current care arrangements were gathered. Additionally, data about the quality of the preschool and alternative care settings were collected again. In Phase V, intensive interviews were conducted with teachers to obtain additional information about the children's peer behaviour, adjustment to school, cognitive and social skills, and personality.

Data collection in Phase VI and Phase VII took place when the children were in the ninth year of school (15–16 years of age), and when they had finished secondary education (21–22 years of age). Measures were chosen to further explore social skills, using self-report measures of relationships with peers, personality development, school performance, behaviour problems, and self-perception. Parents also summarised the family's current socio-economic circumstances, and major family events (such as childbirth, divorce, separation, death, residential moves), while the parents and the adolescents independently described the parents roles and responsibilities.

Overall, the results showed no effects of type of care on social, emotional, or intellectual development. The most important factors in shaping children's development were the quality of care in their own homes, especially the 'emotional climate' in the family. Rather surprisingly, socio-economic factors were of little importance. Some of the structural measures of the quality of alternative care were also predictive of child outcome. These measures included:

1   group size (the fewer the children, the better the outcome);
2   child–staff ratio (the fewer children per adult, the better the outcome);
3   age mixture and age range (the narrower the age range and the more same-aged peers, the better the outcome).

In addition, this longitudinal study has yielded rich insights into aspects of personality development and their relation to external factors such as school performance and psychosocial adjustment (Lamb *et al.*, 2002; Wessels *et al.*, 1997), stability and change in levels of paternal involvement

(Hwang and Lamb, 1997), and relational and assertive self-concepts across social contexts and relationships (Chuang *et al.*, 2004).

The only longitudinal Swedish study that reports distinctive differences between children with different childcare histories is the FAST project (Andersson, 1986, 1989; 1992; 1996). This study of 128 children began when the children were three years old. In follow-up studies, when the children were approaching their eighth birthday, and again when the children were 13 years old, their teachers were asked to assess their cognitive and social competence. Andersson reported that children with early experiences of out-of-home care, whether in centre day care or family day care, developed more favourably (both socially and cognitively) than did children cared for exclusively at home or children who began in out-of-home care after their second birthday. The strongest effects were shown for children who began in out-of-home care in the first year (Andersson, 1989).

Andersson (1996) discusses the impact of childcare and the possible long-term gender effects. Although girls benefited from early day care experience, for boys the benefit was especially marked. Andersson reports that boys entering early day care (at six to 12 months old) adjust well in school, maintain high-school achievement and, at the age of 13, display positive interpersonal skills. Furthermore, relatively few boys displaying learning and/or behaviour problems were in the early entrance group. Girls benefited less from early day care, although they did well in school after any day care experience. In a recent follow-up when the subjects were 25 years of age, Andersson and Strander (2002) reported no significant differences between subjects with early experiences of out-of-home care, whether in centre day care or family day care compared with subjects cared for exclusively at home or subjects who began in out-of-home care after their second birthday.

In sum, Swedish longitudinal research studies on the effects of day care on children's development has not demonstrated any enduring effects of day care or type of day care on children's subsequent development. The one exception found early day care experience to be associated with positive effects during the first 13 years of life. Quality of care, both at home and in day care settings, seems to be a more important determinant of later development than type of care experienced by children.

Conclusion

Sweden is an interesting country to study from the perspective of preschool facilities because of the heavy national funding of preschool services. As a consequence, parents have a high accessibility to preschool services, higher than in most other European countries. Most children under and above the age of three, can receive public day care, which is affordable for parents through the maximum fee system. The high level of training and resourcing of centres also leads to a situation where centres generally provide high quality care and education. This again is different from the situation in many other European countries. The development of research in Sweden needs to be considered within this social context.

To summarise the research in Sweden, it would appear that children attending day care develop at least as well as children cared for at home. Day care policy is supported by and integrated with an extensive system of employment entitlements for parents, which increases their opportunities to provide care for their children. In conclusion, however, a few shortcomings in Swedish day care should be pointed out:

1 *Limited choice* One might argue that Swedish parents have a limited choice of out-of-home care. The policy-makers in Sweden are strongly in favour of public day care. Other forms of childcare, like family day care and so-called open day care centres, are not favoured in a similar way.

2 *Too much homogeneity* Although Swedish public childcare is of high quality, it is also rather homogeneous. Most day care centres look alike and the curriculum is very similar. There is little room for ideas that are out of the ordinary.

3 *Regional and political variation* There are large variations between different parts of the country, both in the total quantity of public day care and the division between centre-based and family day care. In large cities, municipal day care is well developed and the emphasis is on centre day care, and levels of day care are not related to whether municipalities are governed by right- or left-wing parties.

Returning to the introduction to this chapter: Swedes may be lazy, unable to enjoy the good things in life, and have bad cars. However, Swedish family policy is amongst the most extensive in the world, and, despite some shortcomings, satisfies the needs of most Swedish parents and children.

References

Andersson, B-E. (1986). Home care or external care: A study of the effects of public childcare on children's development when 8 years old. *Reports on Education and Psychology, No. 2.*

Andersson, B-E. (1989) Effects of public day care – a longitudinal study. *Child Development, 60,* 857–867.

Andersson, B-E. (1992). Effects of day care on cognitive and socioemotional competence of thirteen-year-old Swedish schoolchildren. *Child Development, 63,* 20–36.

Andersson, B-E. (1996). Children's development related to day care, type of family and other home factors. *European Child and Adolescent Psychiatry, 5,* 73–5.

Andersson, B-E. and Strander, K. (2002). *Framtiden blev vår. 101 sjuttiotalister följda under sina 25 första år* (The future is ours. 101 individuals born during the 70's followed during 25 years). Individ, omvärld och lärande/Forskning nr 11.

Bjurek, H., Gustafsson, B., Kjulin, U. and Kärrby, G. (1996). Efficiency and quality when providing social services: The examples of public day care in Sweden. *Scandinavian Journal of Educational Research,* September.

Broberg, A.G., Hwang, C.P., Lamb, M.E. and Ketterlinus, R.D. (1989). Childcare effects on socioemotional and intellectual competence in Swedish preschoolers. In J.S. Lande, S. Scarr and N. Gunzenhauser, (Eds), *Caring for children: Challenge to America* (pp. 49–75). Hillsdale, NJ: Erlbaum.

Broberg, A.G., Wessels, H., Lamb, M.E. and Hwang, C.P. (1997). Effects of day care on the development of cognitive skills in 8-year-olds: A longitudinal study. *Developmental Psychology, 33,* 62–69.

Chuang, S.S., Lamb, M.E. and Hwang, C.P. (2004). Internal reliability, temporal stability, and correlates of individual differences in paternal involvement: A 15-year longitudinal study in Sweden. In R.D. Day and M.E. Lamb (Eds), *Conceptualizing and Measuring Father Involvement.* Mahwah, NJ: Erlbaum.

Cochran, M.M. (1977). A comparison of group day care and family child-rearing patterns in Sweden. *Child Development, 48,* 702–707.

Cochran, M.M. and Gunnarsson, L. (1985). A follow-up study of group day care and family based childrearing patterns. *Journal of Marriage and the Family, 47,* 297–309.

Ekholm, B., Hedin, A. and Andersson, B.E. (1995). Climates in Swedish day care centres: A methodological study. *Journal of Research in Childhood Education, 9 (2).*

European Commission Network on Childcare (1996). *A Review of Services for Young Children in the European Union 1990–1995.* Bruxelles: DGV.

Gunnarsson, L.O. (1978). *Children in day care and family care in Sweden: A follow-up.* Research Bulletin, No 21, Department of Education. Göteborg: University of Göteborg.

Gunnarsson, L., Andersson, B-E. and Cochran, M. (1987). Barnomsorg utanför hemmet – forskning kring utvecklingseffekter. In H. Dahlgren, L. Gunnarsson and G. Kärrby, *Barnets väg genom förskola, skola och in i vuxenlivet.* Lund: Studentlitteratur.

Gustavsson, J-E. and Myrberg, E. (2002). *Ekonomiska resursers betydelse för pedagogiska resultat: en kunskapsöversikt/Economic resources impact on pedagogic results./Skolverkets monografiserie.* Stockholm: Liber.

Haas, L. and Hwang, C.P. (2000). Programs and policies promoting women's economic equality and men's sharing of childcare in Sweden. In L. Haas, C.P. Hwang and G. Russell (Eds) *Organizational Change and Gender Equity.* Thousands Oaks, CA: Sage, pp 133–161.

Hårsman, I. (1984). The emotional and social adjustment of infants to day care centres. Paper presented at the International Conference on Infant Studies, New York.

Hedin, A., Ekholm, B. and Andersson, B-E. (1997). Climates in Swedish day care centres: Children's behaviour in differing centres. *Journal of Research in Childhood Education, 11 (2).*

Hwang, C.P. and Broberg, A.G. (1991). Swedish parents' preferences for childcare. *Journal of Reproductive and Infant Psychology, 9*, 79–90.

Hwang, C.P. and Lamb, M.E. (1997). Father involvement – stability and perceptions. *The International Journal of Behavioural Development, 21*, 621–632.

Kärrby, G. (1996). Sweden. In *European Commission Network on Childcare (1996). A Review of Services for Young Children in the European Union 1990–1995*. Bruxelles: DGV.

Kärrby, G. and Giota, J. (1994). Dimensions of quality in Swedish day care centres: An analysis of Early Childhood Environment Rating Scale. *Early Child Development and Care, 104*, 1–22.

Kärrby, G. and Giota, J. (1995). Parental conceptions of quality in daycare centres in relation to quality measured by the ECERS. *Early Development and Care, 100*, 1–18.

Lamb, M.E., Sternberg, K., Hwang, C.P. and Broberg, A.G. (1992). *Childcare in context*. Hillsdale, NJ: Erlbaum.

Larner, M. (1982). *Effects of day care on social development*. Cornell University, unpublished paper.

Pramling, I. and Sheridan, S. (2004). Recent issues in the Swedish preschool. *International Journal of Early Childhood, 36*, 1.

Prodromidis, M., Lamb, M.E., Sternberg, K.J., Hwang, C.P. and Broberg, A.G. (1995). Aggression and non-compliance among Swedish children in center-based care, family day care, and home care. *International Journal of Behavioural Development, 18*, 43–62.

Rostguard, T. and Fridberg, T. (1998). *Caring for children and older people: A comparison of European policies and practices. Social Security in Europe 6*. Copenhagen: The Danish National Institute of Social Research 98:20.

Rudebrandt, S. and Thörn, S. (1979). *Barn pa daghem, familjedaghem och hemma – en uppfoljningsstudie (Rapport 6)*. Stockholm: Instituten för Pedagogik, Högskolan för larrutbildning i Stockholm.

Skolverket (2004). Beskrivande data 2004. *Förskoleverksamhet, skolbarnsomsorg, skola och vuxenutbildning. (Deskriptive data 2004. Day-care, after school care and adult education) Rapport 248*.

Söderlund, A. (1975). *Spädbarn på daghem, familjedaghem och hemma. Spädbarns utveckling i tre tillsynsformeren jämförelse (Rapport 14)*. Stockholm: Instituten för Pedagogik, Högskolan för lärrutbildning i Stockholm.

Statistics Sweden (1997). *Barnomsorgsundersökningar/Child care investigations*. Stockholm: Statistics Sweden.

Statistics Sweden (2004). *Statistical Yearbook of Sweden*. Stockholm: Statistics Sweden.

Svenning, C. and Svenning, M. (1979). *Daghemmen jämlikheten och klassamhället*. Lund: Liber.

Wessels, H., Lamb, M.E., Hwang, C.P. and Broberg, A.G. (1997). Personality development between one and eight years of age in Swedish children with varying childcare experiences. *International Journal of Behavioural Development, 21*, 771–794.

7 Early childhood care and education in Aotearoa–New Zealand

Anne B. Smith and Helen May

This chapter provides an historical, policy and curriculum context to the diversity of early childhood provision in Aotearoa–New Zealand and its integrated model of care and education. This is a story of advocacy, shifting state interest and increasing government investment. Currently, a raft of policies are being implemented towards improving quality participation as part of a ten-year strategic plan, *Pathways to the Future: Ngā Huarahi Arataki 2002–2012* (Ministry of Education, 2002). The unique interplay of research, pedagogy and policy in the advocacy, implementation and evaluation of early childhood care and education is appraised.

Historical context

Polynesian migrants from the Western Pacific discovered the archipelago of Aotearoa approximately 800 years ago. European exploration led to colonisation by Britain in the nineteenth century. During early contact, the use of the terms Māori (defined by Māori as being 'ordinary') and Pakeha (defined by Māori as 'extraordinary' and 'white') emerged. The Treaty of Waitangi between Māori and the Pakeha Crown was signed in 1840. This was intended to protect tino rangatiratanga (governance), taonga (treasured sites and objects) and land for Māori, and establish British rule for Pakeha settlers. The Treaty was soon breached when settlers continued to arrive and Māori were unwilling to sell more land. By 1940, Māori had little land left, and their language was in decline. During the postwar years these issues became pertinent to early childhood education, as Māori preschoolers became visible in suburbs and cities and the occasional kindergarten. Early childhood institutions established over the latter part of the century, both for Māori and by Māori, were at the forefront of struggles over power and powerlessness, land, language and culture for Māori and Pakeha. Issues of European colonisation and tino rangatiratanga were at the heart of the argument. Immigration accelerated during the postwar years and came to include people from Pacific Island nations and, more recently, migrants from Asia and Africa. Issues of biculturalism between Māori and Pakeha are now combined with the realities of multicultural diversity.

This paradigm of diversity characterises early childhood provision in Aotearoa–New Zealand. Government policy currently provides direct funding support to centres for children from birth to school age, at five years, in a range of institutions licensed to provide integrated care and education. These might be: teacher-led or parent-led; community operated or privately owned; part day or full day; Māori language immersion or Pacific Nations bilingual; kindergarten or childcare; home-based, centre-based or for remote rural children by correspondence. Both integration and diversity are supported through funding policies, teacher education programmes and the national curriculum called Te Whāriki (Ministry of Education, 1996).

Early childhood institutions were first established in Aotearoa–New Zealand in the late nineteenth century. Government interest in the preschool child was limited to kindergartens, whose programmes fitted with the rationales for emerging state investment and/or intervention in the lives of children such as moral reform, child rescue and child health (May, 1997). Early childhood care and education underwent a dramatic transformation during the second half of the twentieth century. The government promised more support for mothers at home, and its progressive education policies promoted preschool for three- and four-year-olds as a benefit for children as they approached school entry at five years. The postwar years were characterised by huge growth in the early childhood sector and political constraint to contain and/or manage the demand (May, 2001).

Current context

In 2004, there were 184,000 children attending 4,374 early childhood centres/services receiving government funding, with 98 per cent of all four-year-olds and 20 per cent of under-twos attending an early childhood programme (Ministry of Education, 2005c). Participation in early childhood programmes is uneven across the community and improving access for children in Māori and Pacific communities has been a concern since the 1960s. In both contexts participation continues to increase, particularly with a mix of community activism and endeavour and targeted government support. Unlike schools, no early childhood service is fully incorporated into the state sector. A partnership of community or private management and government support and regulation has been the model. Historically, each kind of service emerged to meet a new need, usually through 'do-it-yourself' activism. Each service brought a new rationale for broadening the state's investment in the early years. Some, such as day care, challenged the dominant ideology of the time before eventually becoming incorporated into the mainstream. Since 1989, government policy has sought to incorporate the diversity of early childhood services and to redress earlier divides, for example between care and education, majority and minority cultures, as well as privately owned and community-based services.

Inevitably, some divides are deep and difficult to bridge and new divides have emerged. Recent funding policy (Ministry of Education, 2005a) differentiates between teacher-led and parent-led services. The real costs of the former are now recognised in a policy commitment that, by 2012, will require all staff working in teacher-led services (currently 75 per cent of all services attended by children) to be qualified teachers. Implicit too is the acknowledgement that early childhood teachers will not only have the same level of qualification as school teachers, but also have pay parity (May, 2005). The implementation of pay parity is underway, although not yet guaranteed in the private childcare sector. Parent-led services such as play centres that emerged in the 1940s and Kohanga Reo, Māori immersion language centres that started in the 1980s, are still valued despite the policy divide. To receive government funding, a proportion of the parents whose children attend must be trained or undergo training to implement the national curriculum within their particular service.

Contexts of advocacy and change

Early childhood policy in New Zealand is characterised by periods of effective and cohesive advocacy that has not been afraid to take its case to the streets, alongside the strategies of persuasion, personal presence and the pen. There have been three 'windows' for substantive policy shifts in the government's investment in the early years: the late 1940s, the late 1980s and currently in the 2000s. Each 'window' has been the culmination of sometimes decades of persuasion and been successful owing to links into broader social and education policy reform. Each policy 'window' has been the initiative of a Labour government on the political 'left of centre' and usually the policy was incomplete before the Labour government was ousted from power by a National – 'right of centre' – government. To understand the dynamics of early childhood policy in Aotearoa–New Zealand it is useful to look further at the respective reports that heralded the 'windows' for change.

In 1947 the government released its postwar blueprint, the *Report of the Consultative Committee on Preschool Education Services*. The benefits of preschool were perceived to provide:

- companionship for children;
- stimulating play environments;
- parent education.

The benefits were not just for children and provided:

- relief for mothers from the emotional strain of full-time parenting;
- support for mothers to have more children.

Overall, the 'stabilising' life of the kindergarten was viewed as a benefit to the mental and physical health of the community (*Report of the Consultative Committee,* 1947, p. 6). This paradigm drew upon new under-standings from research in developmental psychology.

From the late 1960s, sociological and political understandings in relation to the rights of minority groups, women and children came to the fore. One example was the policy exclusion of childcare from any substantive govern-ment funding. As a result of ongoing advocacy regarding this separation of childcare from so-called educational (preschool) services, New Zealand became the first country in the world to integrate responsibility for all early childhood services within the education system (Moss, 2000). Changes towards an integrated system of care and education began in the late 1970s. There was a strong emphasis placed in the forums of the time on *the rights of a child to a quality early education* no matter which early childhood set-ting they participated in, how old they were, or whether their mother worked or not. There was also a belief that children had the right to gov-ernment contribution to the cost of their early childhood education. The combination of women's aspiration to participate in the workforce and teachers' wish for a professional image, a career structure and a living wage helped get early childhood issues onto the political agenda. In 1986, early childhood services were brought within one department (the Education Department). An integrated diploma-level training, comparable to primary teaching qualifications, of early childhood teachers was introduced into col-leges of education in 1987. This replaced separate kindergarten and childcare training.

Almost two decades of activism and persuasion by women and the early childhood organisations culminated in the 1988 *Before Five* report (Lange, 1988), which was the government's response to *Education to be More* (Meade, 1988). The report emphasised the holistic nature of early child-hood care and education. Essential elements of the proposed model comprised features addressing the interests of children, the interests of women and the interests of cultural survival.

Overall, the *Before Five* reforms were intended to:

- acknowledge diversity in services in terms of philosophy, culture, struc-ture and ownership;
- improve participation, access, and affordability;
- integrate care and education;
- support quality for children;
- improve the status of teachers;
- enable women to work in paid employment with improved childcare support.

Despite resistance from the Treasury, the early childhood sector won addi-tional funding to implement the new policy directions. Meade wrote that the reforms enabled, 'Women and young children [to] gain a foot in the door' (1990, p. 96).

Disappointment followed as the 'door' did not open fully (Dalli, 1993). A change of government and a philosophical shift articulating small government were reasons. One consequence was a rise in the private childcare sector and a 'market forces' approach to provision that sharpened the historic divide between community and private sector interests. Similarly, there was a deregulation of training providers that led to a plethora of different training programmes that are not always inclusive or integrated (May, 1996). There were still many divisions and distinctions in the funding and working conditions for different kinds of early childhood centres. Nevertheless, by the 1990s some crucial groundwork had been laid concerning: a unified administrative umbrella for all services under a Ministry of Education that was inclusive of centre and home-based childcare services; an integrated holistic 'educare' philosophy; teaching diploma and degree qualifications of the same status as required for the school sector; and the integration of teachers in both the kindergarten and childcare sector into a combined industrial union with primary school teachers (May, 2005).

In 1999, a Labour-led government came to power, with a strategic plan for early childhood provision. The new government immediately introduced a policy of 'equity funding' for centres based on factors such as rural location, low income areas, and/or children with special needs and/or cultural and language needs. The funding was linked to an election policy of 'closing the [economic] gaps'. In 2000, the government appointed a working party to develop a 10-year strategy for early childhood provision (Strategic Plan Working Group, 2001a, b). The focus was on achieving quality participation for all children. This was an acknowledgement that some of the tenets of the *Before Five* policies were flawed and not working equitably for children, the staff or the early childhood services. It was also a tribute to the tenacious work of the organisations, teacher unions, researchers and activists who monitored the shortcomings of the implementation of the *Before Five* policies (Meade, 1990; Dalli, 1993; Wells, 1991).

The working group outlined a range of strategies intended to improve the infrastructures of quality participation. There was a new emphasis given to the Articles of the United Nations Convention on the Rights of the Child, the Treaty of Waitangi and the principles of Te Whāriki (Strategic Plan Working Group, 2001a, b). The working group put a new demand onto the political agenda, 'for whanau [extended family] and families to have a universal entitlement to a reasonable amount of free, high quality early childhood education' (2001a, p. 5). The Minister of Education's reaction was that this was 'blue skies thinking' (Mallard, 2001).

In 2002, the Prime Minister Helen Clark launched *Pathways to the Future: Ngā Huarahi Arataki* (Ministry of Education, 2002). Free early childhood education for children did not materialise, but the government did make a commitment to:

- new funding and regulatory systems to support diverse early childhood education services to achieve quality;
- better government support for community-based early childhood education services;
- the introduction of professional registration for teachers in teacher-led early childhood education, such as those applying in schools and kindergartens.

Since 2002, the government has invested considerable resources towards realising its teacher-led policy. The role of teachers has been articulated as the key to ensuring quality outcomes for children. The research community played a crucial role in demonstrating these understandings. In the field though, there has been some resistance, particularly since new funding policy benefits those centres that employ teachers (Ministry of Education, 2005a). In some locations qualified teachers have been hard to find, but more specifically, some private childcare owners have been reluctant to employ more teachers than the regulatory requirement.

In 2004, in a surprise announcement, the Labour-led government promised the introduction, in 2007, of 20 hours a week free early childhood education for three- to four-year-old children in all teacher-led community-based centres. This would be in addition to existing funding subsidies that were sufficient for an 'almost free' early childhood education for 15 hours a week in a part-day kindergarten. The announcement was welcomed with surprise by many, although it was a more targeted policy than the earlier 'demands' for a 'child's right to a free education'. The private sector, however, saw this as another divisive policy, and in August 2005 Labour made a late election promise to extend this policy to private centres. The National Party promised to revoke the 'free early childhood' policy if it won power, offering instead a policy of tax cuts for childcare costs of working parents. This was an ideological debate between left and right that has periodically characterised both policy and advocacy in Aotearoa–New Zealand. In September 2005, a Labour-led government was elected by a narrow margin.

Curriculum context

During the 1990s, rationales for government investment in the sector were influenced by economic agendas and framed around the discourse of quality. Here we outline the political and cultural context of the development of the first early childhood national curriculum. Previously, the early childhood curriculum was a concern, not of government, but of the respective early childhood services. Aotearoa–New Zealand, as a country, might have been a great distance from other populations but its peoples had always travelled. Many curriculum ideas had rapidly found their own unique expression in local programmes. Amidst the different emphases of the respective programmes there were also shared values, particularly concerning the importance of play and the involvement of parents. The curriculum experience for children, though, depended on the training of staff. The sector had (and still has) a range in terms of quality.

In the early 1990s, the government's agenda was to develop an early childhood curriculum parallel to the New Zealand School Curriculum (Ministry of Education, 1991). These developments were part of an international trend to orchestrate the connections between the economic success of the nation and education. Early childhood organisations were wary at the idea of a national curriculum, and concerned that it would constrain their independence and cut across the essence of their diversity. The alternative, of not defining the early childhood curriculum, was a dangerous one: the national curriculum for schools might start a downward move.

Helen May became part of the story in 1991 when, with Margaret Carr, she was contracted to coordinate the development of a curriculum that could embrace diverse early childhood services and cultural perspectives; articulate a philosophy of quality early childhood practice; and make connections with a new national curriculum for schools. The story of this development spans the 1990s (Carr and May, 1994, 1997, 1999, 2000). This was a policy development that the government wisely did not rush.

In 1996, the Prime Minister launched the final draft of Te Whāriki, the national early childhood curriculum (Ministry of Education, 1996). This was the first time a prime minister so explicitly had stamped government approval on what children might do on a daily basis in early childhood centres. The development and wide acceptance of Te Whāriki as a curriculum within the early childhood sector was a surprising story of collaboration between a right-wing National government and this sector. There was both accommodation and resistance to government agendas. The Ministry of Education funded research projects towards developing appropriate frameworks for evaluation and assessment based on Te Whāriki (Carr, 1998a, 1998b, 2001; Mara, 1998; Podmore *et al.*, 1998; Ministry of Education, 2005b). The links between research and policy were both strong and strategic.

The development of Te Whāriki involved a wide consultative process. More specifically, the writers wanted the curriculum to reflect the Treaty of Waitangi partnership of Māori and Pakeha as a bicultural document, and be grounded in the contexts of Aotearoa–New Zealand. A collaboration with Te Kohanga Reo National Trust and the foresight of Dr Tamati Reedy and Tilly Reedy, who developed the curriculum for Māori immersion centres, made this possible. The theme of empowerment was important for Māori, and 'empowering children to learn and grow' became a foundation principle. Tilly Reedy emphasised the maxim for Māori that 'Toko rangatiratanga na te mana-matauranga – knowledge and power set me free' (Reedy, 1995, p. 6). A set of parallel aims for children in Māori and English was developed, not as translations but as equivalent domains of empowerment in both cultures. They are:

Mana atua	Well-being
Mana whenua	Belonging
Mana tangata	Contribution
Mana reo	Communication
Mana ao turoa	Exploration

The title Te Whāriki was a central metaphor. The early childhood curriculum was envisaged as a whāriki, translated as 'a woven mat for all to stand on'. The principles and aims provided the framework, which allowed for different programme perspectives to be woven into the fabric of the curriculum. There were many possible 'patterns' for this depending on the age and interests of children, the cultural, structural or philosophical context of the particular service, or the interests of parents and staff. This was a curriculum that provided signposts for individuals and centres to develop their own curriculum, weaving through a process of talk, reflection, planning, evaluation and assessment.

The conceptualisation of Te Whāriki around aims for children was different from the traditional developmental curriculum map of physical, intellectual, emotional and social skills that dominated Western curriculum models. Te Whāriki also made a political statement about children: their uniqueness, ethnicity and rights in New Zealand society. For people from the Pacific Island Nations (and other cultures), Te Whāriki provided a curriculum space where language and cultures could be in the foreground and not an add-on (Mara, 1998). For Māori, Te Whāriki was about self-determination. Tilly Reedy told a mainly Pakeha audience: 'Our rights are recognised and so are the rights of everyone else ... Te Whāriki recognises my right to choose, and your right to choose too' (Reedy, 1995, p. 16).

Transforming a national curriculum into practice to make a difference for children has been a challenge. By 2000, the visual presence of Te Whāriki was apparent in most centres but implementing the document was complex, partly because it resisted telling staff what to do, by requiring each programme to 'weave' its own curriculum pattern. The challenges have been ongoing. First, there was the assumption that early childhood centres would have the funding and the qualified staff capacity to operate quality programmes. This was not realised in the early years but is being addressed by the strategic plan. Second, the holistic and bicultural approach to curriculum of Te Whāriki, inclusive of children from birth, was a challenge to staff more familiar with the traditional focus on play areas and activities for preschool children in mainstream centres. Third was a political climate of accountability that made increasing demands on early childhood staff particularly in relation to assessment. Margaret Carr's research on assessment, described later, became a crucial interface mediating between policy and practice.

There was international interest in the rationale of Te Whāriki as a national curriculum statement (Olsen, 1996). Nutbrown (1996), from

Britain, highlighted its emphasis on children's rights as a source of curriculum and also the respect for children as learners. Bruce urged her British colleagues to speak out and clarify for the politicians, 'What we want for our children in early childhood. This has been done in New Zealand ... the radicals have been allowed to speak' (Bruce, 1996 p. 2). The framework of multiple curricula too was of interest (Sobstad, 1997).

It is almost a decade since the launch of Te Whāriki (Nuttall, 2003). To ensure that early childhood staff are skilled and confident with the new language of learning development and culture it has been important that curriculum development be accompanied by research and by professional development, and become embedded in teacher education. There are still challenges ahead. The metaphor of Te Whāriki has become powerful. The key factor underpinning successful policy collaborations with government has been the ability of the diverse groups within the early childhood sector to find common ground – a whāriki, a mat 'for all to stand on' but allowing different patterns. Despite its differences, the sector has found a formula for unity. The harder task has been to persuade governments to demonstrate the kind of political courage that gives real substance to political rhetoric of empowerment and putting children first.

Research context

The strongest influences on New Zealand's research programmes in twentieth-century theory have been from ecological and socio-cultural perspectives on development. Much of the early research was designed to define and elaborate the process features of quality within early childhood microsystems. There was also an interest in looking at whether different types of early childhood centres differed in providing care and education. The coverage of research in this section of the chapter is selective because of space limitations, and mainly looks at research on issues of early childhood quality.[1]

New Zealand research fits into the metaphor of three waves of research on early childhood education (Lamb and Sternberg, 1992; Rosenthal, 1994; Scarr and Eisenberg, 1993). The first wave of research emerged out of experimental early childhood programmes developed in the United States, which included initiatives in early childhood designed to break the cycle of disadvantage and to give poor children a good start at school. The second wave of research concerned the provision of childcare for infants or young children during the day, and emerged from the controversy about whether the daily separations involved in longer day care, especially during infancy, adversely affect bonding with the mother and subsequent social behaviour in early childhood education and school. Research on the nature of quality in early childhood education is part of the third wave of research that represented a move from the crude, 'Does early childcare have harmful outcomes for children?' question, towards identifying specific variations in the early childhood setting and how they affect outcomes for children.

First wave research

There was very little first wave research in New Zealand. Jane Ritchie (1978), however, set up a programme, entitled Te Kohanga, for children of low-income Māori families, to provide them with experiences designed to prepare them for school entry, and to encourage language and social development. The programme used language kits and shared reading to teach language to children in a lesson format. Children's test scores, knowledge of concepts, attention span and ability to follow instructions were reported to have improved after participation in the programme. Such so-called 'deficit-based' programmes are now criticised for not using culturally valued practice, concentrating on teaching children passive skills, and failing to stimulate exploration and creativity. Ritchie, however, questioned the success of traditional play-based curriculum for Māori children.

Second wave research

Second wave research in New Zealand incorporated a strong ecological perspective. Bronfenbrenner came to New Zealand in 1979 in the same year that his book, *The Ecology of Human Development,* was published. His influence can be linked to the development of early childhood policy, and especially to the importance of support for caregivers/teachers, the inseparability of care and education, the influence of wider environments outside the immediate home or early childhood education context on the development of the child, and the development of ecologically valid assessment.

In the late 1970s there was a division between centres that were perceived to be educational (kindergartens and play centres) and custodial (childcare centres). The 'care-type' centres were assumed to have an adverse effect on early attachment, whereas 'education-type' (preschool sessional) programmes were not. One early study (Smith and Bain, 1978) comparing children in childcare centres and play centres, concluded that there was no evidence of adverse effects of childcare experiences, and that attendance at childcare could enable the development of close relationships between peers, and between children and adults.

Third wave research

There has been interest in the processes of interaction that take place in early childhood centres. 'Process quality' involves those aspects of an early childhood education programme that children actually experience, such as teacher–child and child–child interactions and joint activities. Two studies (Smith and Bain, 1978; Smith and Haggerty, 1979) showed that it was impossible to separate out caring affective elements, and cognitive stimulating aspects of early childhood environments. Later research confirmed that administrative auspices were not a good predictor of quality (Smith, 1988), and that there was more overlap than difference between care and education centres. Relationships with teachers and peers were, however, somewhat closer in childcare centres than in education centres but this could well have been due to structural features (ratio and group size). When they reached school the children with more extensive (earlier starting and longer duration) childcare experiences were rated slightly more positively by their teachers than children who had been in sessional preschools, and were doing better academically (Smith *et al.,* 1993).

While previous studies had emphasised staff–child and child–child relationships, another study looked at contrasting staff relationships (Smith *et al.,* 1992). Harmonious relationships with a new teacher developed in a climate where staff spent time in reflective practice, but serious differences in viewpoint and unresolved conflict occurred in other kindergartens. The 'successful' kindergartens worked through consensus and negotiation, while the 'unsuccessful' kindergartens worked through the authority of the head teacher or the majority view.

Research was beginning to influence official views of the nature of quality in early childhood education. The idea of integrating care and education into one department (education) instead of (as was then the case) having a fragmented system with half-day programmes administered through education, and childcare through social welfare, was beginning to gain momentum. Education and care were coming to be seen as integral and related, rather than alternative and separate, and the previous judgemental and disapproving view of parents who made use of childcare centres for their children being questioned (Smith, 1987).

Curriculum

A curriculum model is a very important component of process quality, and a source of principles to guide practice, professional development, a shared language, and a framework through which assessment could be designed. In New Zealand we have been fortunate that the development of a national curriculum was followed by action research, which guided the practice that emerged out of it. Based on socio-cultural theory (Smith, 1993) our early childhood curriculum, Te Whāriki, is 'a cultural site whose social reality is constructed by, and in turn constructs, the communicative interactions amongst teachers and students' (Carr, 1996, p. 9). The emphasis is on encouraging an orientation towards learning that can lead to an ongoing disposition to learn and persevere with difficulties rather than giving up.

An ethnographic and interpretive method of formative assessment, Learning Stories, was developed which was appropriate for Te Whāriki (Carr, 1998a, b). This holistic, transactional model of assessment seeks ways to focus on behaviours that are central to children becoming competent, confident learners and communicators, and focuses not on isolated skills, but on the coalescence of skills, knowledge and attitudes into learning strategies, attitudes and dispositions. A narrative genre and multiple voices are used in Learning Stories, to foreground children's strengths and interests, and what teachers do to build on these. Subsequently, a parallel framework for evaluation entitled Teaching Stories was developed (Podmore *et al.*, 1998). The whole framework (Teaching and Learning Stories) was trialled in six centres for a year (Carr *et al.*, 1999). The generation of reflective discussion, allowing peer observation, being grounded in the child's perspective and being easily read and understood by staff and the community were suggested as criteria for effective assessment. This research informed the development of guidelines for improving quality, and the professional development of teachers (Ministry of Education, 1999).

Including children's voice and perspective in curriculum and assessment is an ongoing focus in New Zealand early childhood research. There is an emphasis on learning rather than performance goals, and engaging children's motivation and interest in meaningful learning tasks. Recent and ongoing research continues to explore the development of dispositions to learn in early childhood settings (Carr and Claxton, 2002; Smith *et al.*, 2005). A government policy response to this research, spearheaded by Margaret Carr, has been to develop a resource of assessment exemplars to guide quality practice for teachers, rather than prescribe particular tools of assessment (Ministry of Education, 2005b).

Studies on structural aspects of quality

Structural quality consists of 'the characteristics which create the framework for the processes that children actually experience' (Cryer, 1999, p. 40). Improving structural quality has been advocated for many years by New Zealand researchers, based on overseas and local research.

Staff training, education and experience

Training and education is a major issue in policy and research for early childhood education internationally. It provides early childhood teachers with a framework of knowledge and supervised experience, which allows them to provide quality early childhood opportunities, as well as preparing them to be professionals who can plan, manage, assess and reflect on the effectiveness of their work with children and families.

Smith surveyed a national sample of 100 childcare centres catering for under-twos, and assessed various aspects of quality (Smith, 1996a; Smith *et al.*, 1995; Smith, 1999). The study showed moderate to strong correlations between staff training and education and measures of quality. The impact of early childhood training on high-quality interactions was strongest when staff had three years of training (Smith, 1996a). Centres with more staff with no school-leaving qualifications (lower levels of general education) tended to be of lower quality.

Engagement with skilled social partners is an important aspect of process quality, and this was examined by looking at joint staff–child attention episodes with under-twos in relation to staff training (Smith, 1999). There was more joint attention in centres where staff had diploma (three-year) levels of training, implying that a more advanced level of training directly influenced the quality and number of interactions between children and teachers.

Teacher–child ratio

A natural experimental study looked at the effect of improving the teacher–child ratio by introducing an extra teacher in kindergartens (Smith *et al.*, 1989). The strongest effect of the introduction of the third teacher was a significant reduction (by more than half) in children's negative behaviour (e.g. arguments and aggressive behaviour) towards peers. The greater availability of adults to mediate and moderate children's aggressive behaviour appeared to be an important effect of improving teacher–child ratios.

Group size

Teacher perceptions of increases in group size in New Zealand kindergartens were examined by Renwick and McCaulay (1995). Teachers working in kindergartens with 45 children listed negative consequences for children, staff and the quality of programmes, from having to work with such large groups. Children were overwhelmed by the numbers of other children and having to compete for equipment, space and teacher time. Teachers found one-to-one or small group work with children difficult, were less able to provide varied learning experiences, and their interactions lacked quality and continuity. Other problems were noise – quiet children getting less attention – safety, and frustration for children in trying to gain teacher attention. Teachers felt that their role had become mainly supervisory, that their workload had increased, that they did not have time to get to know families, and that they were constantly interrupted.

Smaller group size was shown to promote staff–child joint attention, and predict positive child initiations and total child initiations (Smith *et al.*, 1995). Centres with group sizes of 14 or less had three times the number of joint attention episodes between children and staff than occurred in groups of 26 or more (Smith, 1999). Joint attention episodes allow the teacher to work in the child's zone of proximal development, providing opportunities for extension of language, mediation of social interactions between peers, encouragement of exploration and problem-solving, and support for the extension of children's physical skills.

Staff wages and working conditions

Staff wages and conditions are an important structural component of quality, and Smith (1996a) found that the best predictor of quality for infants was staff salary. Job benefits (such as sick leave, holidays, breaks, grievance procedures, etc.) were also important, and thus the higher the wages and job benefits for staff, the higher the quality.

Parental attitudes and values

The relationship between early childhood education centres, parents and the community is a valued component of quality in New Zealand. In 1990, Farquhar, in a New Zealand study of parental and professional perspectives on quality in early childhood, commented that 'what one means by quality in early childhood education and care is problematic due to philosophical and practical assessment issues' (Farquhar, 1990, p. 81). Farquhar questioned the view that defining quality was simply a matter of linking environmental variables with key indicators. She showed that there were many different perspectives on quality, and introduced the important notion that quality is multi-dimensional and dynamic, and should not be dominated by a child development perspective alone. Her work moved early childhood policy-makers and researchers towards taking into account both objective and subjective measures of quality (Smith, 1996b).

Farquhar (1995) also drew attention to the need for more research on the decision-making surrounding the selection of childcare by parents, for women with infants returning to work. Women were generally satisfied with the care they had chosen, whether it was home based or centre based. The women who chose centre-based care viewed it as safer and less likely to exploit women childcare workers. For all women, childcare costs were experienced as a drain on their work incomes, but childcare was viewed as necessary for women's work and career advancement. Most women did not prioritise education for infants but valued good communication from staff.

Barraclough and Smith (1996) analysed whether parents choose and value quality in childcare. The authors found that parents were more positive and uncritical than the researchers about childcare programmes, and that 86 per cent of the parents were using a centre that had been their first choice. There was no correlation between research-based measures of quality and parent satisfaction, and only modest correlation between quality and socio-economic status, parental education and family income. Some parents, because of their cultural capital, may be better able to choose quality. Background and demographic factors (i.e. education, income, etc.) were not good indicators of whether parents choose quality care, however. Parents appear to make passive choices about the care they use for their children, and therefore parental choice about a childcare centre is not a viable means of controlling quality.

The effects of early childhood education and types of centre

Smith *et al.* (1995) showed that there were differences in quality depending on the auspices of childcare centres – either private, community or institution/employment-based (e.g. tertiary institution or company) care. Employment-based centres were of highest quality, followed by community centres, and then private centres. Community centres were not superior to private centres on all measures of quality, but employment-based centres consistently were, possibly due to subsidies from employers, such as for buildings and equipment.

New Zealand's largest and most comprehensive study of the impact of early childhood centre experiences on children's development, initiated by Anne Meade, is the *Competent Children* study, which followed 307 children from four years of age, and has continued until the children are 12 years old. It looks at the contribution which early childhood centre experiences and other variables (such as family and school) make to children's competency in literacy, mathematics, logical problem-solving, communication, curiosity, perseverance, social skills with peers and adults, individual responsibility and fine motor skills. Quality was rated for staff–child interactions, programme-activity focus, and physical environment.

The first report (Wylie *et al.*, 1996) concluded that children's competencies were affected by the length of their early childhood education experience and that more was better for early mathematics and motor skills. The second study (Wylie and Thompson, 1998) reported that a year after they left early childhood centres, the early childhood experience continued to make a contribution to children's competency levels. Associations with literacy and mathematics remained and new associations emerged: perseverance, communication and logical problem-solving. The third report (Wylie *et al.*, 1999) showed that children with at least three years of preschool experience scored higher on competency measures for mathematics, communication, word recognition, fine motor skills, individual responsibility and logical problem-solving. Early childhood education experience was shown to have enduring and concurrent effects on children's competencies. Children who started before the age of two had higher scores, and children from low-income families with four years of early childhood education experience achieved as well as children from high-income families for literacy and communication.

The type of centre only predicted 3 per cent of the variance on reading and mathematics scores at age eight (Wylie *et al.*, 1999). A large proportion of the variance was accounted for by the socio-economic mix of children attending centres. The socio-economic composition of the group of children was therefore shown to be far more important than the type of centre in predicting academic outcomes. The items associated with quality which had the strongest associations with competency outcomes at age 10, included asking open-ended questions, a print-saturated environment, children selecting their own activities, staff joining children in play, children being allowed to complete their work, children cooperating with each other and provision of age-appropriate resources (Wylie and Thompson, 2003). This large and continuing study has had an ongoing influence on the New Zealand government's willingness to support and fund early childhood education in New Zealand.

Conclusions

This chapter reports on developments in policy and research in New Zealand early childhood education services. Aotearoa–New Zealand is a small country with a very diverse early years sector. Our small size has probably helped to nurture the close and continuing relationship between practice, policy and research, but our heterogeneity has sometimes made it hard to bridge historical discontinuities and different aims. Nevertheless, New Zealand has benefited from vigorous advocacy by its supporters in the academic practice and policy world towards improving quality and provision, and encouraging participation by all New Zealand children in some form of early childhood education. A cumulative body of systematic research has directly influenced government policies towards increasing the status, recognition and funding for early childhood education services. The administrative integration of early childhood services in the 1980s and 1990s was based on philosophy and research showing that education and care for young children are inseparable. Integrated early childhood services provided a framework for the ongoing development of improved early childhood centre quality, nurtured children's early learning, and provided options for most parents. These developments have all been integrally linked to both international and national research, which has clarified the important criteria of good-quality early childhood education. The status and recognition of early childhood education has increased, and attitudes towards it are now largely positive, perhaps because research has supported the value of participation in early childhood education for children and their families.

Improving both process and structural quality has become a priority for early childhood education policy. We have come a long way towards the recognition, and incorporation in policy, of the importance of qualifications and training for all early childhood teachers. An associated and equally important development is the gradual recognition and implementation of the policy that early childhood teachers deserve to be paid at the same level as teachers of older children. Our national early childhood curriculum Te Whāriki is, uniquely of New Zealand, bottom-up, and has biculturally developed and shared sets of values and principles. When properly implemented in practice, it helps unify the early childhood education field but does not restrict our diversity. Te Whāriki and Learning Stories provide the foundation for children's lifelong engagement in learning, and shared pleasure among children, families and staff in those achievements. We still have some way to go before all families have equal access to affordable and high-quality early childhood education for their children but, if history is any guide, inexorable if sometimes slow progress will be made towards achieving this goal.

Note

1. Some parts of this section of the chapter are based on an extensive literature review carried out under contract to the Ministry of Education (Smith *et al., 2000)*.

References

Barraclough, S.J. and Smith, A.B. (1996). Do parents choose and value quality childcare in New Zealand? *International Journal of Early Years Education, 4(1)*, 5–26.

Bronfenbrenner, U. (1979). *The ecology of human development.* Cambridge: Cambridge University Press.

Bruce, T. (1996). *Weaving links between New Zealand and the United Kingdom.* Beyond Desirable Objectives seminar, Pen Green Research, Development and Training Base, November 1996, p. 11.

Carr, M. (1996). Don't call me wrong: Aspects of a disposition to learn in early childhood. Paper presented at the NZARE Annual Conference, Nelson, December.

Carr, M. (Ed.) (1998a). *Assessing children's experiences in early childhood: Final report to the Ministry of Education. Part two: Case Studies.* Wellington: Ministry of Education.

Carr, M. (1998b). Technological practice in early childhood as a dispositional milieu. Ph.D. thesis, University of Waikato.

Carr, M. (2001). *Assessment in early childhood settings: learning stories.* London: Paul Chapman.

Carr, M. and Claxton, G. (2002). Tracking the development of learning dispositions. *Assessment in Education, 9(1)*, 9–37.

Carr, M. and May, H. (1994). Weaving patterns: developing national early childhood curriculum guidelines in Aotearoa–New Zealand. *Australian Journal of Early Childhood Education, 19 (1)*, 25–33.

Carr, M. and May, H. (1997). Making a difference for the under-fives? The early implementation of Te Whāriki, the New Zealand National Early Childhood Curriculum. *International Journal of Early Years Education, 5 (3)*, 225–236.

Carr, M. and May, H. (1999). Te Whāriki: curriculum voices. In H. Penn (Ed.), *Early Childhood Services. Theory, Policy and Practice.* Buckingham: Open University Press, pp. 53–73.

Carr, M. and May, H. (2000). 'Empowering children to learn and grow.' Te Whāriki, the New Zealand National Early Childhood Curriculum. In J. Hayden (Ed.), *Landscapes in Early Childhood. Cross-National Perspectives on Empowerment.* New York: Peter Lang, pp. 153–170.

Carr, M., May, H. & Podmore, V. (1999). *Learning and teaching stories: Action research on evaluation in early childhood.* Wellington: New Zealand Council for Educational Research.

Cryer, D. (1999). Defining and assessing early childhood program quality. *Annals of the American Academy of Political and Social Science, 563,* 39–55.

Dalli, C. (1993). Is Cinderella back among the cinders? A review of early childhood education in the early 1990s. In Manson, H. (Ed.) *New Zealand Annual Review of Education, 3.* Wellington: Faculty of Education, Victoria University of Wellington, pp. 223–254.

Farquhar, S.E. (1990). Quality in early education and care: What do we mean? *Early Child Development and Care, 64,* 71–83.

Farquhar, S.E. (1995). Who cares for baby: Women's preferences. Paper presented at the NZARE, Palmerston North.

Lamb, M.E. and Sternberg, K.J. (1992). Sociocultural perspectives on nonparental childcare. In M.E. Lamb, K.J. Sternberg, C.P. Hwang and A.J. Broberg (Eds), *Childcare in context* (pp. 1–23). Hillsdale, NJ: Lawrence Erlbaum Associates.

Lange, D. (1988). *Before Five: Early childhood care and education in New Zealand.* Wellington: Department of Education.

Mallard, T. (2001). Minister of Education speech notes, Wellington, 10 July.

Mara, D. (1998). *Implementation of Te Whāriki in Pacific Island centres. Final report to the Ministry of Education.* Wellington: New Zealand Council for Educational Research.

May, H. (1996). Training, qualifications and quality: The costs of compromise. In A.B. Smith & N.J. Taylor, *Assessing and improving quality in early childhood centres.* Dunedin: Children's Issues Centre, University of Otago, pp. 65–72.

May, H. (1997). *Discovery of early childhood.* Auckland: Bridget Williams Books, Auckland University Press and New Zealand Council for Educational Research.

May, H. (2001). *Politics in the playground. The world of early childhood policy in postwar New Zealand.* Wellington: Bridget Williams Books and New Zealand Council for Educational Research.

May, H. (2005). *Twenty years of consenting parties: The politics of 'working' and 'teaching' in childcare 1985–2005.* Wellington: New Zealand Educational Institute – Te Riu Roa.

Meade, A. (1988). *Education to be More.* Wellington: Department of Education.

Meade, A. (1990). Women and children gain a foot in the door. *New Zealand Women's Studies Journal, 6 (1/2),* 96–111.

Ministry of Education (1991). *The national curriculum framework: A discussion document.* Wellington: Learning Media.

Ministry of Education (1996). *Te Whāriki: He Whāriki matauranga mo nga mokopuna o Aotearoa. Early childhood curriculum.* Wellington: Learning Media.

Ministry of Education (1999). *The quality journey: Improving quality in early childhood services.* Wellington: Learning Media.

Ministry of Education (2002). *Pathways to the future: Ngā huarahi arataki.* Wellington: Learning Media.

Ministry of Education (2005a). *Early childhood education funding handbook.* Resourcing Division, Wellington: Ministry of Education.

Ministry of Education (2005b). *Kei Tua o te Pae. Assessment for learning: early childhood exemplars.* Wellington: Learning Media.

Ministry of Education (2005c). *Education statistics for NZ, 2004.* Data Analysis and Management Division, Wellington: Ministry of Education.

Moss, P. (2000). *Training and education of early childhood education and care staff.* Report prepared for the OECD, Thomas Coram Research Unit, Institute of Education, University of London.

Nutbrown, C. (1996). *Respectful educators – Capable learning. A framework for practitioners.* London: Paul Chapman.

Nuttall, J. (2003). *Weaving Te Whariki. Aotearoa New Zealand's early childhood curriculum document in theory and practice.* Wellington: New Zealand Council for Educational Research.

Olsen, S.O. (1996). *Verdens Bedste Folkskole! – vi kan loere af det New Zealandske Skolesystem.* Denmark: Dafolo Forlag.

Penn, H. (Ed.) (1999). *Early Childhood Services. Theory, Policy and Practice.* Buckingham: Open University Press.

Podmore, V., May, H. and Mara, D. (1998). *Evaluating early childhood programmes using the strands and goals of Te Whāriki, the national early childhood curriculum.* Wellington: New Zealand Council for Educational Research.

Reedy, T. (1995). *Knowledge and power set me free.* Proceedings of the Sixth Early Childhood Convention, Auckland, Convention Committee, 1, 13–32.

Renwick, M. and McCaulay, L. (1995). *Group size in kindergartens: issues arising from changes to group size and other policy developments in the Wellington Region Free Kindergarten Association.* Wellington: New Zealand Council for Educational Research.

Report of the Consultative Committee on Preschool Educational Services (1947). Wellington: Department of Education.

Ritchie, J. (1978). *Chance to be equal.* Christchurch: Cape Catley Ltd.

Rosenthal, M.K. (1994). *An ecological approach to the study of childcare.* Hove: Lawrence Erlbaum Associates.

Scarr, S. and Eisenberg M. (1993). Childcare research: Issues, perspectives, and results. *Annual Review of Psychology* 44: 613–644.

Smith, A.B. (1987). Recent developments in early childhood 'educare' in New Zealand. *International Journal of Early Childhood, 19 (2):* 33–42.

Smith, A.B. (1988). Education and care components in New Zealand childcare centres and kindergartens. *Australian Journal of Early Childhood, 13(3):* 31–36.

Smith, A.B. (1993). Early childhood educare: Seeking a theoretical framework in Vygotsky's work. *International Journal of Early Years Education, 1(1),* 47–61.

Smith, A.B. (1996a). *The quality of childcare centres for infants in New Zealand.* New Zealand Association for Educational Research, State-of-the-Art Monograph No. 4.

Smith, A.B. (1996b). Is quality a subjective or objective matter? In A.B. Smith and N.J. Taylor (Eds), *Assessing and improving quality in early childhood centres.* Dunedin: Children's Issues Centre, pp. 81–90.

Smith, A.B. (1999). Quality childcare and joint attention. *International Journal of Early Years Education, 7(1)*, 85–98.

Smith, A.B. and Bain, H.M. (1978). Dependency in day care and playcentre children. *New Zealand Journal of Educational Studies, 13(2)*: 163–173.

Smith, A.B., Grima, G., Gaffney, M. and Powell, K. (2000). *Early Childhood Education: Literature Review Report to Ministry of Education.* Dunedin: Children's Issues Centre (146 pages).

Smith, A.B., and Haggerty, M. (1979). An evaluation of caregiver behaviour in a child-care centre. *New Zealand Journal of Educational Studies, 14(2)*: 152–163.

Smith, A.B., Inder, P.M. and Ratcliff, B. (1993). Relations between early childhood centre experience and social behaviour at school. *New Zealand Journal of Educational Studies, 28*: 13–28.

Smith, A.B., McMillan, B.W., Kennedy, S. and Ratcliff, B. (1989). The effect of improving preschool teacher/child ratios: An experiment in nature. *Early Child Development and Care, 42*, 123–138.

Smith, A.B., McMillan, B.W., Kennedy, S. and Ratcliff, B. (1992). Early childhood teachers: Roles and relationships. *Early Child Development and Care, 83*, 33–44.

Smith, A.B., Ford, V., Hubbard, P. and White, J. (1995). *Working in infant childcare centres: Final Research Report to Ministry of Education.* Dunedin: University of Otago.

Smith, A.B., Duncan, J. and Marshall, K. (2005). Children's perspectives on their learning: Exploring methods. *Early Child Development and Care 175(6)*, 473–487.

Sobstad, F. (1997). National Program for the Kindergarten in Norway: a framework for reflection in action. Unpublished paper presented at a a curriculum seminar, Queen Maude College of Early Education, Norway, December, p. 11.

Strategic Plan Working Group (2001a). *Consultation document for the development of the Strategic Plan for early childhood education.* Wellington: Ministry of Education.

Strategic Plan Working Group (2001b). *Final version. Strategic Plan for early childhood education.* Wellington: Ministry of Education.

Wells, C. (1991). The impact of change: against the odds. In Foote, L., Gold, M. and Smith, A.B. (Eds), *Fifth early childhood convention papers.* Dunedin: Early Childhood Convention, pp. 115–127.

Wylie, C.J. and Thompson, J. (1998). *Competent children at 6: families, early education and schools.* Wellington: New Zealand Council for Educational Research.

Wylie, C.J. and Thompson, J. (2003).The long-term contribution of early childhood education to children's performance – evidence from New Zealand. *International Journal of Early Years Education, 11(1)*, 69–78.

Wylie, C., Thompson, J. and Hendricks, A.K. (1996). *Competent children at 5.* Wellington: New Zealand Council for Educational Research.

Wylie, C., Thompson, J. and Lythe, C. (1999). *Competent children at 8: families, early education and schools.* Wellington: New Zealand Council for Educational Research.

8 Early childhood care and education in Israel

Miriam K. Rosenthal

This chapter discusses early childcare and education in Israel from a socio-cultural and ecological perspective. It opens with some facts concerning young children in Israel and the health, welfare and educational services available to them. These are presented in the historical and cultural context of Israel. The chapter then describes the early childcare and education systems and focuses on research on infants and toddlers in childcare. It concludes with the implications of present-day research findings for social policy and future research.

The ecology of young children in Israel

A recent report (Ben-Arieh, Tzionit and Kimchi, 2004) indicates that Israel has a young society with a proportionally larger population of children than most Western countries. Yet, as in many Western countries, the number of children per family is getting smaller. At the close of 2004, the 2.2 million children in Israel comprised 33.4 per cent of the general population.

Approximately 70 per cent of children in Israel are Jewish, of whom 8 per cent are born into ultra-orthodox families. Most other children are born into Arab (mostly poor) families: 23 per cent Moslem, 2 per cent Christian, 2 per cent Druze and 3 per cent without religious identity. In addition, Israel has a growing population of children without Israeli citizenship (approximately 6 per cent), born to foreign workers and into 'unrecognised' Bedouin tribes.

Most of the children in Israel, both Jews and non-Jews, live in urban areas. Whilst 73 per cent of mothers of Jewish children under four years of age are in work, only 16.7 per cent of mothers of Arab children of the same age are in work (Ben-Arieh *et al.*, 2004).

As a result of recent social and economic changes, increasing unemployment and reduction in government funding for social and educational programmes, one finds more young children living below the poverty line (Tzionit and Tamir, 2002).

Historical and cultural background

During centuries of exile from their homeland, Jews struggled to survive as a people and maintain their cultural identity. This struggle led to the development of a rich, intricate and interdependent community life. Jewish communities assumed responsibility for the welfare of their members and developed educational and welfare institutions to strengthen the links between the individual, the family and the community. However, the main goal of these services was to strengthen and maintain the community identity, continuity and community ties, rather than meet the needs of individuals (Jaffe, 1982).

Several major historical processes in the past hundred years laid the foundations of modern Israeli society. They include the persecution of Jews in Europe and the evolution of political Zionism as a national liberation movement, striving for the establishment of a sovereign Jewish state as a haven for Jews either fleeing hostile environments and/or seeking to live in their old homeland.

At the time of the Declaration of Independence in 1948, the Jewish community in what was then Palestine comprised 650,000 members, mostly of European background. Their goal was to establish a productive, self-sufficient Jewish society based on socialist principles (Smilansky *et al.*, 1960). These ideals shaped the health, social and educational policies for the children of the new state of Israel. This young generation was expected to realise a major cultural transformation and become the 'New Israelis', strong, healthy, free and proud Jews, living in their own land and speaking their own language.

Within 10 years of independence Israel more than doubled its population by absorbing 325,000 concentration camp survivors and nearly half a million Jewish refugees from Moslem countries (Israel Foreign Ministry, 1994). Significant immigration continued in the 1970s and 1980s. The most recent wave of mass immigration in the 1990s has increased Israel's population by more than 15 per cent (Dolev *et al.*, 1996).

Many immigrants came with limited economic resources and limited (Western) educational background. The move into a radically different society together with traumatic life histories made adjustment into the new society more difficult for some and hindered their achievement of economic and social success. Poverty, large families, and a high percentage of single-parent families among some immigrant groups have been identified as some of the risk factors associated with immigration. The absorption of immigrants has been a major challenge to Israeli society.

Social, health and education services for young children

The social, health and education services for young children that were developed at the turn of the twentieth century by the Jewish community in

Palestine were designed to meet the *survival needs* of young children, as well as *acculturate* them into the values and norms of this new Jewish society. During 50 years of statehood these services were modified, extended or limited, but essentially maintained the same basic goals and structural features.

As a democratic society this community of 650,000 Jews vowed in its Declaration of Independence (1948) to establish 'equal rights for all citizens regardless of sex, religion or race'. This vow referred not only to the 800,000 Jewish newcomers but also to the 150,000 non-Jewish Arabs who remained in its territory. Yet the fact that many of the services designed for children were historically developed by the Jewish community for its children led to inequality in the provision of services to non-Jewish minorities (Bar-On, 1994).

Health-related services

Community-funded health services for young children were introduced in 1916 when the first Family Health Centre (Tipat Halav) was established to promote the health of pregnant women, infants and toddlers. With a staff of doctors and public health nurses these centres provide immunisation and early diagnosis of health and developmental problems. The nurses also advise mothers in pre- and postnatal care and in nutrition and hygiene.

The Ministry of Health accepted responsibility for these centres and assumed a national responsibility for public health services for *all* young Israeli children. In recent years many of these centres also began to employ simple screening devices for early detection of developmental risk. These centres serve approximately 95 per cent of Jewish and non-Jewish Israeli families alike (Palti, 1995).

The government's commitment to the provision of health services to children, however, has been undermined recently with the growing privatisation of Israel's economy and the implementation of the National Health Insurance Law (Doron, 1995). The Ministry of Health has shifted its responsibility from *providing* health services to *supervising* them. Nevertheless, for the time being, the Ministry is still responsible for operating all Family Health Centres and all health services for children in hospitals, including child abuse units (Dolev *et al.,* 1996).

The welfare system

Present-day welfare services for young Israeli children are likewise based on the social services developed by the Jewish community in the pre-state era. Social services expanded considerably following statehood. A National Insurance Law (1953) was passed that included two universal maternity supports: a maternity grant, which covered the costs of hospital birth and the initial costs for the baby; and a maternity leave allowance of 75 per cent of the mother's income before giving birth, for a period of 12 weeks (Doron and Tamir, 1986). Over the years, the maternity allowance has been extended to cover 100 per cent of the mother's income and fathers can also receive the allowance (instead of mothers) from the forty-second day after birth. Children's allowances and other social security supports are also paid for by the National Insurance Institute. The children's allowance programme was made universal in 1975, became selective again in the 1980s and was reinstated as universal in 1992.

The Ministry of Welfare is responsible for setting the social policy as well as funding about 75 per cent of social services' costs (Efrat *et al.*, 1998). The Service for Children and Youth is responsible for the welfare of children in two ways: for services to children who are abused or neglected, or are otherwise at risk; and for placing children away from their families and choosing adoptive parents. Seventeen per cent of Israeli children under the age of 17 need the help of these services (Tzionit and Tamir, 2002). These are identified as children 'at risk'. The services offered include intervention programmes for children at home (e.g. day care, afternoon programmes, parenting programmes) as well as adoption, residential care and foster care for children who need to be removed from their families.

Early childcare

As for other services, early childcare was introduced some 50 years before independence. Two basically different sub-systems evolved to serve the needs of children under school age: one system serves children aged from 0–3 years ('day care'), the other serves children aged three to six ('early education'). The two systems have different goals, and different ministries set their policies. Their funding comes from different sources and is based on different priorities.

THE DAY CARE SYSTEM

This was developed as a branch of the welfare system, along with orphanages, to provide shelter for needy children or a service for working mothers whose husbands were enlisted during the Second World War and required all-day care for their children. It was expected to meet family welfare goals, and focused on providing basic custodial care.

From the 1970s, this system was assigned new goals, leading to a rapid increase in day care facilities. The main goal was to promote the participation of mothers in the labour market. Another goal was to address the educational gap of disadvantaged children by providing educational enrichment through day care (Rosenthal, 1992). While the Finance Ministry was willing to allocate funds to facilitate reaching the first goal, no funds were allocated to turn custodial care offered by day care centres into educationally enriching programmes. The Division for the Status of Women is responsible for day care centres and a sponsored system of family day care.

EARLY CHILDHOOD EDUCATION

This was developed as a service independent of day care. Influenced by its commitment to the absorption of Jewish immigrants, the early childhood education system, which had been developed in the pre-state era, was now expected to acculturate its extraordinarily diverse population of refugees from post-Holocaust Europe, Middle Eastern Arab countries and Eastern Europe (Rosenthal, 1992). Acculturation was supposed to enable these new immigrants to share equally in the opportunities of a society rapidly moving toward increased industrialisation (Lombard, 1973). The system was charged with the responsibility of developing the 'new Israeli', the Sabra. It aimed at creating a new cultural identity, reaching out to immigrant parents through the education of their children. In line with Jewish tradition it aimed to strengthen the *community identity,* rather than meet the developmental needs of individual children.

The commitment of the new Jewish state to education was exemplified by the Compulsory Education Law in 1949, less than eight months after the election of the first Israeli parliament (Kleinberger, 1969). Today, education in Israel is free for all children aged five to 18 and is compulsory to age 15. The inclusion of at least one compulsory year of kindergarten was seen as a necessary prerequisite for the later success in school of children whose immigrant parents neither spoke Hebrew nor were familiar with modern education (Lombard, 1973). These laws applied to all citizens of Israel, including non-Jewish minorities.

Within less than 20 years of statehood it became clear that the early childhood education system was not adequately preparing the young of Jewish immigrant communities for school. In the early 1970s a Committee for Children and Youth in Distress, appointed by the Prime Minister's Office (1972), led a public inquiry into policies affecting children's poverty and educational disadvantage. The work of this committee, the growing public awareness of the importance of the early years to the child's intellectual development, together with the poor performance of many five-year olds, resulted in a *selective provision of free preschool education* to three- to five-year-old children from 'disadvantaged' (mostly first-generation Jewish immigrant) families residing in 'development areas' and poor neighbourhoods. Early childhood education was now charged with the responsibility of closing the educational gap between Jewish immigrant children and the veteran Jewish-Israeli population. The goal of 'acculturation' gave way to the goal of 'school readiness'.

It should be noted that the effort concentrated on poor and disadvantaged children from Jewish immigrant families, in the attempt to integrate them into the mainstream, and not on Arab children (Bar-On, 1994). An amendment to the Compulsory Education Law in 1999 indicated that compulsory and free education will be extended to *all* three- to five-year-olds, over a 10-year period. The first few years saw a surge in the number of non-Jewish children attending preschool. However, because of budgetary considerations the implementation of the law dwindled after the first few years.

Current early childcare and education in Israel

The goals and policies of educational services for children aged three to six are different from those offered to younger children.

Education and care for the 0–three age group

A recent analysis (Fichtelberg-Burmatz, 2004) of the education and care of children aged three months to three-and-a-half years shows that 35.6 per cent of children are cared for at home by their mothers. Another 10.2 per cent are cared for by a family relative (without pay). The remaining 54.2 per cent of children are in some form of childcare for which parents pay. Most of these children spend their days in a group setting (day care centre, family day care and others). Only 35.9 per cent of children in this group are in settings entitled to government support. All the rest are placed in private settings such as with a nanny, childminder or in a day care centre. These childcare settings are not supervised, licensed or registered.

The data on paid childcare reveals that Jewish parents tend to place their infants in out-of-home care at a very young age (the mean age is 10.2 months). Over 50 per cent of the children in paid care were placed there by the age of 12 months, and nearly 90 per cent were placed there by the age of two years. The mean age of placement in paid childcare among the Arab population is 19 months (Fichtelberg-Barmatz, 2004).

Only the registered childcare settings are entitled to receive government funds. Most of the registered operators are run either by non-profit organisations or local authorities (e.g. voluntary-run women's organisations, community centres, churches, kibbutzim). The government provides subsidy on a sliding scale based on characteristics of parents using the service: the type and hours of maternal work/study; a means test (income, area of residence, family size, the date of immigration); and developmental risk (Ministry of Labour and Social Affairs, 1996).

Service operators are required to adhere to regulations on group size, number of staff and maximal costs, to qualify for government funding. Low-income parents pay only 28 per cent of the cost for each child, while high-income parents pay 98 per cent of the cost (Fichtelberg-Barmatz, 2004). Operators are obliged to take in a certain number of children from lower-income/immigrant families.

The government has never articulated its policy regarding *access* to and *quality* of education and care for this age group. The Day-care Supervision Law (1965) requires the relevant ministry to supervise all out-of-home childcare and license only that meeting basic standards. The government, however, never developed standards of quality for education and care settings, nor did it allocate funds to pay supervisors, inspectors or a licensing authority. The Division for the Status of Women developed a list of requirements (e.g. minimal space per child, group size, confirmation of payment of city tax, approval of the Ministry of Health). This list does not reflect an awareness of the standards required to assure quality of care and education. It is neither exhaustive nor is it appropriate for many settings.

Studies on the quality of care in the day care system were used in an attempt to influence policy-makers to consider issues of quality, especially in childcare offered to infants and children from poor and socially distressed families (Rosenthal, 1988; Rosenthal *et al.*, 1987; Rosenthal *et al.*, 1986). Unfortunately, the results of these studies have been traditionally ignored by policy-makers. The drive to meet public demand and provide large numbers of affordable and safe childcare programmes conflicts with the drive to meet professional demands to offer quality care that supports children's development. This is a conflict common to childcare policy across Western societies (Melhuish and Moss, 1991; Lamb *et al.*, 1992). This conflict is likely to remain as long as the perception of day care by policy-makers and society at large remains that of a system designed to meet the needs of working mothers rather than to address general cultural or national goals.

Recent attention has been drawn to childcare conditions through fatal accidents in childcare settings, the media exposure of several incidents of child abuse in some childcare settings, and the extensive media coverage of research data on the poor quality of care and its implications (see below). At the same time, the government has adopted the 'welfare to work' social policy, with the assumption that improving access to childcare will facilitate the implementation of this policy. There is, however, a growing awareness among parents of young children that 'care' and 'education' are inseparable and there is a growing demand for affordable quality education and care for all infants and toddlers.

These developments have recently led the Ministry of Industry, Commerce and Employment, into a more active involvement with policy related to childcare for the 0–three age group. In December 2004, this ministry appointed a professional committee to develop standards to improve the quality of childcare and education. The committee will also suggest ways of enforcing standards (through effective licensing and supervision) throughout all childcare, registered or not. The question as to who will bear the costs of this move has remained unresolved. The Finance Ministry is willing to support changes that result in greater access to childcare for unemployed mothers. It objects, however, to allocating funds to improve the quality of education and care. It is expected that a pilot implementation of the new standards and regulation procedure, alongside a reassessment of the subsidy system, will start in 2006.

The Israeli day care system serves children aged three months to four years. These day care programmes usually operate eight hours a day (8am–4pm), six days a week, although some programmes now offer half-day or five-day arrangements. The rooms in the registered centres are generally well equipped with adequate furniture and toys. However, groups tend to be very large and the education and training of staff working with children under three is very low. While groups with children older than three years must have a trained nursery school teacher for at least half a day, this regulation does not apply to groups with younger children.

Various surveys of day care centres revealed that over 70 per cent of the staff were non-professional with a very low level of education and without formal training in either child development or the principles of education (Livnat, 1971). Only 5.7 per cent had college training in *any* subject (Koren-Karie *et al.*, 1998). Yet, a proposal to develop a country-wide standardised and regulated training programme (Rosenthal *et al.*, 1987) met with strong objections from the Ministry of Finance, expecting such standardisation to lead to unionisation of caregivers and demands for better pay.

However, in 1975 a graduate programme was established at the Hebrew University for the trainers of care providers in early childhood settings. This programme has trained the current research and professional leaders in early childhood in Israel. Its graduates play an important role in the development of innovative programmes and new methods of training and supervision in childcare, and in preparing teaching materials, as well as working with policy-makers (Rosenthal and Shimoni, 1994).

Family day care homes

The subsidised and registered day care centre service is supplemented by a system of subsidised family day care (FDC) homes. In each FDC home a woman cares for (at most) five infants and toddlers. These homes are sponsored either by the local community centre or social services department and should be supervised regularly by a social worker or early childhood professional. The care providers are expected to have pre-service training. However, with the cut in budgets little training is now offered and often professional supervision is minimal. This service has grown very rapidly, from 25 homes in 1977 to approximately 2,025 in 1999, and 2,300 in 2005. About 43.5 per cent of the FDC homes operate in Arab and Druze communities (Almog, 2005).

Preschool education for the three to six age group

Attendance in preschool settings in the Jewish population is 99.4 per cent for four-year-olds or older, and 95.4 per cent for three-year olds. Although the attendance figures are considerably lower in the non-Jewish population, they are continually rising. Attendance in nursery schools of Arab three- to five-year-olds has risen from 30 per cent in the 1980s (Al-Haj, 1995) to 69 per cent in 1996 (Bar-On, 1994). This is close to the Jewish rate for the five- to six-year-old group. The change is related to socio-economic and cultural changes in the Israeli Arab community. As more Arab mothers work outside of their homes, and the Arab recognition of the need to invest in early childcare grows, the pressure has been mounting on the government to better allocate resources for Arab early education provision.

While day care programmes run all day, usually six days a week, the typical preschool for three- to six-year-olds consists of a half-day programme. The classrooms contain 30 to 35 children. The public ones are usually housed in specially constructed buildings and are adequately equipped with child-size furniture, play equipment and educational materials. The classroom activities tend to be oriented to the group rather than the individual, with an emphasis on the child as a member of the group (Furman, 1994). The daily schedule is controlled by the teacher, yet within a given period children may select the task and the group with which they will be involved (Lombard and Jasik, 1983). The staff consists of one trained teacher and one non-professional aide. Teachers undergo three years of college training. This pre-service training is supplemented by ongoing training sessions on curriculum topics. Many teacher training colleges now offer an academic BA degree.

The initial major goal for the early education system was acculturation. The curriculum was then predominantly focused on the acquisition and enrichment of Hebrew and on cultural content. In the early 1970s it was realised that more than 50 per cent of children entering school were 'educationally disadvantaged', with poor prognosis of academic achievement. This led to a change in goals. The current goal of the Ministry of Education is 'to ensure that all children are provided with the necessary conditions and opportunities for effective functioning and personal achievement'. More specifically, it aims at ensuring the intellectual development and skill acquisition necessary to educational success. The primary objective of kindergartens is likewise focused on school readiness (Efrat *et al.*, 1998). To reach its goals the Ministry of Education has published guidelines, outlining the areas considered important for a child's optimal growth and school-readiness (Efrat *et al.*, 1998). These guidelines are supplemented by in-service training offered to preschool teachers.

From the late 1970s to 2000, the Ministry of Education took some important steps to support the quality of education in preschools under its supervision. This support included the training and supervision of private nursery schools serving two-year-olds. However, since 2000, following severe budget cuts, the Ministry of Education has cut its efforts to support quality in preschools. These cuts have almost completely stopped the implementation of the free-and-compulsory education law for all three- to four-year-old children.

Research on quality of childcare in Israel

Research on quality of childcare is generally based on the understanding that children's experiences in early childhood settings influence their well-being and development. It also assumes that early childhood programmes are perceived as responsible for their effects on children's development.

Preschool programmes for three- to five-year-olds were generally assumed to be of adequate to good quality. Parents, even though perturbed by the very large groups of children in these settings, rely on the supervision of the Ministry of Education and tend to select a setting mostly on the basis of hearsay and proximity to home or work. Unfortunately, very little, if any, research on the *quality* of preschool and its effects has been carried out and/or published.

There is, however, a growing body of research on the quality of care in the day care system in Israel. Assessments of both *structural* and *process* aspects of quality of care in Israeli day care centres make it clear that the goal of providing care of a satisfactory quality could not possibly be achieved within the existing system (Rosenthal *et al.*, 1987; Rosenthal, 1994a).

Structural aspects of quality

These aspects generally refer to dimensions such as group size, adult-to-child ratio, caregivers' education and training, and staff turnover. Group size in Israeli day care centres tends to be large with a relatively poor adult-to-child ratio. Thus, a typical centre has between 60 and 150 children in age-homogenous groups (Rosenthal, 1992). What is further discouraging is the increase in group size, with a doubling between 1978 and 1998 for the under-twos, and substantial increase in group sizes for older children. These figures have been recently confirmed by a study of infant day care: 65 per cent of the infants sampled were in groups of between 16 to 27 infants (Koren-Karie *et al.*, 1998).

As studies have shown over the years, the potential of the Israeli day care system to provide enrichment or even good-quality care is further reduced by the fact that staff are not adequately qualified. Koren-Karie and her colleagues have shown that 57 per cent of caregivers had 11–12 years of education and 31 per cent had only four to ten years of education. Moreover, 39 per cent had no training whatsoever. Furthermore, nearly 62 per cent had either no supervision, or met with a supervisor once every few months (Koren-Karie, *et al.*, 1998).

Until the mid-1990s there was a relatively low staff turnover in Israeli day care. Caregivers tend to be older women. More than 76 per cent are between 36 and 62 years old; 49 per cent have been working in childcare for six to 15 years and 30 per cent for 16–32 years (Koren-Karie *et al.*, 1998). These are women who agreed to work eight hours a day with two weeks' annual leave for one of the lowest salaries in the labour market (Rosenthal, 1992, 1994a). These conditions have worsened over the years. Recent reports from non-profit organisations running day care centres reveal growing concern over staff turnover (Rosenthal, 2005). A recent study investigated caregivers' perceptions of their role as well as their ability to cope with ethical dilemmas in their daily work. While these women indeed perceived themselves as educators and guardians of children's well-being, the main theme underlying their ability to cope with daily dilemmas was that of survival. This referred to their concern over their ability to physically safeguard the children as well as their own survival in the workplace, while maintaining their sanity and integrity as human beings (Zadok, 2005).

These structural problems reflect the low priority given by Israeli policy-makers to early childhood care and education. They further reflect a public understanding of what constitutes 'quality care', which is different from that generally accepted by early childhood experts. For example, most parents accept large groups and non-individualised care as the norm for early childhood care.

Process-related aspects of quality

These generally refer to the interactions of children with their caregivers, peers and the educational environment. Rosenthal (1991a) compared these interactions in three types of out-of-home care settings in Israel: day care centres (DCC), family day care (FDC), both in towns in the centre of Israel, and children's houses in kibbutzim. The study shows that there were no differences between DCC and FDC in towns on most caregiver characteristics, in the educational programme, and in the educational quality of the physical environment. However, DCC offered poorer quality interaction with the caregivers and the emotional tone of the programme was less relaxed than in FDC. Presumably the larger groups in DCC and the poor adult-to-child ratios enhanced the tension of both caregivers and children and led caregivers to more frequent expressions of anger towards the children.

Frequent negative control (e.g. scolding children) was reported by Koren-Karie and her associates during mealtimes with infants in 44 day care centres. They found very little sensitive and positive responsiveness to infants during various activities. Only during half of the observations were infants greeted personally upon arrival in the centre. Only 25 per cent of the time were they addressed upon departure at the end of the day. Nappy-changing took on average 2:05 minutes (minimum time is 0:15 seconds). Only in 32 per cent of changes did infants receive personal and warm attention. Similarly, during bottle-feeding, 20 per cent of the time infants did not receive any personal attention. The average feeding time was 4:35 minutes, with a record minimum time of 0:35 seconds! Putting an upset infant to sleep in a cot took, on average, 0:47 seconds, with a minimum time for a non-upset baby of 0:01 seconds (Koren-Karie *et al.,*1998).

Observing the same children in these settings, Sagi and his colleagues reported a relatively high frequency of insecure attachment, as compared to infants reared in non-group settings, either at home or by a private caregiver (Sagi *et al.,* 1998).

In contrast to the DCC and FDC in towns, the kibbutz childcare settings rated highest on 'structural quality': small groups; high adult-to-child ratios; better educated, trained and experienced caregivers; and a better physical environment. Although no differences were found between kibbutz and FDC in the behaviour of caregivers, kibbutz children engaged more frequently in both positive learning experiences and social behaviour than FDC or DCC children. This supports the contention that it is the quality of the educational environment rather than the type of childcare that determines the differences in 'learning experiences' (Rosenthal, 1991a).

Rosenthal's study highlighted differences between two independent dimensions of 'quality care': the caregiver's spontaneous interactions and their educational programme (Rosenthal, 1990, 1991c), in common with other research by Hestenes *et al.*, 1993. Rosenthal's data shows that while the quality of interactions was related to the frequency of supervision the caregiver received, and the degree of autonomy the caregiver had, the quality of the educational programme was related to the age and social background of the children in the group. Caregivers are generally untrained and poorly educated and the more supported and entrusted they feel, the greater quality of care they offer (Tizard, 1974).

Supervision for caregivers was further investigated by Gatt (2004). In order to foster sensitive and responsive care-giving, a model of *individual video-aided supervision* was developed at the Graduate Programme for Early Childhood Studies at the Hebrew University of Jerusalem. Forty family day care providers participated in this study. Twenty participated in a video-aided supervision programme. The other 20 formed a control group that received regular supervision (without video observations) from the same supervisors. Video-aided supervision was found to enhance differentiated responses to children's signals of distress as well as positive behaviours (such as positive speech, stimulation, touch and mutual affection). Moreover, these caregivers displayed less restrictive and controlling behaviour following the video-aided supervision programme. Furthermore, even when restricting a child, caregivers in this group incorporated more positive behaviours.

Rosenthal (1994b, 1995) investigated the relationship between the caregivers' interactions with toddlers in their FDC homes, the characteristics of the childcare environment, and toddlers' social and non-social play behaviour. Two aspects of young children's play were investigated in the first study (Rosenthal, 1994b): *play with objects* and *play with peers*. The sensori-motor interaction of children with objects was classified as fine motor and gross motor forms of play. Their social interactions were coded as positive, agonistic, and a form of social play we called 'joint play', that is characterised by group participation in a common activity with repetitive sounds and laughter (Budwig *et al.*, 1986). Both aspects of children's play were rated for complexity. The social and linguistic contexts of play were related to each type of children's play. Although the two forms of play were interrelated, both reflecting the child's competence, they were affected differently by the child's characteristics and by the childcare setting. Family background had little effect on the children's play. The child's characteristics (age, sex and separation difficulties) affected social play rather than play with objects.

Three elements of the childcare setting were considered: the social environment (adult caregiver and peer group characteristics); the educational content of the daily programme; and the educational quality of the physical environment.

Two aspects of the caregiver's attitudes and behaviour influenced children's play: her developmental expectations and the extent to which she interacted positively with the children. Children in FDC homes with caregivers who frequently engaged them in positive interactions spent more time in positive interactions with their peers than did children in homes with less frequent positive interactions. Moreover, children in the homes of caregivers with expectations of early cognitive achievement spent more time in fine motor play with objects and less time in gross motor play or alone. It is likely that the caregiver's expectations indirectly affected children's play with objects through her arrangement of the physical environment and the daily programme. However, it seems that caregivers with expectations of early achievement in the social domain expected young infants and toddlers to be competent enough socially to 'manage on their own'. The children in their homes spent more time alone and less time in social or fine motor play.

The educational quality of the physical environment and the daily programme were the best predictors of children's play. An emphasis on educational content, and on more varied play equipment, resulted in more frequent fine motor play. This form of play with objects brought children into close contact with each other, providing joint themes and leading to more social joint play. Moreover, although overcrowding limits children's opportunity to engage in gross motor play with objects, it does create more social contact resulting in more frequent joint play. These young children, probably because of the group context, spent more time in social interaction than in play with toys. Both the mean age and the age homogeneity of the group affected the competence level of play. All children played at a higher level in groups with a higher age mean, but only the under-twos were affected by the age mix of the group.

In moderately heterogeneous age groups (13–24 months between youngest and oldest), young children played more competently with toys and peers than in more homogenous or more heterogeneous groups. Only the fine motor play of older children was affected by the age heterogeneity of the group. They displayed more frequent fine motor play in either extremely homogenous or extremely heterogeneous groups.

The results suggest that while the presence of older children facilitated a high level of play in younger children, the presence of younger children did not affect the competence of older children's play. This study (Rosenthal,

1994a) highlights the contribution of the social composition of the *group* to the daily experiences of even very young children in childcare. Discussions of quality of childcare should address this issue alongside concerns about the influence of caregivers' behaviour on children's development.

Although psychologists and education experts generally highlight the importance of 'stimulus shelter' (Wachs *et al.,* 1979) or 'space to be alone' (Prescott, 1981) in the physical planning of a childcare environment, our findings raise questions as to the validity of this assumption. Space to be alone in a small, mixed-age group of infants and toddlers, in a home-like environment, may distance children from each other. In this study children spent more time alone or in agonistic interaction rather than in positive social interaction or 'joint play'. They also played with objects at a lower level of competence.

'Joint play' is an interesting form of social interaction among young peers, which, although easily identifiable, has not been the subject of much research. This study suggests that it is related to sociability and communication skills, and tends to come at the expense of the child's fine motor play with objects. It is not related to any child or family characteristic. It was observed more frequently in more homogeneous age groups, regardless of age, with a lower socio-economic level, and in crowded homes of caregivers with more authoritarian socialisation beliefs, who placed greater emphasis on educational aspects, and who did not provide 'space to be alone'. It seems that bringing children of similar ages and competence into close contact facilitates this form of social interaction. Caregivers tend to be wary of such 'joint play' lest they lose control over the children's behaviour, and yet this form of social play happens more frequently with the more controlling caregivers.

Rosenthal and Zur (1993) investigated toddlers' emotional exchanges with peers, and especially expressions of concern for each other, in relation to the caregivers' interventions during children's peer interaction, and to the toddlers' gender, age and social competence. Toddlers aged 22–28 months were observed in 30 FDC homes after preliminary observations in DCC failed to obtain enough of a record of prosocial expressions of concern among toddlers. The data supports the hypothesis that child factors as well as caregivers' behaviour contribute to toddlers' emotional exchanges. Socially competent toddlers engage more in positive and prosocial, as well as in agonistic, interactions with peers. Boys engage more frequently than girls in agonistic interaction. Toddlers' emotional exchanges were unrelated to scores of the overall quality of care in these FDC homes.

Agonistic interaction and vicarious personal distress at the sight of a peer in distress were associated with forceful and controlling caregiver behaviour as well as with her lack of interest in children's distress. Caregivers' interventions were moderated by toddlers' characteristics, and controlling behaviour was associated with vicarious personal distress more frequently among competent toddlers and among boys.

These studies raise questions as to the developmental and educational goals in early childhood settings and their relationship to 'quality of care'. It has been suggested that 'concern for others' may be an important educational goal in some cultural contexts, and aspects of care and education that contribute towards such a goal should be included in the definition of quality of care (Rosenthal, 1995, 1999, 2003).

Conclusions

This review of research on early childcare and education in Israel highlights the importance of a contextualised, ecological and culturally valid approach to the study of childcare and education. Thus the differences between childcare and preschool settings, or the differences between the Jewish and the Arab sectors in Israel, can be understood only in the historical and cultural contexts of their evolution. Recent anthropological observations suggest that the daily routines observed in early childhood settings in Israel reflect a strong collective, as opposed to individualistic, orientation with emphasis on 'shared national' rather than 'personal' experiences (Furman, 1994). It is possible, therefore, that the large groups in Israeli early childhood settings, as well as the relatively infrequent individualised care and education in these settings, should be understood in the historical and socio-cultural context of this country.

References

Al-Haj, M. (1995). *Education, Empowerment and Control: The case of the Arabs in Israel*. NY: State University of New York Press.

Almog, T. (2005). Personal communication. Jerusalem: Ministry of Industry, Commerce and Employment.

Bar-On, A. (1994). Citizenship, social rights, and the ethnic state: The case of structural discrimination against Arab children in Israel. *Journal of Social Policy, 23(1)*, 1–19.

Ben-Arieh, A., Tzionit, Y. and Kimchi (2004). *Children in Israel: Statistical Yearbook*. Jerusalem: The National Council for the Child. (Hebrew).

Budwig, N., Strage, A., and Bamberg, M. (1986) The construction of joint activities with an age-mate: The transition from caregiver–child to peer play. In J. Cook-Gumperz, J. Streeck, and W. A. Corsaro, *Children's worlds and children's language* (pp. 83–108). New York: Monton de Gruyter.

Dolev, T., Aronin, H., Ben-Rabi, D., Clayman, L., Cohen, M., Trajtenberg, S., Levy, J. and Yoel, B. (1996). *An overview of children and youth in Israel: Policies, programs and philanthropy*. Baltimore, MD: International Youth Foundation.

Doron, A. (1995). *In favor of universality: The challenges of social policy in Israel*. Jerusalem: Magnes. (Hebrew).

Doron, A. and Tamir, Y. (1986). *Social policies towards families of working parents with children of early childhood*. Jerusalem: The Center for Social Policy Research in Israel. (Hebrew).

Efrat, G., Ben-Arieh, A., Gal, J. and Haj-Yahia, M. (1998). *Young children in Israel.* Jerusalem, Israel: The National Council for the Child.

Fichtelberg-Barmatz, O. (2004). *Childcare arrangements for very young children.* Jerusalem: Ministry of Industry, Commerce and Employment; Department of Planning, Research and Economics.

Furman, M. (1994). *The new children: Violence and obedience in early childhood.* Tel Aviv, Israel: HaKibbutz HaMeuhad. (Hebrew).

Gatt, L. (2004). The effect of video-aided supervision on caregivers' quality of care and on infants and toddlers' experience in family daycare. Paper presented at the SRCD meetings in Atlanta, Georgia.

Hestenes, L.L., Kontos, S. and Bryan, Y. (1993). Children's emotional expression in childcare centers varying in quality. *Early Childhood Research Quarterly, 8,* 295–307.

Israel Foreign Ministry (1994). *Facts about Israel: An overview of the state of Israel.* Jerusalem.

Jaffe, E.D. (1982). *Child welfare in Israel.* New York: Praeger.

Kleinberger, A.F. (1969). *Society, schools and progress in Israel.* London: Pergamon Press.

Koren-Karie, N., Egoz, N., Sagi, A., Joels, T., Gini, M. and Ziv, Y. (1998). The emotional climate of center care in Israel. Paper presented at the ISSBD meetings in Bern, Switzerland.

Lamb, M.E., Sternberg, K.J., Hwang, C. and Broberg A.G. (1992). *Childcare in context: Cross-cultural perspectives.* Hillsdale, NJ: Erlbaum Associates.

Livnat, Y. (1971). *Survey of Day Care Centers.* Jerusalem: Prime Minister's Office.

Lombard A.D. (1973). Early schooling in Israel. In N.D. Feshbach, J.I. Goodland and A. Lombard (Eds), *Early schooling in England and Israel* (pp. 63–102). New York: McGraw Hill.

Lombard, A.D. and Jasik, L.S. (1983). The education of young children in Israel. In G.R. Lall and B.M. Lall (Eds), *Comparative early childhood education* (pp. 19–31). Springfield, Ill: C.C. Thomas.

Melhuish, E.C. and Moss, P. (1991). *Day care for young children: International perspectives.* London: Routledge.

Ministry of Labour and Social Affairs (1996). *Instructions for Tuition in Day Care Centres and Family Day Care for Children of Working Mothers.* Jerusalem: The Division for the Status of Women. (Hebrew).

Palti, H. (1995). *National Health Insurance Law – Implications on preventative health services for the mother and child.* Jerusalem: National Council for the Child. (Hebrew).

Prescott, E. (1981). Relations between physical setting and adult/child behaviour in day care. In S. Kilmer (Ed.), *Advances in Early Education and Day Care* Vol. 2, (pp. 129–158). London: JAI Press.

Rosenthal, M.K. (1988). Childcare in Israel: Current status and efforts toward change. *The Networker, 9(3),* 1–6.

Rosenthal, M.K. (1990). Social policy and its effects on the daily experiences of infants and toddlers in family day care in Israel. *Journal of Applied Developmental Psychology, 11(1)*, 85–103.

Rosenthal M.K. (1991a). Daily experiences of toddlers in three childcare settings in Israel. *Child and Youth Care Forum, 20(1)*, 39–60.

Rosenthal, M.K. (1991b). The relation of peer interaction among infants and toddlers in FDC to characteristics of the child-care environment. *Journal of Reproductive and Infant Psychology, 9*, 151–167.

Rosenthal, M.K. (1991c). Behaviours and beliefs of caregivers in family daycare: The effects of background and work environment. *Early Childhood Research Quarterly, 6*, 263–283.

Rosenthal, M.K. (1992). Nonparental childcare in Israel: A cultural and historical perspective. In M. Lamb, K. Sternberg, C. Hwang and A. Broberg (Eds), *Childcare in context: Cross-cultural perspectives* (pp. 305–330). Hillsdale, NJ: Lawrence Erlbaum Associates.

Rosenthal, M.K. (1994a). An ecological approach to the study of childcare: Family day care in Israel. Hillsdale, NJ: Lawrence Erlbaum Associates 163 pgs.

Rosenthal, M.K. (1994b). Social and non-social play of infants and toddlers in family day care. In H. Goelman and E. Jacobs (Eds), *Children's play in childcare settings* (pp. 163–192). Albany, NY: SUNY Press.

Rosenthal, M.K. (1995). Is the 'concern for others' an educational objective in early childhood? Paper presented at the 5th European Conference on the Quality of Early Childhood Education, Paris, France.

Rosenthal, M.K. (1999). Out-of-home child-care research: A cultural perspective. *International Journal of Behaviour Development, 23*, 477–518.

Rosenthal, M.K. (2003). Family day care in Israel: Policy, quality and daily experiences of children. In A. Mooney, J. Statham and D.C. Farm (Eds), *International perspectives on policy, practice and quality* (pp. 93–110). London: Jessica Kingsley Publishers.

Rosenthal M.K. (2005). Childcare for infants and toddlers in Israel: lessons from research. In P. Klein (Ed.), *Infants today and tomorrow*. Tel Aviv: Bar Ilan University. (Hebrew).

Rosenthal, M.K. and Shimoni, R. (1994). Issues and evaluation of an Israeli early childhood leadership training program. In S. Reifel (Ed.), *Advances in Early Education and Day Care* (pp. 155–187). Greenwich, CT: JAI Press Inc.

Rosenthal, M.K. and Zur, H. (1993). The relationship between caregivers' interventions during peer interaction and toddlers' expression of concern for others. Paper presented at the SRCD meetings in Atlanta, Georgia.

Rosenthal, M.K., Biderman, A. and Luppo, M. (1987). *The Day Care Standards Committee. Final Report*. Jerusalem: Ministry of Labour and Social Welfare. (Hebrew).

Rosenthal, M.K., Shimoni R. and Simon, Z. (1986). *Family day-care in Israel: Social policy and its implication*. Jerusalem: Akademon, Hebrew University. (Hebrew).

Sagi, A., Koren-Karie, N., Ziv, Y., Joels, T. and Gini, M. (1998). Shedding further light on the NICHD study of early childcare: The Israeli Case. Paper presented at the ICIS meetings in Atlanta, Georgia.

Smilansky, M., Weintraub, S. and Hanegbi, Y. (1960). *Child and youth welfare in Israel*. Jerusalem: The Szold Institute.

Tizard, B. (1974). Do social relationships affect language development? In J. Connolly and J. Bruner (Eds), *The growth of competence*. London: Academic Press.

Tzionit, Y. and Tamir, Y. (2002). Children in Israel: Current picture. *Social Security, 63*, 5–34. (Hebrew).

Wachs, T. D., Francis, J., and McQuiston, S. (1979). Psychological dimensions of the infant's physical environment. *Infant Behaviour and Development, 2*, 155–161.

Zadok, I. (2005). Ethics, values and survival: A caregiver's role as seen by caregivers in early childhood settings in Israel. PhD thesis, The Hebrew University, Jerusalem.

9 Early childhood care and education

An Indian perspective

Shraddha Kapoor

India is the ninth most industrialised country in the world, undergoing rapid industrialisation and economic and social change, but early childhood care and education has been a low priority. According to UNICEF, the average Indian child has a poor start to life. Only one in three has the opportunity to be in an early learning programme.

The 2001 census indicates that only 40–45 per cent of the 157.9 million children aged 0–6 years old have access to any early childhood care and education programme. State childcare programmes only provide for 22 per cent of children aged 0–6, and private-sector programmes provide for the remaining 18–23 per cent. The private sector remains unchecked and no figures either of numbers of programmes, or levels of attendance, are available. In fact, not only is there no regulatory body to enforce standards or norms, there are no standards or norms to enforce because there is no national curriculum and no official early childhood programme guidelines (Sharma, 2005).

India's National Policy for Children declares that the child is the nation's most important asset. While most of the care of young children takes place in the home, even statistics for formal programmes, mandated or organised (commercial, government or non-governmental organisation (NGO)), are difficult to find. According to Swaminathan (1985), only about 1 per cent of Indian children are formally enrolled in listed day care centres. The state has amended its constitution to legally recognise entitlement to education as a fundamental right, but it confines its new guarantee of free and compulsory education to the 6–14 year age group, ignoring the needs of children under six years old. Although about 25 per cent of children aged three to six are enrolled in non-formal preschool programmes, children under the age of three are rarely prioritised even in the government programmes for the underprivileged.

Early childcare continues to be the responsibility of the family rather than the state. The belief that individual families should solve their children's problems is deeply ingrained. Traditionally, the child is thought to develop naturally and, therefore, little conscious effort is made to provide a structured learning environment. Though young children are well cared for, learning is seen as incidental (Sachidananda, 1965). These attitudes are reflected in a government policy that does not provide outlines for even the most basic early childhood care and education infrastructure. Historical and socio-cultural frameworks can be seen to have deeply influenced the development of policies and programmes concerning the care and education of young children. Early childhood care and education in India can therefore be best understood through an exploration of its historical, ethnic and socio-cultural contexts.

Historical perspective

The earliest documents on the care of young children in India are from the early seventeenth century; these suggest that the majority of childcare was provided by the family. In preschool years, discipline was permissive and the emphasis was on learning by imitation, using parents and elders as role models. Though confined to upper-caste boys, a beginning in education was made by placing young children under the tutorship and guidance of respected gurus (Khalakdina, 1998).

During the colonial era, the famous Minutes of Lord Macaulay institutionalised the British system of primary education alongside the gurukuls and madrasas in the early nineteenth century. The Scottish missionaries taught simple reading, writing and arithmetic, essentially for recruits to the clerical class of the British bureaucracy. Since the masses had no contact with the British, the indigenous systems, with their informal, socio-religious teachings, continued (Antonova *et al.,* 1979).

The first formal institutions for young children in India were based on Froebel's philosophy and were set up by missionaries. These visionary beginnings were continued through the work of several key pioneers in early childhood education. Maria Montessori came to India in 1939 after accepting an invitation from some theosophists. The Second World War kept her in India for seven years and during that time she conducted a large number of preschool education courses. Even today there are several nursery schools in India loosely following the Montessori system of preschool education. The Indian pioneers of the time, Gijubhai Badheka, Tarabai Modak and Anutai Wagh, were from the western region of India. Gijubhai Badheka was influenced by ancient Indian methods of teaching and opposed a conventional schooling system. He wrote the path-breaking book '*Divaswapna*' ('Daydreaming') and set up Dakshinamoorthy balmandir ('temple for children'), which influenced the thinking of early childhood educators for generations. The Nutan Bal Shikshan Sangh (New Child Education Society) was run by Modak in the 1920s in Bombay, and Anutai Wagh developed the concept of Anganwadi ('courtyard garden'), a simple childcare centre run in a tribal area.

Newer forms of education, especially for the young, emerged from the non-violent movement for independence. Great stalwarts of that time included:

Swami Vivekananda's humanitarian approach towards reforming Indian thought, Lokmamya Tilak's and later Ram Manohar Lohia's concept of harmonising the diversities in Indian culture, and Tagore's philosophy which initiated environmental learning, all focusing educational efforts towards the deprived masses. These efforts culminated in the concept of Basic Education. This was an offshoot of Gandhi's philosophy: that all are equal, that living by one's manual skills and learning by doing, were the bases of education for the young.

(Khalakdina, 1998, p. 166)

The major thrust for childcare at that time came in the form of philanthropic or voluntary efforts from dedicated visionaries who worked for the disadvantaged. These early efforts for child welfare were: Guild of Services (1923), the Balkanji Bari (1927), the Parsi and Hindu residential orphanage, the Children's Aid Society (1927), the All India Women's Conference (1926), the National Council of Women (1925), the Andhra Mahila Sabha (1937), and Kasturba Gandhi Memorial Trust (1942), (Khalakdina, 1998).

Early childhood education, despite these initiatives, did not take a formal shape until independence. According to Swaminathan (1992), early childhood education and care remained restricted to certain regions of the country, was concentrated in urban areas, and was confined to those who could afford it. Though India boasts a rich tradition of community and family-based childcare for the young, traditional care is now threatened by several factors, including the break-up of the joint family, changes in labour markets, the restructuring of business, and the increasing pressures of modern living.

Post-independence initiatives

At independence in 1947, preschool education was primarily in the hands of schools started by either Scottish missionaries or voluntary organisations. The government's role in reaching out to the poor and needy of the population was minimal as its priority was to revitalise the political and judicial systems and agricultural sector.

The first step of the government was to set up a Central Social Welfare Board (CSWB) in 1953. The board was visualised as an interface between government and voluntary organisations. Dr Durgabai Deshmukh, its founder and chairperson, understood the importance of providing voluntary workers with status and responsibility and a committee was set up to study the problems of children under six years old. This committee recommended the evolution of a comprehensive plan for the care and education of young children. It suggested that, with governmental financial assistance, responsibility for running preschool education should be left to voluntary agencies. The committee also emphasised the need for a cadre of adequately trained child welfare workers. CSWB encouraged the voluntary sector to set up *balwadis* (houses for children) as the locus for childcare activities.

The objective of the programme was to shift the focus towards rural areas and the poor and to emphasise the integral development, rather than the education, of the child. In 1961, the Indian Council for Child Welfare launched the Bal Sevika training programme for early childhood education workers. However, by the early 1970s, there were only about 2000 balwadis in the entire country. Balwadis, though a valuable initiative, did not successfully contribute to formal education plans as their emphasis was too diluted, focusing, as they did, on a simplified version of child development (Swaminathan, 1992).

India's integrated childhood programmes

Once early childhood education was understood as a strategy for community development, rather than as a step in the educational ladder, government interest and involvement in early education increased. Early childhood education could now be seen as more than a voluntary sector service or a facility for the rich. The government recognised that the average Indian child had a poor start to life and set up the nationwide integrated childhood programme to try to reach, and improve the lives of, the most vulnerable sector of the population. With 250,000 centres nationwide (Sharma, 2005), the Integrated Child Development Service (ICDS) is the world's largest integrated childhood programme, modelled in part on the US Head Start programme (Bhavnagri, 1995). Started in 1975 with financial and technical assistance from UNICEF and the World Bank, ICDS aims to improve the health, nutrition and development of children. It offers:

- health, nutrition and hygiene education to 4.8 million expectant and nursing mothers;
- non-formal preschool education to over 23 million children aged three to six years;
- supplementary feeding for all children and pregnant and nursing mothers;
- child growth monitoring and links to primary healthcare services such as immunisation and vitamin A supplements.

ICDS covers families in urban slums, tribal areas and remote and backward rural regions. A particular emphasis is placed on reaching female children. In addition to health care and nutrition, ICDS centres provide opportunities for structured and unstructured play, and learning experiences to promote the social, emotional, mental, physical and aesthetic development of the child. ICDS is experimenting with different strategies. Programmes are located so that they are accessible to the children of poor working mothers. Many ICDS centres are attached to primary schools. The government intends to expand the coverage of ICDS considerably in the years ahead.

Every year, the ICDS programme costs an average of $10–22 per child. The services are delivered at childcare centres called Anganwadi by one Anganwadi worker and one helper. The worker is usually a local woman earning approximately $5–7 each month, who has three months of institutional training and four months of community-based training. The course, like the programme, focuses on the importance of health and nutrition whilst also offering basic training in skills for the promotion of children's cognitive, social and emotional development (Department of Women and Child Development, 1995).

Initially, preschool education was secondary to health education. However, as child survival rates increased in the early 1990s, preschool education, as preparation for school, assumed greater importance. ICDS centres adopted a non-formal play-intensive method. In practice, there is little evidence of this shift in focus across ICDS centres nationwide (Upadhyay *et al.*, 1998; Cleghorn and Prochner, 2003). Even today, most ICDS programmes have a paediatric orientation with a primary focus on nutrition. Kaul *et al.* (1993) found that children with preschool experience were more likely to stay in primary education than children with direct entry into primary school. The drop-out rate for the preschool group was 31.8 per cent compared to 48.2 per cent for direct entry children. Studies carried out by NIPCCD (National Institute of Public Cooperation and Child Development) and NCERT (National Council for Educational Research and Training) indicate higher enrolment in primary school among children from ICDS programmes, suggesting that a well-functioning Anganwadi (childcare centre) does contribute to ensuring universal schooling.

Surveys in India reveal that children often drop out of school after being beaten and terrorised by the teacher for failing to grasp basic concepts (Cleghorn and Prochner, 2003). Teachers, when asked why they beat children, blame the child's lack of interest and comprehension. Both the inability to concentrate and the failure to cope with studying may have their roots in the neglect of early childhood development. Children who have not had good early childhood development tend to be slow learners. The Indian education system pays little attention to slow learners, making it likely that they will be pushed out of schools.

ICDS has demonstrated its effectiveness over the past three decades, despite unevenness in the quality of services. A national study in 1992 by the NIPCCD reported the positive impact of ICDS programmes. ICDS has reached 62 per cent of children, focusing particularly on children in rural and tribal areas, improving their nutrition and health status, increasing school enrolments and reducing school drop-out (NIPCCD, 1992; Sriram, 1998). Another study found that the programme had an impact on the psycho-social development of children. Though there have been no cost benefit studies (Sharma, 1993) on ICDS, its role in early childhood development is recognised.

For the urban middle class there are several preschool institutions following the modern Western system that have emerged over the past two decades. These are high-fee programmes sometimes attached to elementary schools, preparing the children of ambitious and upwardly mobile parents to get admission into select schools (Chaudhary, 1983). The quality of these programmes is variable and can be exploitative, where children are taught to compete from a very early age. These private institutions are downward extensions of primary education and have a heavy emphasis on formal teaching. With no licensing requirements, these programmes follow no government regulations or national curriculum. Many programmes are run by untrained personnel, with inadequate facilities. They perpetuate 'mis-education' in the name of early childhood education (Kaul, 2002). Such programmes are out of reach for India's majority of poor and rural children who must use government primary schools, thus reducing their capacity for future learning (Sharma and Khosla, 1995).

Childcare facilities for working mothers

Day care is a recent phenomenon in India, and childcare services are of four kinds: statutory, governmental, voluntary and private. Statutory childcare is provided by employers for workers in mines, factories and plantations, and for tobacco workers, contract labourers and migrant workers. There are several acts of legislation meant to ensure that employers provide childcare for working women. However, the laws have not been amended over the years and have several loopholes. Many employers evade the law either by employing less than the minimum number of female workers needed to make the law applicable or by employing unmarried women. Both in qualitative (custodial) and quantitative (50,000 out of 650,000 eligible children) terms the childcare provision is highly inadequate (Sriram, 1998).

There are commercial day care centres for children of middle-class, double-income families and both the government and non-governmental organisations run crèches for the underprivileged. However, it is now recognised that childcare is essential for working women. The inadequacies of the current system have been reiterated in almost every forum addressing the needs of working women in India (Bardhan, 1987). According to Swaminathan, a stalwart in the area of early childhood care and education (ECCE) in India:

> the history of day care ... shows a very slow growth, and failure to meet the needs of working mothers, in terms of extent, content and quality. There are roughly 90 million women in the workforce, of which about 24 million are estimated to have children in the age group of birth to six years. Nearly 90 per cent of these women are in the unorganised sector and do not have access to childcare according to the statute.
>
> (Swaminathan, 1998, p. 26)

The government's initiative to provide day care to working mothers is only 30 years old. In 1974, CSWB introduced a grant-in-aid scheme for crèches providing childcare for ailing and working mothers. This scheme is still in existence and provides financial assistance to organisations to set up crèches for the children (0-five years) of low-income working and ailing mothers. Each unit consists of 25 children who are provided with sleeping facilities, healthcare, supplementary nutrition, immunisation etc., and caters to very low-income groups. Children of many working women are neglected, as there are simply not enough crèches in the cities. The absence of appropriate childcare forces poor families to leave infants to the care of siblings barely old enough to look after themselves.

The voluntary sector has developed some innovative programmes for children and infants providing nutrition, healthcare and childcare. Voluntary agencies like mobile crèches, self-employed women's association (SEWA), society for the integrated development of the Himalayas (SIDH), Mahila Samakhya and Bal Niketan Sangh have offered childcare to mothers who need it the most. Where these NGOs function, communities have benefited. They provide effective examples of the ECCE programme in India.

In recent years, limited research has been conducted into the scope, reach and quality of childcare in India (Anandalakshmy, 1989; D'Souza, 1979; Gopal, 1998; Saraswathi, 1994; Swaminathan, 1985). The government has no policy or regulation to monitor childcare quality. However, a monitoring study was carried out by Lady Irwin College to investigate the extent to which organisations in and around Delhi have been successful in implementing CSWB programmes. The findings revealed that crèches supported by CSWB were crowded and run in unsanitary buildings. Staff were not paid properly and were untrained. Nutritional components were also not satisfactory and community participation was negligible (Anandalakshmy, 1989). The coverage of this scheme was surprisingly inadequate. Many crèches were found to exist only on paper (Khullar, 1991) and to cover less than 10 per cent of the children in need of care.

Research on childcare arrangements for children of urban, middle-class working mothers (Datta, 1995; Sharma, 1996; Kapoor, 2005), found that day care was not the childcare of choice. The care and education of young children was seen as a family responsibility. It seems that it is this feature of Indian society that has been responsible for the lag in state support in the care, education and development of Indian children.

Socio-cultural perspective

In every society young children are dependent on adults for their survival and care. Traditions regarding child-rearing vary from community to community. In most cases, the child's natural mother and father play leading roles. The most important adults in the child's life are her/his parents. In almost all cases the mother is the primary caregiver. The discourse surrounding motherhood in the twentieth century has continued to emphasise the centrality of the mother–child relationship. An unequal share in parenting can also be seen in Indian middle-class, double-income families (Ramu, 1989; Kapoor, 2005).

Traditions also vary with regard to the accepted substitutes for the mother. In many non-Western communities, people live in extended family groups of three or four generations. Relatives – grandmothers, aunts, older sisters – are thus always at hand to take the maternal role. In India's metropolitan areas, a growing number of educated middle-class women are going out to work. Yet, according to an international research project on the two-income couple, the transition from single- to two-income families is not causing the same level of turmoil in Indian society as in other developed countries (Lewis *et al.*, 1992).

In principle, one would expect parents and communities to arrange childcare that is consistent with their beliefs and goals in a relatively stable society (Super & Harkness, 1997). The choice of childcare would be dependent not only on what is available to the parents but also on what parents believe is the most appropriate care for their child in the absence of the mother. Levine (1977) conceptualised childcare as a universal hierarchy of parental goals. These goals define what parents want for their children, ranging from ensuring basic survival to the acquisition of economic capabilities, and finally to the attainment of locally relevant cultural values. The centrality of the mother–child relationship typifies the Western attitude to childcare. The same is not true for non-Western societies, particularly India. Feminists have cited anthropological research from around the world to show that the image of the mother as the sole caregiver of the child is a recent Western invention. In a study conducted in Simla (a hill station in northern India), it was found that one-third of the sample employed servants to care for their children in their absence, a very small number sent their children to day care, and the rest had a mother or mother-in-law taking care of the child. The common alternative care for children in middle- and upper-income families is domestic helpers. Children from India's richest families often have a maid (ayah) who takes care of them (Khalakdina, 1979), either alongside the mother and other family members, or alone when the mother is away at work. The maid is often employed to perform other household tasks alongside their childcare responsibilities (Kapoor, 2005). This care arrangement is totally informal. Indian ayah or domestic helpers are very similar, in terms of their childcare experience, to au pairs in the West. They are usually from crowded homes where the advent of a new baby is a fairly common occurrence. They have seen babies being born, seen them nurse, live and grow up. They have probably cared for a younger sibling or cousin. Therefore, babies are neither an object of interest, nor an object of anxiety (Minturn *et al.*, 1966).

Women were least troubled about childcare if they could leave their children in the care of a relative either living in the same household or in the same neighbourhood (Sharma, 1996). Grandmother care is the predominant childcare choice of Indian working mothers (Kapoor, 2005). A resident grandmother may contribute economically to the family, which in turn could affect her parenting involvement. She may exert more control over house-hold decisions that include child-rearing (Wilson, 1986). In the Indian joint family the status and position of the grandmother in the family would influence her caregiving role. Who owns the house is similarly important (whether the parents of the child are living with the grandparents or the grandmother is residing in the parents' home).

The nuclear family system commonly observed in the West is only one among diverse forms of the family. The structure of the family has a large impact on child-rearing and care. Parenting and child-rearing often occur in very different conditions in different societies and cultures (Levine, 1977). Extended families are an important feature of Indian child-rearing, even when resources are not limited. Many cultures, including Indian, view extended-family child-rearing as an integral and important part of their culture. It is believed to provide a buffer against the stresses of everyday living. It is also important for cultural heritage transmission from generation to generation. In many communities, extended families mean that relatives are always at hand to take the maternal role in an emergency. A report from the Indian census of 2001 has shown that the Indian family unit has an average of six members who all live in one room and that the majority of newly married couples do not live independently (Office of the Registrar General, 2003). Given these circumstances, it seems natural that childcare in India is still predominantly provided by the extended family.

Even Bowlby (1973) suggested that near-relatives should care for children when natural parental care has failed for any reason. However, he observed that it was rarely relatives who took over the caregiving role. He listed five reasons why relatives were unable to care for children in these families: all relatives were deceased, aged, or ill; relatives lived too far away; relatives were unable to help for economic reasons; relatives were unwilling to help; or the children's parents grew up in a foster home and never had relatives. An extended family network of caregivers is therefore usually not available to parents in the West. A major contributor to this family isolation amongst all social class groups in industrialised societies is age segregation. The fragmentation of institutions according to age, and the high mobility within modern societies, has meant that interaction between people of different age groups occurs less and less frequently and is of diminishing social significance. Most societies will never again experience the mutual responsibilities and obligations of close inter-generation relationships like those that prevailed in pre-industrial societies or those that still exist in non-Western societies (Corsaro, 1997). Another approach to understanding this phenomenon would be to focus on the socio-psychological construct known as 'individualism versus collectivism'. Cultures value individualism when they foster the individual's needs, wishes and desires over the needs, wishes and desires of the group (Matsumoto, 1993). Extended families are often observed in societies that value collectivism, or at least the interdependence of their members, rather than individualism.

However, participation in child-rearing through extended families is often seen as a consequence of poverty rather than a desirable state of affairs. Extended families differ from one culture to another, but they have in common the sharing of resources, emotional support and caregiving.

Unlike in the West, educated middle-class mothers in India choose the care of a family member over day care. In the West, parents only tend to choose family-member childcare under the pressures of poverty, social isolation and lack of government financial support (Kontos *et al.*, 1995). However, there are exceptions. Australian families typically use the informal care of relatives, babysitters and nannies, especially during the first two years of their child's life, even though Australian families are eligible for financial assistance (Love *et al.*, 2003). This suggests that the decision to use informal care may be based on personal preference rather than cost, as in middle-class India. Also families may shy away from formal programmes that appear to promote different social practices, preferring care that emphasises collective forms of obligation.

Unfortunately, existing research pays little attention to caregivers outside of the nuclear family (e.g. the mother's mother-in-law and sister-in-law in the joint family) (Roopnarine *et al.*, 1990). There is no systematic alternative theory of Hindu child-rearing practices, which is essentially group mothering (Kurtz, 1992). There is a prescriptive belief in India that children should be cared for by their mothers, or by others from within the family, and not sent out to external childcare agencies.

Indian mothers are used to sharing childcare responsibilities with other family members and domestic helpers, even when they are at home. Indian children grow up within an extended family network and young mothers expect childcare assistance from family members and domestic helpers. Family members step in naturally and informally to care for children when their mother goes out to work and grandmothers become caregivers by default. Indians are family-oriented and marriage and child-bearing are absolute necessities for most (Chaudhary, 2004; Trawick, 2003). Children are desired in Indian families and young married couples are cajoled into having children as soon as possible. When a working woman expresses concerns about the care arrangements for her future child, she is usually reassured that the family will come forward and care for the child. Sometimes concerns do not even need to be expressed in extended families, as they will care for their young without being asked. Multiple mothering is a truism in India. When a mother works, she does so not just for self-fulfilment, but also for the sake of the wider family who encourage her to continue working after the birth of her child and who therefore provide childcare to make returning to work easier (Roland, 1988). According to Mullati (1995), most Indian families follow a joint-nuclear-joint cycle, i.e. childcare cycles between the extended and nuclear family. Wherever possible parents organise their lives to ensure that their child is cared for by a family member. Even when families live in different countries, the grandparents may move temporarily to ensure the appropriate care for their grandchild. If a mother marries into a family that does not support her work outside of the home, her natal family may come forward to help. Family members (grandmothers, aunts) are substitute caregivers in the Indian tradition. As *Sanskar* (family values) are only passed from one generation to another through family members, it is only when no family members are available to care for their young that the family looks for outside help. Non-familial caregivers are seen as alternative caregivers and not as substitute caregivers. Sometimes families even organise domestic helpers for their children's nuclear unit rather than entrust childcare to those outside of the household.

Kapoor (2005) found that mothers were most comfortable with childcare provided by family members, their own mothers in particular. Day care and domestic help were only used when there was no extended family available. If a family member was not available for childcare, the nuclear family income affected the choice of substitute care. Higher-income families chose domestic help, the more expensive option, over and above day care. Only when all of the above arrangements failed did Indian middle-class families turn to day care. Domestic helpers are preferred over day care, because helpers can be directly instructed in the family's childcare agenda and they are more economically viable as they may also perform other household chores. Unlike day care teachers who are viewed as strangers, domestic helpers can be trained to follow the unique care-giving instructions of the family. The fact that group care also involves travel, and provides less individual care and attention for the child, are further deterrents. Mothers seemed to feel least guilt when leaving their child with its grandmother, and most guilt when sending their child to day care.

In India, the mother is very rarely the sole caregiver. All family members usually share the responsibility for children although the mother may be a central figure (Sharma, 2003). Caring for children is not seen as being helpful to the mother; instead, childcare is seen as the family's shared responsibility. The sharing of care among adults in the family and beyond can provide a context for normal child development unexplored by existing developmental theories based on the 'individualistic' Western model (Sharma and LeVine, 1998). In India, the extended family is key to the psychological growth of the Indian child (Bisht and Sinha, 1981). The extended family is a near-universal feature, certainly in the emotional, if not physical, sense (Bassa, 1978). Children belong to the family and not to their parents (Khalakdina, 1979). Childcare is the shared responsibility of the extended family. An important feature of family life in India is familism. The term implies that an affiliation to the family is a predilection that pervades all social interactions (Anandlakshmy, 1984).

To understand Indian child-rearing, one has to look beyond the mother–child dyad. Typically, the Indian mother is in an extended family that deindividualises her relationship with the child (Vatuk, 1982). The ties between mother and child are forced into the background. The task of mothering is shared like food and space. Extended family is a source of support for parents (Matsumoto, 1993). Sharing a household with relatives, characteristic of extended families, is seen as a good way of maximising a family's resources for successful child-rearing. When the mothers of this generation move away from the Indian concept of multiple mothering and towards the Western idealised concept of exclusive mothering – a move encouraged by their exposure to Western life and literature – they start experiencing the guilt of leaving their child in the care of another person. By accepting the social and cultural construct of sharing the task of childcare, the mothers of this generation could avoid experiencing the turmoil of their Western counterparts.

Conclusions

Government and popular support for early childhood care and education in India is nothing like that seen in Western developed nations. As India is a developing nation, there are financial constraints on the development of early childhood care and education, but more important is the failure to recognise the crucial role of early childhood care and education for positive child outcomes such as learning, school readiness, nutrition and health. In a country where the family is held responsible for early childcare, the governmental drive to provide state childcare services is understandably minimal. Family care is seen as the best for the child even when a mother goes out to work. Institutional care is largely believed to be a violation of young children's primary needs and numbers of studies seem to support the argument that women do not want or need organised alternative care. It is perhaps this feature of Indian society that has been responsible for the lag in providing state education and care for young children. The belief that individual families should solve their children's problems has also influenced the policy for disabled children (Sharma, 2004). Even in the provision of a basic educational infrastructure for children, the same apathy has been experienced. The idea that government, business and the community have broader social responsibilities for providing family support has been slow to take, even in the developed nations.

In India it is commonly believed that caring for family members (whether a baby, an ailing or an older person) is one of the primary responsibilities of the family. Mostly, where families are large, relationships are congenial, and money is not a problem, these situations are dealt with in the course of everyday family life. Any condition under which one or more of these features are disturbed becomes problematic and stressful for individuals and families. Domestic helpers are also becoming scarce, expensive and undependable. Small, urban, nuclear, unprivileged families therefore would be at maximum stress risk. In Germany and Sweden, for instance, the young parent confidently looks to the state for support (both economic and institutional) on the arrival of a new baby. There is no such provision in India and it is therefore time to review welfare policy in the light of contemporary changes in Indian society. Traditional patterns of living should be sustained but state support, in situations where traditional support may be absent, should be available. In a society where girls and women are forced to assume almost the entire responsibility for child-rearing, under-investment in the provision of appropriate childcare facilities unfairly denies women the freedom to pursue education, employment and other economic, political and cultural opportunities. However, it is not only women who need to be supported. Current legislation attempts to deal with female labour in the organised sector, and it must be remodelled not only to enforce more childcare provision for working mothers but for all workers irrespective of gender, organisational sector and labour force.

It is likely that women will continue to work outside of the home and that their children will grow up with a variety of childcare arrangements. The management of these childcare arrangements will impact the lives of children whose mothers work. Government should provide a supportive environment that recognises and acknowledges the needs of working mothers by ensuring support from state, corporate and community institutions. In childcare that is not supervised or under government regulation, the desired trust and accountability may be lacking. The solution lies in having guidelines, regulations, policies and licensing for extra familial childcare.

The country's middle and upper classes pay unregulated nursery schools to provide them with preschool education for their children. Though some high-fee preschool programmes are excellent by any international standards, most preschools are 'rote-learning, school-admission preparatory factories' where even educated middle- and upper-income parents are unable to demand quality. These private early childhood education programmes also need to be regulated. However, it is the underprivileged who suffer the most. ICDS has led to about 25 per cent of all children aged three to six being enrolled in non-formal preschool programmes, but the quality of these programmes is far from satisfactory. Though there is an increased recognition that only quality early childhood programmes result in positive childhood outcomes, and that poor quality programmes can have negative consequences (Sharma, 2005), the recognition has caused little active response. There is still no national curriculum or national guidelines and no national body to enforce quality standards. The training of childcare workers and early childhood educators has also been neglected.

Along with its distinct socio-cultural identity, India is also a country of diversity. Successful early childhood programmes need to be flexible, taking cultural values and the local context and needs into account. They need to make space for the traditional folklore, infant games, child-rearing, nutritional and health practices of the region (Kaul, 2002). The NCERT and Indian Academy of Pediatrics have advocated a Guide to Preschool Education recommending that preschool education should:

- be non-formal education;
- use the mother tongue (English is often the medium of instruction in fee-paying schools);
- base its activities and teacher training on NCERT guidelines;
- become a local priority for businesses, organisations and communities.

The guide also stresses that efforts must be taken to enlighten the public about the advantages of promoting non-formal pre-primary education (Nair, 2004).

India's strength lies in its strong institution of family and the wealth of traditional practices in early childhood education and care. With advocacy, national curriculum and guidelines, trained childcare workers and teachers, culturally appropriate and quality-regulated early childhood care and education, the world's largest population of young children could have a good start in life.

References

Anandalakshmy, S. (1984). Cultural themes in the Indian context. Paper presented at the Summer Institute in Child Development, Lady Irwin College, University of Delhi.

Anandalakshmy, S. (1989). Crèches in Delhi. Conference paper, Lady Irwin College, University of Delhi.

Antonova, K., Bongard-Levin, G. and Kotovsky, G. (1979). *A history of India*. USSR: Progress Publishers.

Bardhan, K. (1987). *Women's work and living in some south and south-east Asian countries*. New Delhi: Centre for Women's Development Studies.

Bassa, D.M. (1978). The child in his family. In J. Anthony & C. Chiland (Eds), *Children and their parents in a changing world* (pp. 333–7). New York: John Wiley.

Bhavnagri, N.P. (1995). An interview with Professor Amita Verma: A leader in early childhood education in India. *Childhood Education, 71*, 156–160.

Bisht, S. and Sinha, D. (1981). Socialization, family, and psychological differentiation. In D. Sinha (Ed.), *Socialization of the Indian child* (pp. 41–54). New Delhi: Concept Publishing.

Bowlby, J. (1973). *Attachment and loss: Separation (Vol. 2)*. New York: Basic Books.

Chaudhary, N. (2004). *Listening to culture*. New Delhi: Sage.

Chaudhary, P. (1983). Keynote address at workshop sponsored by Aga Khan Foundation on cognitive development in early childhood programmes in India. Haryana Agriculture University, Hissar.

Cleghorn, A. and Prochner, L. (2003). Contrasting visions of early childhood education: examples from rural and urban settings in Zimbabwe and India. *Journal of Early Childhood Research, 1(2)*, 131–153.

Corsaro, W.A. (1997). *The sociology of childhood*. Thousand Oaks, CA: Pine Forge Press.

Department of Women and Child Development (1995). *Integrated Child Development Services*. New Delhi: Ministry of Human Resource Development, Government of India.

D'Souza, A. (1979). *Children in Crèches*. New Delhi: Intellectual Publishing.

Datta, V. (1995). Home away from home: Family day care in India. Volume 1 of Suraksha: *Early Childhood Care & Education in India*. Madras, India: M.S. Swaminathan.

Gopal, A.K. (1998). *Crèche services in India – an evaluation*. New Delhi: NIPCCD.

Kapoor, S. (2005). *Alternate care for infants of employed mothers: Experiences in different childcare arrangements*. PhD Thesis, University of Delhi.

Kaul, V. (2002). Early childhood care and education. In R. Govinda (Ed.), *India Education Report: A Profile of Basic Education* (pp. 23–34). National Institute of Educational Planning and Administration: Oxford University Press.

Kaul, V., Ramachandran, C. & Upadhyaya, G.C. (1993*). Impact of ECE on retention in primary grade*. New Delhi: National Council of Educational Research and Training.

Khalakdina, M. (1979). *Early childcare in India*. International Monograph Series on Early Childcare. London: Gordon & Breach.

Khalakdina, M. (1998). Early childhood care and education in India: a perspective. In M. Swaminathan (Ed.), *The first five years: a critical perspective on early childhood care and education in India* (pp. 163–195). New Delhi: Sage

Khullar, M. (Ed.) (1991). *Whither childcare services?* New Delhi: Centre for Women's Development Studies, UNICEF India and Save the Children Fund, UK.

Kontos, S., Howes, C., Shinn, M., & Galinsky, E. (1995). *Quality in family childcare and relative care*. New York: Teachers College Press.

Kurtz, S.N. (1992). *All the Mothers Are One: Hindu India and the cultural reshaping of psychoanalysis*. New York: Columbia University Press.

Levine, R.A. (1977). Child rearing as cultural adaptation. In P.H. Leiderman, S.R. Tulkin and A. Rosenfeld (Eds), *Culture and infancy* (pp. 15–27). New York: Academic Press.

Lewis, S., Izaraeli, D. and Hootsmans, H. (1992). *Dual earner families: internal perspectives*. London: Sage.

Love, J., Harrison, I., Sagi-Schwartz, A., van Ijzendoorn, M.H., Ross, C., Ungerer, J.A., Raikes, H., Brady-Smith, C., Boller, K., Brooks-Gunn, J., Constantine, J., Kisker, E., Paulsell, D. and Chazan-Cohen, R. (2003). Childcare quality matters: How conclusions may vary with context. *Child Development, 74*, 1021–1033.

Matsumoto, D. (1993) *People psychology from a cultural perspective*. California: Brooks/Cole Publishing Company.

Minturn, L., and Hitchcock, J.T. (1966). *The Rajputs of Khalapur, India*. New York: John Wiley.

Mullati, L. (1995). Families in India: Beliefs and realities. *Journal of Comparative Family Studies, 36*.

Nair, M.K.C. (2004). Pre-school Education. *Indian Pediatrics 2004; 41*: 425–7.

National Institute of Public Cooperation and Child Development (NIPCCD) (1992). *National Evaluation of Integrated Child Development Services*. New Delhi.

Office of the Registrar General (2003). *Census of India (2001)*. Office of the Registrar General: New Delhi India.

Ramu, G.N. (1989). *Women, work and marriage in urban India*. New Delhi: Sage.

Roland A. (1988). *In Search of Self in India and Japan: Toward a Cross-Cultural Psychology*. Princeton: Princeton University Press.

Roopnarine, J.L., Talukder, E., Jain, D., Joshi, P. and Srivastav, P. (1990). Characteristics of holding, patterns of play, and social behaviours between parents and infants in New Delhi, India. *Developmental Psychology, 26(4)*, 867–873.

Sachidananda (1965). Cited in Khalakdina, M. (1979), *Early childcare in India*, International Monograph Series on Early Childcare. London: Gordon & Breach.

Saraswathi, T.S. (1994). Women in poverty contexts: balancing economic and childcare needs. In R. Barooah (Ed.), *Capturing complexity*. New Delhi: Sage.

Sharma, A. (1993). Current issues in early childhood care and education. In T.S. Saraswathi and B. Kaur (Eds), *Human development and family studies in India: An agenda for research and policy*. New Delhi: Sage.

Sharma, A. (2005). Towards quality in ECCE: The Indian experience. Presentation at two-day meeting of the ECERS International Networking, University of London, 18 March.

Sharma, A. and Khosla, R. (1995). *Child development in India: Opportunities and challenges*. In *Rotary International – Rotary International Award 1995, Child Welfare and Development*. New Delhi: Rotary Awards for Service to Humanity (India) Trust.

Sharma, D. (2003). *Childhood, family, sociocultural change in India: reinterpreting the inner world*. New Delhi: Oxford University Press.

Sharma, D. and Levine, R.A. (1998). *Childcare in India: a comparative developmental view of infant social environments. New directions for child development. Socioemotional development across cultures. No. 81.* San Francisco: Jossey-Bass Publisher.

Sharma, N. (2004). Understanding childhood disability in India. In J. Pattnaik (Ed.), *Research in global child advocacy: childhood in South Asia*. Greenwich, CT: Information Age Publishing.

Sharma, U. (1996). *Women's work, class, and the urban household. A study of Shimla, North India*. London: Tavistock Publications. The State of the World's Children 2001, A UNICEF Publication.

Sriram, R. (1998). Women's empowerment and childcare: the interface. In M. Swaminathan (Ed.), *The first five years: a critical perspective on early childhood care and education in India (pp. 240–272)*. New Delhi: Sage.

Super, C.M. and Harkness, S. (1997). The cultural structuring of child development. In J.W. Berry, P.R. Dasen and T.S. Saraswati (Eds), *Handbook of cross-cultural psychology, Vol. 2. Basic processes and human development* (pp. 1–41). Boston: Allyn & Bacon.

Swaminathan, M. (1985). *Who cares? A study of childcare facilities for low-income working women in India*. New Delhi: Centre for Women's Development Studies.

Swaminathan, M. (1992) Training for childcare workers in India. *The Coordinators' Notebook No. 12*. The Consultative Group on ECCD.

Swaminathan, M. (1998). Introduction. In M. Swaminathan (Ed.), *The first five years: a critical perspective on early childhood care and education in India* (pp. 15–28). New Delhi: Sage.

Trawick, M. (2003). The person beyond the family. In V. Das (Ed.), *The Oxford India Companion to sociology and social anthropology, Vol 2* (pp. 1158–1178). Delhi: OUP.

Upadhyay, G.C. (1998). *Numeracy and reading readiness levels of entrants to class 1 – a synthesis report*. New Delhi: National Council of Educational Research and Training.

Vatuk, S. (1982). Forms of address in the north Indian family: an explanation of the cultural meaning of kin terms. In A. Ostor, I. Fruzzetti and S. Barnett (Eds), *Concepts of person: kinship, caste, and marriage in India* (pp. 56–98). Delhi: Oxford University Press.

Wilson, M.N. (1986). The black extended family: An analytical consideration. *Developmental Psychology, 22*, 246–258.

10 Development of kindergarten care and education in the People's Republic of China since the 1990s

Li Shenglan

In the People's Republic of China, kindergarten is an institution for the care and education of preschool children (from three to seven years old). This chapter gives an overview of the development of kindergarten care and education in China since the 1990s. I start with a description of how the kindergarten system has developed, with reference to government policy, and then summarise research findings. Four main areas of kindergarten innovation will be discussed: type, size and enrolment; aims, content and approach; attitudes to hiring and training staff; and perceived responsibilities within the wider community.

Type, size and enrolment

Kindergarten types

The Ministry of Education of the People's Republic of China promulgated the Kindergarten Management Legislation in 1990. Under this legislation, education commissions across the country should provide publicly run, and encourage independently managed (i.e. by businesses, resident groups or individuals), kindergarten programs. In 1996, the Ministry of Education issued further legislation that instructs kindergartens run by businesses and the military to extend their services beyond their workers and open their programmes to local children. Encouraged by legislation and profit, the number of kindergartens run by businesses increases yearly. For instance, in Shanghai in 2003, 252,200 children attended 1,014 kindergartens. Of those 1,014 programmes, 321 were independently managed, providing preschool care and education for 71,000 children (Shanghai Municipal Education Commission, 2004). It seems likely that these independently managed programmes will continue to burgeon, providing the majority of kindergarten provision in the future.

Kindergarten care and education programmes

The Kindergarten Work Regulation outlines a range of part-day, full-day, seasonal and boarding programmes (Ministry of Education, 1996).

Generally, full-day programmes operate about eight hours a day (8am to 4pm). Seasonal and part-day programmes operate temporary schedules to accommodate working parents. Boarding programmes are open 24 hours a day, five days a week (not Saturdays and Sundays) for the full year. Though most kindergartens in China are full-day programmes, boarding programmes are more prevalent in the larger cities.

Though the different programmes are tailored to suit parental working patterns, boarding programmes have been criticised by early childhood professionals. Research into boarding kindergartens has shown that they cannot maintain collaborative relationships with each child's family and that they fail to foster children's social-emotional development, specifically healthy emotional development and social attachment (Li, 2000; Wu, 2001). On the other hand, research has shown that boarding programmes encourage children not only to be independent but to think positively about such programmes (Ruan, 2000; Yao, 2001).

Group sizes and staff–child ratios

Most kindergartens are now both nationally and provincially regulated or licensed. Standards of health and safety, nutrition, teacher training, staff–child ratios and group size are maintained through annual inspections. The Kindergarten Work Regulation stipulates the maximum group size based on children's age: groups of three- to four-year-olds must contain no more than 25 children; groups of four- to five-year-olds, or five- to six-year-olds, must contain no more than 30 children. Some kindergartens have mixed-age groups but conform to these size guidelines, though there are separate regulations for smaller group sizes in boarding programmes (Ministry of Education, 1996). Local education departments may stretch the regulations to allow for an extra five children per group.

In practice, group sizes exceed these specifications, as every child is assured entry into kindergarten. This guaranteed enrolment has the desired effect of meeting the needs of working parents, but has an enormous impact on group sizes and staff–child ratios. There are normally 12 groups within each programme. Every group is supervised by two teachers and one teaching assistant, making the staff–child ratio higher than 1:10.

In contrast to other countries, early childhood programmes in China guarantee entry. This contrast stimulated research into Chinese kindergartens, where smaller group sizes and lower staff–child ratios were shown to strengthen positive interactions between staff and children, providing children with more individual care and attention, as well as nurturing children's personalities (Ye, 2004). Recent research has also looked at multi-age groups, and children within these groups showed better developed social skills, especially when interacting with others of different ages (Huang, 2004; Wang, 2005).

Enrolment of young children

The Chinese Children Development Outline: 2001–2010 states that the government will adhere to the principle of Children First, ensuring children's rights to health and education with a focus on preschool childcare. The number of kindergartens is increasing as a consequence and more children have access to kindergartens. In 2001, 20,218,400 children were enrolled in 111,700 kindergartens (Ministry of Education, 2002). In 2002, this increased to 20,360,200 children enrolled in 111,800 kindergartens (Ministry of Education, 2003). These figures rose again in 2004 when 20,894,000 children were enrolled in 117,900 kindergartens (Ministry of Education, 2005). In cities, kindergartens now provide cover for almost all three- to six-year-olds. For example, in Beijing, 205,532 children aged three to six attended 1,422 kindergartens in 2004 (Beijing Municipal Education Commission, 2005). In the same year in Shanghai, more than 95 per cent of children aged three to six were enrolled in kindergarten (Shanghai Municipal Education Commission, 2005).

The Chinese Children Development Outline aims to provide three years of preschool education for almost all children in cities and economically developed areas. Plans for the countryside focus on increasing rural children's enrolment in one-year preschool programmes, and local governments are to provide development plans for children in line with these aims. The Ningxia Huizu Autonomous Region, for example, aimed for 45 per cent of children in the region to receive three years of preschool education and 80 per cent to receive one year of preschool education by 2005. Similarly, Hainan Province aimed for 55 per cent of children in the province to receive three years of preschool education and 80 per cent to receive one year of preschool education by 2005 (Liu, 2002). In 2003, the Office of the State Council proposed national aims for the reformation of preschool education over a five-year period, as follows: by 2007, the percentage of children receiving three years of preschool education should rise to 55 per cent; the percentage of children receiving one year of preschool education should rise to 80 per cent; and all children in urban areas should receive three years of preschool education.

In addition, the Chinese Children Development Outline suggested developing early education for infants and toddlers (birth to age three years). In response, studies into the care and development of 0-three-year-old children have been carried out in Shanghai. They demonstrate that early childhood is a key developmental stage as children learn rapidly from birth to age three. It is obvious that there are some sensitive periods when young children are more susceptible to certain behaviours and can learn specific skills more easily. Children's experiences during early childhood not only influence their functioning in school but can also have effects throughout their life. Studies in Shanghai show that environments and events experienced in early childhood have lasting effects on children's cognitive development (Yang, 2001; Zhang, 2002, 2004; Huang, 2003). This led to the Shanghai Municipal Education Commission publishing the Shanghai 0–three-year-old Children Plan of Care and Education in 2003 and as a result, programmes for 0–three-year-old children are rapidly becoming a part of the kindergarten system in Shanghai. The plan calls for kindergartens to provide new services for children from birth through to three years old. It is a growing trend for parents to enrol children in kindergarten at a younger age.

Aims, content and approach

Aims of kindergarten care and education

The Kindergarten Work Regulation states that kindergarten is an important part of basic education. Kindergartens should care for and educate children, focusing on developing the child as a whole, as well as trying to meet the needs of working or studying parents. This regulation enables early childhood professionals to understand the importance of kindergarten care and education, outlining its major aims:

*   To provide a healthy environment: developing children's motor skills through physical activities; encouraging children to build hygienic habits.
*   To promote cognitive and language development, communication skills and a positive attitude to learning through hands-on activities that explore the different senses and increase awareness of the environment.
*   To nurture children's moral and social attitudes: encouraging love for children's hometowns, their motherland, and the importance of collective labour (both manual and intellectual); developing the attributes of honesty, self-confidence, curiosity, friendship, courage, respect for public property, politeness and self-regulation, amongst others.
*   To develop children's appreciation for the arts and artistic expression.

These educational aims guide kindergarten activities throughout the country. To some extent, these aims vary in different provinces, autonomous regions and municipalities, but the national aims remain the standard upon which all kindergartens are based. For example, the Shanghai Municipal Outline of Kindergarten Education in 2001 directs local education agencies and kindergartens to develop unique programmes tailored to the children, families and communities they serve. Different communities of parents and professionals have diverse views about what additional skills their children need to face the society of the future. This has led to kindergartens increasing areas of specialisation like physical education, art, science and technology or foreign languages.

Content of kindergarten care and education

As we enter the twenty-first century, enormous changes are taking place in the content of kindergarten care and education in China. The Ministry of Education (2001) promulgated the Kindergarten Education Guideline, which proposes that kindergartens should cover all areas of children's development in a straightforward manner. The guideline divides education into five domains: health, language, society, science and art, which replace the eight domains previously listed under the Kindergarten Education Outline published in 1981, namely, physical education, daily life, moral education, language, science, mathematics, music and fine arts.

As children's cognitive, socio-emotional and behavioural development are inter-related, some early childhood professionals have questioned the merits of separating education into domains. They began to study how to integrate across domains. Findings from this research suggest that educational activities should be based around the four seasons (Zhao and Tang, 1994; Ni and Zhao, 1996; Tang, 1999). In recent years many kindergarten teachers have come to realise that the realms of children's development – physical, cognitive, emotional and social – are closely related, and that development in one realm influences development in other realms. On the basis of these research findings, and working within governmental guidelines, teachers try to put these ideas into practice.

Approaches of kindergarten care and education

When planning kindergarten activities, Chinese early childhood professionals need to take into account three sets of legislation: the Kindergarten Management Legislation (Ministry of Education, 1990), the Kindergarten Work Regulation (Ministry of Education, 1996) and the Kindergarten Education Guideline (Ministry of Education, 2001). These laws emphasise the importance of play as a basic tool through which to educate and engage children, and informs the structure for planning daily kindergarten activities.

Daily activities

Kindergarten daily activities are designed to complement the inter-related development of children's cognitive, physical, emotional and social growth. Therefore the balance of individual, small- and large-group activities, child-directed and teacher-directed activities, and indoor and outdoor activities, is carefully organised. The usual schedule for a full-day programme in China is as follows:

7:50   Opening activities: welcome children, health check, free activities
8:20   Morning exercises

8:40   Bathroom, hand-washing, snack
9:00   Large group activities: language/mathematics/science
9:30   Bathroom
9:40   Large group: music/movement/painting/drawing/physical activities
10:00   Bathroom
10:10   Small group: learning centres, free activities
10:40   Clean-up
10:50   Prepare for lunch: hand-washing, helpers set table
11:00   Lunch
11:30   Relaxation: story time, music time, short walk
12:00   Nap
14:30   Get up, bathroom, hand-washing
15:00   Snack
15:20   Outdoor activities
15:50   Clean-up
16:00   Group meeting: recall day's activities, prepare to go home, departure.

OPENING ACTIVITIES

As each child enters, the kindergarten nurse and teacher greet her/him individually. Daily personal greetings provide an opportunity to check every child's health and emotional state as well as allowing the child to practise language skills and build a positive attitude towards kindergarten. Children usually do not arrive at the same time, so the first arrivals can select an activity from a range of quiet activities, such as playing puzzles, playing cards, playing at chess and cutting paper.

MORNING EXERCISES

All children and teachers do morning exercises together in the outdoor playground. Different movements are assigned to each age group. These exercises, accompanied by recorded music, enhance children's physical development and motor skills.

LARGE GROUP ACTIVITIES

Large group activities are educationally focused. Directed by one or two teachers, the whole group studies together for about 30 minutes. Language, mathematics or science are taught in the first session, then music and dance, painting and drawing or sport are taught in the second session. All activities use a variety of teaching materials and equipment and are increasingly based upon a child-centred model of teaching. Large group activities not only allow children to share and demonstrate ideas, they also provide an opportunity to experience a sense of community.

SMALL GROUP ACTIVITIES

Small group activities allow children to choose between several learning centres. The learning centres are designed to enhance children's interests, knowledge and skills in different areas, including science, books/language, block-play, art, physical dexterity and housekeeping, as well as more playful explorations, for example, of water and sand.

CLEAN-UP

Children return all work and play materials and equipment to their labelled places. Most materials in the classroom for children's use are within reach on open shelves. This time helps young children to develop a sense of control and ownership.

BATHROOM, HAND-WASHING, SNACK AND LUNCH

Since the mid-1990s, children are allowed to use the bathroom whenever necessary. Before any activity in which food is prepared or eaten, children must wash and dry their hands. All snacks and lunches are provided by the kindergarten and aim to be both nutritious and attractive to children. The children serve themselves and eat in silence under the supervision of the teacher and teaching assistant who ensure that children finish their food. Then children are involved in cleaning up. In this way, children learn hygiene and self-management.

RELAXATION

After lunch, children have a chance to relax. Relaxing activities include listening to recordings of stories or music, or taking a short walk.

NAP

Midday naps are considered essential for a child's healthy physical development. Therefore, every group has a bedroom with many beds and every child, under adult supervision, must have a nap, or lie still, for about two-and-a-half hours.

OUTDOOR ACTIVITIES

The Kindergarten Work Regulation recognises the importance of outdoor play and exercise. It directs programmes to ensure that children spend at least two hours a day in outdoor activities. Most kindergartens try to fulfil this requirement.

GROUP MEETING

The children in each group sit together with a teacher and review the day's activities. The meeting is devised not only to go over what has been taught, but also to develop listening, speaking and concentration skills, as well as to encourage children to share with others and evaluate their behaviour.

Environment

Providing a safe and nurturing environment is essential to successful kindergartens. Teachers try to create an environment best suited to the promotion of physical, social and intellectual growth, taking into consideration everything from the safety of the neighbourhood, building and facilities, to the provision of well-lit rooms and appropriate and attractive toys and materials.

Play activities

Play activities are at the heart of the Kindergarten Management Legislation (Ministry of Education, 1990), the Kindergarten Work Regulation (Ministry of Education, 1996) and the Kindergarten Education Guideline (Ministry of Education, 2001). They recognise that children learn through play. These play activity sessions are therefore planned by teachers to match children's developmental needs and include a range of physical, cognitive, dramatic, social, outdoor and free play. These play sessions utilise all the teachers' skills. As well as planning the activities, teachers are directly involved in the children's play: supervising, observing and participating.

Hiring and training staff

Kindergartens employ directors, assistant directors, teachers, teaching assistants, doctors or nurses, cooks and other workers. The quality of these employees is related to the quality and success of the kindergarten. In 1996, the Ministry of Education enacted the Kindergarten Work Regulation, which stipulates the qualities necessary for kindergarten employment. Early childhood professionals should:

- have a love and respect for all children
- be willing to increase their professional knowledge and improve their professional skills
- be socially and morally responsible
- possess the physical and mental health required to carry out the responsibilities of their roles and positions.

Qualifications, responsibilities and requirements

The Kindergarten Management Legislation specifies that kindergarten directors and teachers should graduate from Kindergarten Teacher School (Ministry of Education, 1990). The course accepts junior high-school graduates and takes three years to complete.

In 1996, the Ministry of Education, through the Kindergarten Work Regulation, demanded further qualifications, responsibilities and position requirements for kindergarten directors. In addition to graduating from Kindergarten Teacher School, kindergarten directors must also have professional education experience, a Level 2 Teacher Certification, and complete the Training Credentials for the Director Position. The Kindergarten Work Regulation also stipulates the director's major leadership and management responsibilities. Kindergarten directors are not only responsible for planning and implementing the care and education programme, they must also:

- have a working knowledge of the relevant laws, regulations and policies;
- manage children's health, safety and nutrition;
- recruit, supervise, evaluate and motivate personnel;
- manage the kindergarten's finances and facilities;
- support families as valued partners in the educational process;
- establish partnerships with the local community.

Teachers' responsibilities are also stipulated in the Kindergarten Work Regulation. Their prime responsibility is for the children in their class. They should get to know the children in order to organise suitable working environments and activities. They should also establish good relationships with the children's parents. Teachers should follow health, safety and emergency procedures and attend in-house training organised by the directors.

In 2001, the Chinese Children Development Outline called for even higher teacher qualifications and highlighted the importance of ongoing in-house teacher training. The Guideline for the Reformation and Development of Young Children's Education, issued by the State Council in 2003, takes teacher development one step further, ordering kindergartens to build programmes of in-house teacher training, and encouraging teachers to implement localised early childhood research projects.

Training and qualifications

These guidelines instruct the regional education departments to map out professional development programmes. For example, the Shanghai Municipal Education Commission stipulates that kindergarten directors and teachers should be trained in a variety of ways. They should complete an early childhood education degree. In addition, kindergarten teachers and directors must participate in ongoing continuing education: every five years, directors should complete 360 hours of new training and teachers should complete 240 hours of new training. This focus on training motivates directors and teachers to spend their spare time learning more about child health and development, family and community relationships, professional practice and development and research.

In response to this legislation, more and more kindergarten professionals have completed an associate or baccalaureate degree. Fifty-eight per cent of directors and 66 per cent of teachers have an associate degree or equivalent, and 89 per cent of directors and 91 per cent of teachers meet the qualification requirements in Shanghai in the 2003 school year. In addition, the 2004 Educational Development Statistics show that 98 per cent of teachers hold the required educational qualifications, with 79 per cent of teachers and 85 per cent of directors having successfully completed an associate degree, baccalaureate degree or master's degree in Shanghai (Shanghai Municipal Education Commission, 2005).

Directors and teachers are graded from Level 1 (highest) to Level 5 (lowest) depending on their experience, knowledge and skills, degree, performances and research results. Progression through the grades is increasingly difficult, and moving from Level 2 to Level 1 is especially hard. There are few Level 1 positions available and Level 2 teachers and directors must not only meet the requirements for the promotion, but must also pass an evaluation by the local and provincial education commission. There are therefore many teachers and directors graded at Level 2 who are of Level 1 standard. In 2003 in Shanghai, only 5.21 per cent of directors and 0.24 per cent of teachers had received a Level 1 grading.

Teachers and teaching assistants are paid according to their level of training and responsibility. It is believed that children benefit most when their teachers have high levels of formal education and have early childhood professional qualifications. For most teaching staff, continuing education is part of the ongoing process of becoming a professional teacher. This attitude to professional development means that many directors and core teachers are involved in master's degree programmes.

Hence national and local kindergarten policies have led to a dramatic increase in the number of kindergarten professionals in China. In 2001, there were 630,100 directors and teachers in China (Ministry of Education, 2002), with yearly increases bringing this figure to 759,600 in 2004 (Ministry of Education, 2005).

Partnerships within the wider community

Relationships with families

Tasks

The family is critical to children's education and development as parents are children's first teachers. Kindergarten staff can help parents to develop this role by providing useful information about children's learning and development. The Kindergarten Work Regulation stipulates that kindergartens should work in partnership with families, helping parents to establish appropriate home environments and providing parents with information about the care and education of their children (Ministry of Education, 1996). As a result, family involvement programmes and activities have become an essential part of every kindergarten.

In 2000, Li Shenglan investigated parental involvement through a survey of teachers and parents of 141 children from full-day kindergartens in Shanghai. These studies revealed that the higher the level of parental involvement, the higher the developmental level of the child. However, with only 52 per cent of parents becoming involved with kindergartens regularly, the lack of parental involvement in children's kindergarten education remains a serious problem. Li Shenglan suggests that, in order to promote children's social, emotional and academic growth, kindergartens should strengthen relationships with families. They need to encourage parents to take a more active part in educating their children by attracting more parental participation in kindergarten programmes on a regular basis.

Means to achieve tasks

The Kindergarten Work Regulation states that the kindergarten–parent relationship should be reciprocal. On the one hand, kindergartens are directed to inform parents of the content and methods of kindergarten care and education through regular parent–staff meetings, family education consultations and open days. On the other hand, kindergartens must carefully consider parents' ideas and suggestions regarding education and management. Channels of communication between parents and kindergartens should also be managed through parent committees, which should provide a forum for discussion of kindergarten programmes and plans and the nature of child-rearing.

In practice, kindergartens have developed different ways of communicating with parents. Face-to-face communication is the most important and has led to the following approaches: parent–staff meetings, open days, everyday talk, home visits, family education lectures and consultations, parent–child activities and parent volunteering.

PARENT–STAFF MEETINGS

In general, teachers hold parent–staff meetings twice a term. At the beginning of each term, teachers introduce parents to the group plans and activities laid out for that term. At the end of each term, teachers report on the children's progress. In addition, there are conferences for parents of specific age groups.

OPEN DAYS

Every term, half a day is put aside for directors and teachers to welcome parents into the classroom, which provides an opportunity to observe the children's morning activities. To encourage parents to attend, they receive half a day's paid leave from their employers.

EVERYDAY TALK

When parents drop off and pick up children, teachers can engage parents in small-talk. This provides an opportunity for teachers to speak to parents informally about their children's needs, interests and progress.

HOME VISITS

Teachers visit children at home during the holidays to assess the home environment, help parents learn how to support their children's learning, and gain parents' trust.

FAMILY EDUCATION LECTURES/CONSULTATIONS

Every term, kindergartens provide lectures on family care and education. Local paediatricians, psychologists and educators give lectures to parents on child development and child-rearing. Some kindergartens also provide family consultations, which provide an opportunity for parents to ask specialists about their children's development.

PARENT–CHILD ACTIVITIES

Examples of planned parent–child activities are: parents playing games with the children in the playground; parents reading books to the children in the classroom; parents helping children to cook food in the kindergarten kitchen.

PARENT VOLUNTEERING

Some kindergartens invite parents to be volunteers. Parents have particular skills based on their training and experience and with additional teacher training provided by the kindergarten, they can provide help by volunteering as teacher assistants, classroom aides, course mentors, activity tutors, field-trip monitors and homework helpers.

When it is impossible for kindergarten professionals to arrange face-to-face communication with parents, other ways of contacting families come into play: bulletin boards, newsletters, written reports and telephone calls.

BULLETIN BOARDS

General information, announcements, daily schedules and curriculum plans are all posted on bulletin boards outside classrooms for parents to read.

NEWSLETTERS

Kindergarten newsletters are printed monthly and are an excellent way to keep families informed about kindergarten activities.

WRITTEN REPORTS OR NOTES

Some kindergartens use written reports to contact families, typically every two weeks, describing children's recent academic and social development. Teachers may write an additional note if a specific need or difficulty arises. Telephone contact with families also occurs.

These different types of parent involvement often occur together. Li Shenglan investigated 86 directors and core teachers from 80 full-day kindergartens and six boarding kindergartens in Shanghai City, Shandong, Zhejiang and Guandong provinces in 2002–3. The most frequent means of contact with the family was parent–staff meetings (95 per cent), followed by bulletin boards (92 per cent), then talk during drop-off and pick-up of children (86 per cent), then telephone calls (76 per cent), parent–child activities (71 per cent), family education lectures (66 per cent) and open days (62 per cent). Li Shenglan suggests that kindergartens should expand their use of other types of communication, making better use of email and website technology in particular.

In Li's (2000) survey of parents in Shanghai, there were different views on the best method of communication. The most popular methods of parent–kindergarten communication, in order of preference, were: parent–staff meetings, small talk during welcome and departure, home visits, parent–child activities, open-day activities and kindergarten–family notes, and it was suggested that kindergartens should use these preferred forms of contact to engage parents in their children's education.

Kindergarten professionals now believe that the key to effective parent involvement is a two-way flow of information. They help parents to realise that mutual cooperation is in everyone's best interest. Kindergartens, children and families are all part of the education and development process. All three parties can benefit from a positive, well-planned programme of family involvement.

Relationships between kindergarten, the home and the community

The Kindergarten Education Guideline states that kindergartens should cooperate harmoniously with families and local communities, using all kinds of local resources to foster children's development (Ministry of

Education, 2001). Additionally, the Chinese Children Development Outline instructs schools, families and communities to unite to form a single integrated educational system both within, and outside, the school gates. The Guideline for the Reformation and Development of Young Children's Education suggests that kindergartens should form similar ties with families and communities, making use of local resources to improve the quality of family education. It also suggests that kindergartens should involve families and communities in kindergarten management.

In response to this legislation, kindergarten professionals try to develop links between families, the kindergarten and the community, encouraging parents and community members to become involved in kindergarten activities, as well as offering their services to the local community. Good relationships between parents, schools and communities have a positive effect on young children's development, yet Li (2003, 2004a, 2004b, 2004c, 2004d) found that the use of community resources by kindergartens allowed much room for improvement.

Conclusions

The past 15 years have been full of important changes for kindergartens in the People's Republic of China. The State Council and the Ministry of Education have performed leading roles in formulating national legislation, regulations and policies for the development of kindergarten care and education and developing kindergarten services. These regulations ensure the rights, and promote the development, of kindergarten professionals, parents and children.

A high level of government commitment, funding and legislation, at national, regional and local level, ensures extensive kindergarten provision for children from three to seven years of age. Legislation prescribes the characteristics of the children's kindergarten experiences in a manner that is considerably more detailed and specific than that seen in probably any other country. There is also recognition of research findings in the formulation of legislation. Currently, interest has focused on the three-to-seven age range but there is some indication emerging of government interest in the 0-three age range. Clearly, kindergartens are regarded as important by the state, which devotes large resources to their development. Kindergartens are seen as central to the integration of the interests of the child, family community and state, and there is an emphasis on integrating kindergartens into the wider community.

References

Beijing Municipal Education Commission (2005). *2004 Year School Educational Development Statistics*. Beijing: Beijing Municipal Education Commission.

Huang, J.J. (2003). *Researches on kindergarten education*. Shanghai: Shanghai Educational Publishing Company.

Huang, R.Q. (2004). Research on the multi-aged groups. Unpublished research report.

Li, S.L. (2000). How to foster children's social-emotional development. *Family Education*. *8*, 32–33.

Li, S.L. (2001). *Family Education for Young Children and Parents (3rd ed.)*. Shanghai: Shanghai Educational Publishing Company.

Li, S.L. (2003). Researches on Shanghai kindergarten education development. *Preschool Education Research, 6*, 16–20.

Li, S.L. (2004a). *Researches on partnerships of kindergarten, family, and community (rev. ed.)*. Shanghai: East China Normal University Publishing Company.

Li, S.L. (2004b). *Preschool education (rev. ed.)*. Shanghai: East China Normal University Publishing Company.

Li, S.L. (2004c). *Family education in early childhood (rev. ed.)*. Shanghai: East China Normal University Publishing Company.

Li, S.L. (2004d). *Comparative early childhood education (5th ed.)*. Shanghai: East China Normal University Publishing Company.

Li, S.L. (2005). Implications of sociology theory on kindergarten education. *Shanghai Education Research*, 1, 35–38.

Liu, J. (2002). Hainan '10.5' plan of young children's education. *China Education Newspaper, 4, 12, 2.*

Ministry of Education of the People's Republic of China (1990). *Kindergarten Management Legislation*. Beijing: Ministry of Education, People's Republic of China.

Ministry of Education of the People's Republic of China (1996). *Kindergarten Work Regulation*. Available at: http://www.moe.edu.cn/edoas/website18/info687.htm. 10/03/2005.

Ministry of Education of the People's Republic of China (2001). *Kindergarten Education Guideline*. Beijing: Ministry of Education of the People's Republic of China.

Ministry of Education of the People's Republic of China (2002). Report on Educational Statistics. Beijing: Ministry of Education of the People's Republic of China.

Ministry of Education of the People's Republic of China (2003). Report on Educational Statistics. Beijing: Ministry of Education of the People's Republic of China.

Ministry of Education of the People's Republic of China (2005). Report on Educational Statistics. Beijing: Ministry of Education of the People's Republic of China. Available at: http://www.moe.edu.cn/english/basic_b.htm

Ni, R. and Zhao, X. (1996). The curriculum for 4 year old children in kindergarten. *Young Children's Education. 5,* 9–10.

Ruan, A.X. (2000). How to develop children's independence. *Children's Health, 12,* 20–21.

Shanghai Municipal Education Commission (2004). *2003 Year School Educational Development Statistics.* Shanghai Municipal Education Commission. Available at: http://www.shmec.gov.cn/xxgk/attach/627.htm

Shanghai Municipal Education Commission (2005). *2004 Year School Educational Development Statistics.* Shanghai: Shanghai Municipal Education Commission. Available at: http://www.shmec.gov.cn/web/concept/shedu_article_list.php?area_id=262

Tang, L. (1999). The curriculum for 3 year old children in kindergarten. Unpublished report.

Wang, X. (2005). On the development of children's social skills in multi-aged groups. *Young Children's Education, 7,* 10–11.

Wu, X.L. (2001). One Kindergarten Reformation and Development. *Education and Development, 12,* 40–41.

Yang, X.L. (2001). A research report about children's brain development. Unpublished.

Yao, Y. (2001). Boarding kindergarten is a good kindergarten. Unpublished report.

Ye, L.Y. (2004). Research on the smaller group sizes. *Young Children's Education, 3,* 7–8.

Zhang, C. (2002). Children's brain development and its implications. Unpublished.

Zhang, F. (2004). Cooperative Learning. *Young Children's Education, 12,* 14–15.

Zhao, X. and Tang, Z. (1994). The curriculum for 5 year old children in kindergarten. *Early Childhood Education, 2,* 4–5.

11 An international overview of early childhood care and education

Edward Melhuish and Konstantinos Petrogiannis

As indicated in the introduction, and exemplified in previous chapters, ideological and historical context can explain how a system of ECCE develops within a country, and an understanding of the ECCE system and its characteristics can explain how effects upon children can occur (Melhuish, 1991, 2005; Kamerman, 1991). Also it is important to realise that childcare is diverse, and not make the mistake, which is only too common amongst politicians, of regarding day care for under-ones as basically the same issue as kindergarten for three- to four-year-olds.

Some forms of ECCE have explicit educational aims and are usually targeted on children from three years upwards (e.g. nursery schools, kindergartens). Other forms of provision are care-oriented and, while operating for under-threes, also cater for older children (e.g. day care centres). There is an overlap between the care- and education-oriented sections with the distinction becoming increasingly blurred, with recognition of the importance of learning in the first three years for longer-term development. In addition, there is a distinction between childcare as a form of intervention for disadvantaged children and childcare for the general population where enabling maternal employment is often the dominant purpose, and fostering child development may or may not be high on the agenda. Countries have differing policies and experiences with regard to these different types of childcare.

For many countries, childcare has traditionally been considered the private problem of families, which often gives rise to antagonism to increased childcare provision. However, increasingly it is taken for granted that childcare is here to stay given the social changes occurring in developed and developing countries. In industrialised societies ECCE is now being recognised as part of the infrastructure for economic development (Warner *et al.,* 2003) since childcare – with or without the educational elements – is a necessity for modern societies with women as central to the workforce. 'Day care is a fact of modern life, no longer a debatable issue ... like a roller coaster that cannot be stopped' (Blum, 1983, p. 2).

The diversity in ECCE provision across countries reflects the historic and cultural factors affecting the ideology and economic structure of a society, which give rise to the wide range of values, attitudes, beliefs and practices regarding children and childcare (see also Lamb *et al.*, 1992; Melhuish and Moss, 1991; Moss, 1988; Kamerman, 1991). These cultural influences are translated into policy decisions. The resulting public policies with regard to employment law, parental leave and ECCE form the context for parents' decisions about use of ECCE for their children. As Bronfenbrenner (1992) said, 'the course of childcare policy and practice is shaped to a substantial degree by the broader context in time and place'.

International evidence allows cross-national sharing of experience and practice in areas of common interest, while allowing account to be taken of national similarities and differences. Within a country, consideration of such evidence can be a stimulus for policy innovation through enabling countries to learn from each other's successes and failures. Throughout this book a number of issues are raised that reveal similarities and differences between countries in policy and research regarding ECCE.

Social trends and ECCE

Several trends are apparent in industrialised countries. These include an increase of divorce and single parenthood; the withering of the extended family with the result that grandparents or other relatives are becoming less available for childcare; and increasing need for two family incomes to meet material and social aspirations. Such changes together with the increase in maternal employment have led to changes in attitudes toward women's participation in the workforce, and the roles of mothers, fathers, the extended family and childcare. Modern parents may appear less child-oriented and more self-centred than their parents, and increasingly they have views that childcare is not exclusively the mother's duty.

The most important socio-economic change affecting the traditional model of child-rearing and family structure has come through the changing roles of women resulting from the increase in female employment, which has been a universal trend in industrialised countries over the past 30–40 years. Currently, for many countries the fastest growing group in the labour market is mothers of preschool children, particularly under three years of age. In Sweden, for example, the proportion of mothers with children under three who work has risen from one-third to two-thirds over the past two decades. In the USA and UK, the proportion of working mothers of preschool children has doubled since the mid-1960s, and even in southern European countries that have a lower rate of female participation in the labour market, e.g. Italy and Greece, there have been significant increases. Inevitably this results in an increased need for childcare, and the vital role of childcare in facilitating female choice around work–life balance is now universally recognised. Accessible childcare is now viewed as crucial to the facilitation of female labour-market participation, which is increasingly seen as one of the necessary conditions for economic prosperity in modern societies.

Changing patterns of maternal employment in turn have increased the pressures for changes to employment law and parental leave. The provision of maternity leave to enable employed mothers to recover physically from childbirth, and to enable the family to adapt to a new baby, is found in all advanced industrialised countries. However, the extent and conditions surrounding such leave vary enormously. Parental leave policies vary in duration, in proportion to wages replaced, in their applicability to fathers as well as mothers, and in whether any part of the leave is mandatory for mothers. Extending parental leave, particularly if paid, has profound implications for childcare needs, particularly in infancy when high-quality childcare is most expensive. The interdependence of parental leave and demand for childcare is clearly illustrated by Scandinavian experience, e.g. Sweden, where extensions of parental leave have decreased demand for infant day care.

The countries with the most extensive parental leave are those that combine high economic development with an ideology that accepts the care of preschool children and fostering equal opportunity as at least partly a state responsibility. While societal responsibility for children has long been part of Scandinavian tradition, in the UK such ideas have only slowly come to be accepted by government. In the UK's case the recent enhancements of parental leave have resulted from the coincidence of a government committed to increasing opportunities for women with a period of economic success, yet the final push came from research evidence indicating that increased parental leave may well be good for children, and hence improve the long-term human capital of the country. Indeed, there has been increasing attention to research evidence that indicates that the home is where human capital is nurtured.

In societies with traditional views concerning maternal employment, but where nevertheless maternal employment is increasing, home-based arrangements are more likely to be used in preference to centres, as in southern European countries like Italy and Greece. In contrast, among parents in cultures where approval of maternal employment is the norm, centre-based care is more prevalent, but this may also be influenced by the availability of relatives for childcare. Where the role of extended families is changing, as in Italy and Greece, it is likely to lead to a decrease in dependence on home-based childcare.

ECCE and the public sector role

There is variation in beliefs about the extent to which childcare is seen as a public responsibility or a private, family concern. The availability of publicly-funded childcare, especially that of high quality, and related family support policies are indicators of how societies see the balance of responsibility between parents and the wider community (Wise and Sanson, 2000).

Among the countries presented in this book the US represents one extreme, holding that decisions and financing pertaining to childcare should be left to families on their own. This ideology of 'childcare is a private issue' is congruent with the lowest parental leave allowance of any industrialised country and, at a federal level, the notion of state responsibility for childcare only as an intervention for disadvantaged children to compensate for impoverished home lives, although individual states show progress with increasing state provision of preschool education, and some states aiming for universal provision. For the vast majority of working parents, there is no public support beyond a care tax credit. There is state involvement in regulation, but standards vary enormously across the USA.

European countries present a mixed picture, illustrated by four countries in this book. From the mid-1980s, within the European Union (EU), there was widespread demand for greater day care facilities for preschool children, and there were proposals that an EU policy goal should be to establish preschool as a legal 'right' (Moss, 1988). In line with this, the EU summit in Barcelona passed a recommendation that by 2010, member states should provide childcare for at least 33 per cent of children under the age of three, and for at least 90 per cent of children between age three and school age (Neyer, 2003). Several countries have already achieved this goal and others are slowly or rapidly approaching it.

In the UK, childcare has historically been viewed as a private matter. Until recently, most publicly funded centres were meant for children at risk. However, since 1997, a new government became the principal driver in the childcare field and promised to develop high-quality, affordable childcare. UK provision, which began from a low base, is now benefiting from significant public funding and a radical reform of policy. The current governmental aim is to entrench childcare provision within the mantle of the established welfare state, which would make removal of government support for childcare by a future government politically unacceptable. As part of this aim there is now universal state-funded preschool provision for all three- and four-year-olds. The Scandinavian experience supports this view that once parents have a service they value it such that it becomes electoral suicide to try to remove it.

Sweden represents another extreme where the state is regarded as the parents' partner in child-rearing. Publicly funded day care is seen as a right and day care is generally high quality and homogeneous. Increasingly, childcare is centre-based, but relatives or childminders, especially organised childminding schemes, are also used. The decrease in the role of private childminders and relatives in Sweden (as well as in other countries) is partly a response to the increase in publicly funded services, but also, with increasing female employment, the number of female relatives willing to offer childcare is reducing.

Whereas Scandinavian countries managed to combine generous day care provision and parental leave, other European countries have failed to respond similarly to increased maternal employment. In Greece, for example, public childcare is considered inadequate and the number of families using the facilities is very limited. Most children receive private day care, mostly from relatives, with the remainder coming from private nurseries, which have been growing rapidly over the past 15 years. In Italy, with similar trends regarding maternal employment, there is ambivalence in attitudes to childcare. Traditional ideas about the role of the extended family are still revered yet they are coming into conflict with the realities of modern life where high levels of female employment, including maternal employment, are normative. There is large regional variation reflecting the high level of autonomy of regional government, and many regions provide extensive publicly funded childcare, often reflecting collectivist ideas, but, overall, private provision predominates, particularly childcare by relatives.

The ECCE services in Israel were originally developed with two main objectives: to meet the survival needs of young children and to acculturate them into Jewish society. There is a dual system of ECCE: a day care system, for children aged 0–three years, to promote the participation of mothers in the labour market as well as to address the educational gap of 'disadvantaged' children; and an 'early education' system for children aged three- to six-years-old with the main target being to acculturate the diverse population of refugees returning to Israel and to strengthen community identity, rather than meet the developmental needs of individual children. Also this system should ensure 'school readiness' for disadvantaged children. In 1999, a new law extended preschool education to all three- to five-year-olds, but severe budget cuts effectively halted further implementation of the law after the first few years.

In a multicultural society such as New Zealand, there are culturally based differences in attitudes toward early childcare and toward community support for parenting. The history of negotiation revealed in the chapter by Smith and May shows how multiple perspectives can be resolved in a consistent government policy. The current policy is for early childhood programmes facilitating the provision of affordable and accessible childcare to all children over three years old, which has been influenced by research.

In China, central government planning of services is usual. In line with this there has emerged a government development plan for preschool childcare provision. Most government attention has focused on childcare for the over-threes, and is clearly influenced by notions of developing the human capital of the nation. The government has set the target of preschool education for almost all children between three and six years of age through kindergartens. Until recently, interest in the under-threes appeared minimal, although there are some indications that this may be changing. In addition, and in order to assist working parents, new preschool schemes have been developed such as the 'boarding programmes' that are open 24 hours a day, five days a week, for the full year.

In India, early care and education of young children continues to be the responsibility of the family rather than the state. For the under-threes in particular, India's strong tradition of childcare provided by the extended family still prevails. For the three- to six-year-olds there is increasing demand for preschool education with nearly half of all preschool children attending some kind of ECCE, and the state provides ECCE for 22 per cent of children. The ideology that individual families should solve their children's problems and that the child is to develop naturally is reflected both in governmental policy to provide a limited structured learning environment and limited ECCE facilities.

Education or care

The split between childcare as education versus routine care is reflected in the frequent division of responsibility for ECCE services between government departments of education and social welfare or health. Education is seen as serving intellectual needs, and care as serving physical and emotional needs. Hence, there is a model for preschools under educational auspices and another model for day care emphasising basic welfare and safety under welfare auspices. Yet modern developmental theory acknowledges that education begins at birth and separating education and care ignores the fundamental nature of development, where every experience of the child is a potential learning experience. New Zealand was the first country to integrate responsibility for all early childhood services under education, and the notion of 'educare' integrating childcare and education and recognising their indivisibility, is wholeheartedly accepted within New Zealand. Similar thinking in Sweden led to responsibility for childcare being transferred to education auspices from 1996. In recent years, the UK has followed the same route. However, the majority of countries retain a 'split' ECCE model that is reflected in the formulation of two parallel structures: one for early childhood care and one for early childhood education. Hence those developed countries currently making greatest advances in ECCE adopt an integrated model for ECCE services, while a split model reflects more traditional provision.

Quality of ECCE services

It is highly probable that the quality of ECCE services is more consistent and better on average in countries like Sweden and New Zealand, which have developed national systems of publicly funded and relatively well-resourced services, than in countries like Greece, Italy, India or the US, where there is no central system of quality evaluation. The research evidence appears to support this proposition. The UK and China are moving toward a central system of quality regulation for ECCE.

With regard to quality of the learning experience within ECCE, there are significant differences across the countries. In general, there has been increasing recognition that children's early years are an important time of learning and education, as well as a preparation for a life of change. Most countries have worked to develop curriculum guidelines. Curricula across countries tend to look forward, have a purpose, set expectations, and be goal-oriented. Key differences are found in responsibility for curriculum development, the ages covered by the curriculum, which services it applies to, the type, principles and content of the curriculum and the degree of prescription or autonomy in implementation. In most of the countries the educational curricula have been developed under educational auspices. In some other countries, the curriculum is extended from infancy until the beginning of school, as in the case of New Zealand and Sweden, reflecting their age-integrated provision. Finally, there are countries that place particular emphasis on the ethnic identities and language of the children attending the ECCE programmes, for example, New Zealand's highly innovative ECCE approach.

ECCE *as infrastructure for economic development*

The few cost–benefit analyses undertaken of preschool education are unambiguous in showing substantial benefits (see Melhuish, 2004, for review). These analyses have been applied where high-quality childcare has been used as a form of intervention for disadvantaged families. A striking feature of these results is that the size of the benefits allows a very substantial margin of error and interventions would still be economically worthwhile. Barnett (1996) undertook a cost–benefit analysis of the Perry Preschool Project in the US, which followed equivalent groups of disadvantaged children, who had or had not received high-quality preschool education. At age 27 the benefits in terms of savings in schooling, taxes on earnings, welfare savings and reduction in crime produce a benefit–cost ratio of 7:1. By age 40 the benefit–cost ratio had increased to 17:1 (Schweinhart *et al.*, 2005). A benefit–cost ratio of 7:1 at age 21 is reported for a large-scale preschool programme for disadvantaged children in Chicago (Reynolds *et al.*, 2002). Both of these projects involved half-day preschool for disadvantaged three- to five-year-olds. However the applicability of these indications of savings to the general population is open to doubt in that so much of the benefit derives from reductions of negative outcomes, e.g. crime, remedial education and unemployment, where the incidence of these negative outcomes is dramatically less in the general population and therefore the scope for savings is similarly dramatically less. Nevertheless, when considering poor child outcomes such as learning difficulties or behaviour problems, the 'prevention paradox' is relevant in that while the rate of incidence is greater for disadvantaged populations, the absolute number of cases is greater in the general population. Hence there is likely to be considerable long-term economic benefit accruing from universal preschool provision.

The extensive evidence of the benefits of preschool education, and the cost–benefit evidence, support the proposition that preschool education is an important part of the infrastructure for economic development (Heckman, 2000). Preschool improves the development of human capital. With higher levels of human capital being needed to sustain economic growth in ever more technologically dependent economies, preschool is a cost-effective way to increase human capital and hence provide a precondition for later economic development. This argument has been influential in winning the support of politicians and government finance departments who fund preschool education in a number of countries. This has occurred in the UK, New Zealand and states within the USA. It is also interesting that two of the strongest growing economies in the world, India and China, are increasing investment in preschool education, which indicates that as their economies develop, the requisite human capital will come onstream to maintain their economic development for many years to come. China in particular is taking preschool education very seriously. It is close to providing universal preschool education from three years upwards, and the state is undertaking heavy involvement, from maintaining high levels of provision, legislating on quality and training of staff, right down to specifying daily activities for children. China appears to recognise ECCE as part of the infrastructure for economic development and is determined to get it right.

Research on early childhood care and education

When children enter childcare they are entering another world, one that offers experiences different from the home. The world of childcare and the world of home may make different demands on children. For example, a child may receive more individual attention at home than in a day care centre. The child must learn to share attention. Children's experiences in one world could affect how they behave in their second world and vice versa. So, children who are more accustomed to undivided attention at home may find childcare more difficult. Thus to understand children's experiences we need to study children both at home and in childcare and to see how the two worlds interact.

Countries do not follow the same path in the way that they have researched ECCE and children's development. Most evidence comes from English-speaking countries. The United States has by far the most extensive research. New Zealand, Sweden and the UK have similar but much smaller traditions of research. Italy and Greece have a tradition in pedagogical research that is largely limited to considering the childcare experience with little work incorporating child outcomes. In India, research attempts to 'persuade' the government to look more closely at ECCE, whereas in China research appears to be a procedure for developing practice and testing the implementation of ECCE, and appears to be used by government in formulating policy.

We can attempt to summarise the research from the various countries covered in this book. While the research on preschool education (three-plus years) is fairly consistent, the research evidence on the effects of childcare for 0-three-year-olds upon development has been equivocal, with some studies finding negative effects, some no effects and some positive effects. Discrepant results may relate to age of starting and also probably at least partly to differences in the quality of childcare received by children. In addition, childcare effects are mediated by family background with negative, neutral and positive effects occurring depending on the relative balance of quality of care at home and in childcare. Recent large-scale studies in the USA and UK find effects related to both quantity and quality of childcare. Quality of childcare is seen as potentially affecting children's development in the research of several of the countries covered in this book. Also there is evidence from the USA and UK that high levels of group care, particularly, may elevate the risk for developing antisocial behaviour.

Research in the USA, UK and Sweden finds evidence that the effects of childcare factors are about half those for family factors. Factors such as mother's sensitivity, family income and quality of the home environment are found to have a stronger association with child outcomes than are childcare factors (including the amount, type, stability and quality of care).

For provision for three years onwards the evidence is consistent that pre-school provision is beneficial to educational and social development for the whole population. The effects are greater for high-quality provision. The evidence on childcare in the first three years for disadvantaged children indicates that high-quality childcare can produce benefits, particularly for cognitive and language development. Low-quality childcare produces either no benefit or negative effects. Also UK and Israeli evidence indicates that disadvantaged children benefit more in socially mixed groups than they do in homogeneously disadvantaged groups.

Research lessons

Research related to the quality and characteristics of childcare is common across many of the countries covered here. Extrapolating from research done across several countries the following characteristics of early years provision are most important for enhancing children's development:

- Adult–child interaction that is responsive, affectionate and readily available
- Well-trained staff who are committed to their work with children
- Facilities that are safe and sanitary and accessible to parents
- Ratios and group sizes that allow staff to interact appropriately with children
- Supervision that maintains consistency
- Staff development that ensures continuity, stability and improving quality
- A developmentally appropriate curriculum with educational content.

Policy lessons

At the level of policy, the lessons of international experience are that high-quality early childhood care and education requires:

- Policy development that integrates care and education
- Universal access
- Public investment in infrastructure
- Integrated participatory approach to quality of services
- Appropriate training and working conditions for staff
- A long-term framework for research and evaluation.

Within this book there are examples supporting all of these points.

References

Barnett, W.S. (1996). *Lives in the balance: Benefit-cost analysis of the Perry Preschool Program through age 27.* Monographs of the High/Scope Educational Research Foundation. Ypsilanti, MI: High/Scope Press.

Blum, M. (1983). *The day care dilemma.* Lexington, MA: Lexington Books.

Bronfenbrenner, U. (1992). Child care in the Anglo-Saxon mode. In M. Lamb, K. Sternberg, C. Hwang and A. Broberg (Eds), *Child care in context.* Hillsdale, NJ: Lawrence Erlbaum.

Heckman, J. (2000). Policies to foster human capital. Working Papers of Harris School of Public Policy. Chicago: University of Chicago. Available at www.harris school.uchicago.edu/About/publications/working-papers/pdf/wp_sup_14.pdf

Kamerman, S.B. (1991). Child care policies and programs: An international overview. *Journal of Social Issues, 47,* 179–196.

Lamb, M., Sternberg, K., Hwang, C. and Broberg, A. (Eds) (1992). *Child care in context.* Hillsdale, NJ: Lawrence Erlbaum.

Melhuish, E.C. (1991). Editorial: Cross-national comparisons and the interpretation of day care effects. *Journal of Reproductive and Infant Psychology, 9,* 63–65.

Melhuish, E.C. (2004). *A literature review of the impact of early years provision upon young children, with emphasis given to children from disadvantaged backgrounds: Report to the Comptroller and Auditor General.* London: National Audit Office. Available at http://www.nao.org.uk/publications/nao_reports/03–04/268_ literaturereview.pdf

Melhuish, E.C. (2005). Day-care. In B. Hopkins *et al.* (Eds) *Cambridge Encyclopaedia of Child Development.* Cambridge: Cambridge University Press.

Melhuish, E.C. and Moss, P. (Eds) (1991). *Current issues in day care for young children.* London: Routledge.

Moss, P. (1988). *Childcare and equality – Consolidated report to the European Commission.* Brussels: Commission of the European Communities.

Neyer, G. (2003). *Family policies and low fertility in Western Europe.* MPIDR Working Paper. Rostok: Max Planck Institute for Demographic Research.

)

Reynolds, A.J., Temple, J.A., Robertson, D.L. and Mann, E.A. (2002). *Age 21 cost-benefit analysis of the Title 1 Chicago Child-Parent Centers.* Madison, WI: Institute for Research on Poverty. Available at www.irp.wisc.edu/publications/dps/pdfs/dp124502.pdf

Schweinhart, L.J., Montie, J., Xiang, Z., Barnett, W.S., Belfield, C.R. and Nores, M. (2005). *Lifetime effects: The High/Scope Perry Preschool study through age 40.* Monographs of the High/Scope Educational Research Foundation, 14.

Warner, M.E., Ribeiro, R. and Smith, A.E. (2003). Addressing the affordability gap: Framing child care as economic development. *Journal of Affordable Housing and Community Development Law, 12(3),* 294–313.

Wise, S. and Sanson, A. (2000). *Child care in cultural context: Issues for new research.* Research Paper No. 22. Canberra: Australian Institute of Family Studies.

Index